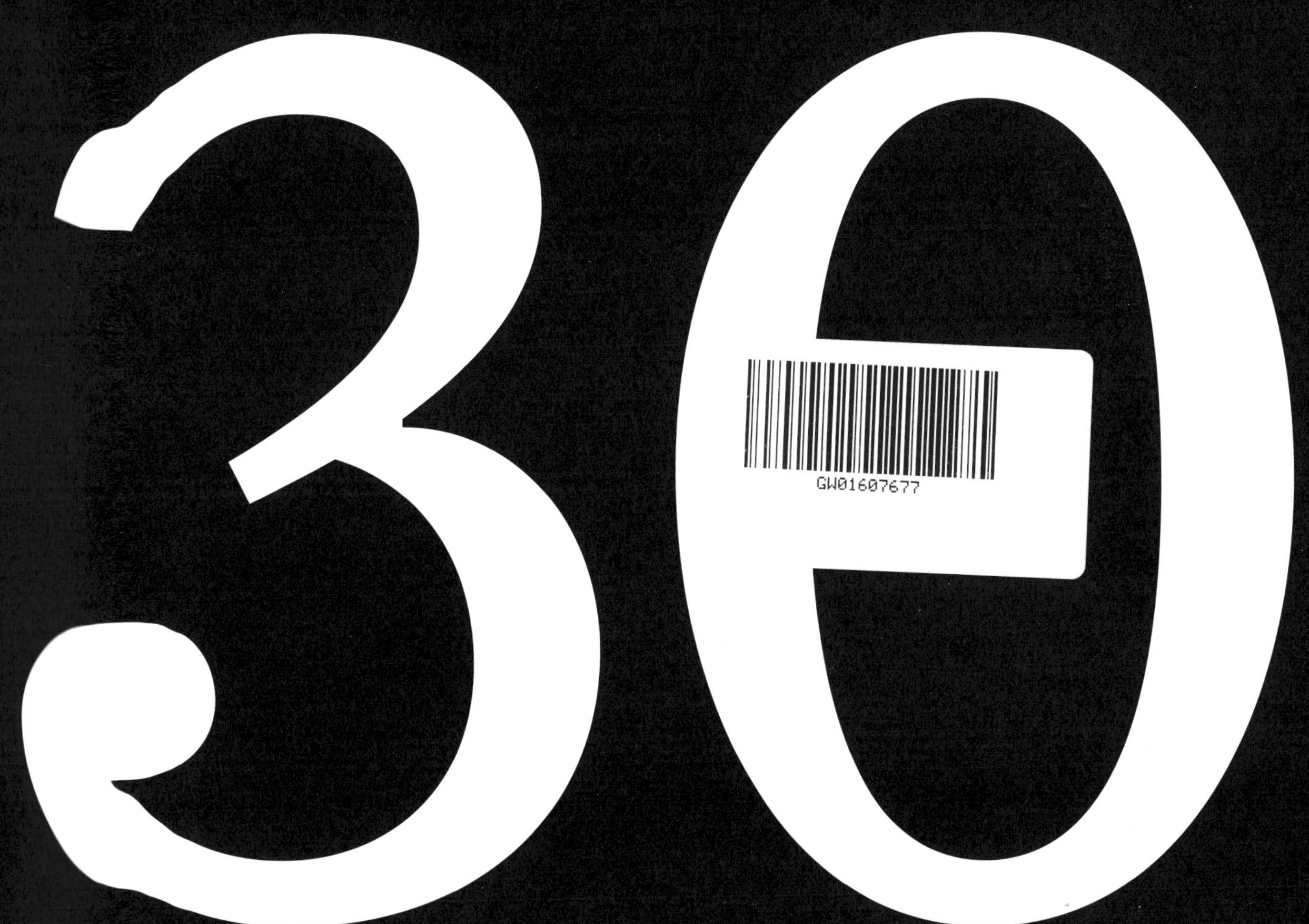

GW01607677

Photoworks

30 YEARS OF PHOTOWORKS

PAST PERFECT

PRESENT CONTINUOUS

DESERT ISLAND PICS

FUTURE TENSE

PHOTOWORKS AT 30
LOUISE FEDOTOV-CLEMENTS

Established in 1995, Photoworks has played a pivotal role in shaping the landscape of contemporary photography in the UK, and contributed significantly to the global dialogue on visual culture, storytelling and the power of the photographic image. As the director of Photoworks, I have the honour of leading this distinguished institution into its 30th year, a momentous milestone in its journey as one of the most influential and forward-thinking photography organisations in the world.

Over the past three decades, Photoworks has become synonymous with developmental innovation, supporting photographers whose work challenges, informs and redefines how we understand our collective and individual identity. From thought-provoking exhibitions to groundbreaking commissions, residencies and awards, from nurturing emerging talent to engaging with global issues, Photoworks has consistently positioned itself as a catalyst for creativity and a champion of photography's role in both art and society. Our commitment to excellence has resonated far beyond the UK, influencing the international arts community and engaging audiences worldwide. Photoworks would not be here without the dedication and vision of our staff, audiences and communities, and we appreciate everyone who has engaged and worked with, created and supported Photoworks over its history to date.

As a team, we are deeply aware of the rich legacy we have inherited, one that has cultivated a unique platform for artists, audiences and communities to come together through photography. From the early days of exhibitions and commissions to our expanding role in education, publishing and public engagement, Photoworks has grown in both its ambition and impact. This edition of our annual publication shares important highlights from our past, with a long history of developmental work we reflect on a collection of commissions with photographers that demonstrate the depth of past collaborations. Expertly brought together by our Annual editor Diane Smyth, the publication charts the histories, present and future of our connections. It begins with a series of conversations with the directors, editors and curators who have shaped Photoworks since the beginning, followed by features on new photography talents and then onto speculative futures of the medium.

As we reflect on this extraordinary past, it is clear that our impact reaches across borders, touching diverse communities, perspectives and cultures. The anniversary is not just a moment for reflection, but also an opportunity to look forward – to embrace changing global dynamics, to acknowledge the challenges we face as a community and to understand how photography continues to shape the way we view, document, create and respond to the world around us.

Within the past 30 years, we have witnessed the rise and fall of the internet, the increase, decline and re-emergence of the darkroom, the establishment of photography as an artform and the mass transition from analogue to digital, the invention of social media, the rise of the mobile phone and the globalisation of communications.

To reference a wider context, at this moment we are facing unprecedented change. A funding collapse is happening throughout the creative and public sector; arts provision in schools is sorely diminished; the cost of living is in crisis, and we are in the midst of a climate emergency. Conflict, inequity, insecurity and uncertainty are affecting us all. As a riff on Mark Fisher's quote in *Capitalist Realism*, it's easier to imagine the end of the world than the creation of a better society. However, we are not just critics of the status quo; we are architects of the future as it could be.

This Annual recognises not only our history but also the possibilities ahead. The next chapter for Photoworks is one that I am excited to navigate, as we build on our legacy while expanding our reach and impact on the international stage. We will continue to empower artists and audiences from all corners of the world, fostering enduring collaborations, championing diverse voices, facilitating dialogue and exploring the most urgent issues of our time. Photography's ability to speak truth to power, to document history, to imagine and to inspire change remains more vital than ever, and at Photoworks, we will ensure that it continues to be a medium that resonates deeply, both locally and globally.

A BRIEF HISTORY OF PHOTOWORKS

A BRIEF HISTORY OF PHOTOWORKS

An organisation 30 years – and more – in the making, Photoworks has evolved and endured with energetic teams, finds Diane Smyth, committed to supporting those who make and think about photographs

2025 is Photoworks' 30th anniversary, but the organisation's roots go back to the Cross Channel Photographic Mission, which was set up in 1987 and managed by Leo Stable to document the impact of the Channel Tunnel, then under construction. As the name suggests, the CCPM was a partnership across the Channel, with the French Centre Regional de la Photographie (CRP) des Hauts-de-France, which instigated the whole idea. Between them, CCPM and CRP made 24 commissions exploring landscapes and communities in France and England as the tunnel was built.

In 1993, with financial backing from Kent County Council and South-East Arts, CCPM employed Anne McNeill to run workshops and events around the commissions. McNeill, who had started her career with radical magazine and gallery Camerawork, soon got involved with the commissions, supporting artists such as Anna Fox (who worked with Val Williams), Julian Germain and Janine Weidel to make idiosyncratic documentary projects. In 1994, CCPM published a book, *Soundings*, to mark the opening of the Tunnel, gathering together work by many of the artists. For McNeill, this publication showed how important CCPM's work was, and what a waste it would be to let it die.

"It was, like, 'Oh, what's going to happen now?!'" McNeill says. "There hadn't been any plans or legacy narrative, but I was very clear that something really good had happened in the commissioning, and that it must carry on. There was a need for commissioning. There wasn't a catalyst in place for a commissioning agency, so that's when we came up with the idea for Photoworks. The idea was that we would commission photographers in the UK and France, but we had to be based in Kent, because we were dependent on funding from Kent."

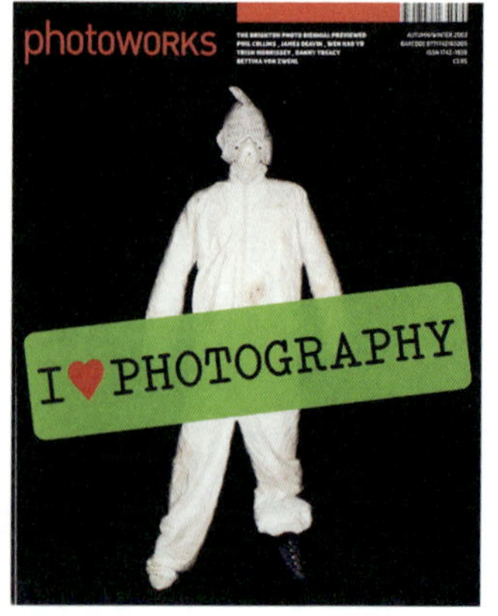

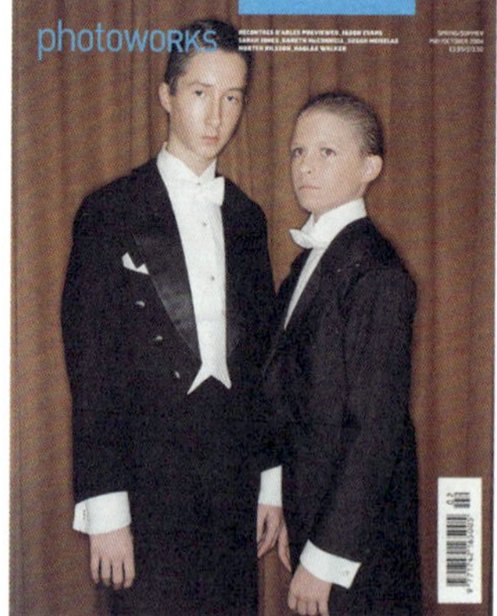

Photoworks magazine was launched in 2003 and ran biannually until 2013.

Photoworks was born in 1995, in an office on the top floor of Maidstone County Hall; much of McNeill's work was in setting up the organisation and establishing it as a charity, but she also had to carve it out as a concept. Magazines and Sunday supplements still had healthy budgets for documentary work at this time so the idea of a commissioning agency for photography was new; documentary was also perceived in terms of editorial, so installing it in galleries was unusual and few non-photographic or local authority galleries were set up to do so.

Thinking in terms of touring exhibitions, and without a Photoworks exhibition space, McNeill looked to Kent's network of library galleries. "The library galleries were good because then you reach a non-photographic audience," she says. "But then you also didn't have control. You didn't have control over what the front-of-house might say about the work, for example. I remember the feeling at the time was that photography wasn't art – or it could only be art if it was done by artists, or photography was for documenting work by artists.

"So part of the work was about changing perceptions, educating people that photography was a valid art form. Slowly, slowly things began to change. The growth of degree courses helped in that – people getting educated in visual literacy, educated in photography."

Photoworks had some early successes, including *The Country Life* series, in which curator Val Williams commissioned artists to respond to the George Garland Collection. Archived at the West Sussex County Records office, this collection gathered thousands of prints made from the 1920s to 1978, in which Garland documented a vanishing rural England. Susan Lipper, Joachim Schmid and David Johnson were commissioned, and the resulting work published as a series of small publications.

INTO THE 21ST CENTURY

1998 was the UK Year of Photography and that marked a sea change in attitudes, says McNeill; it also signalled her departure from Photoworks, because she left in December 1996 to become artistic director of Photo 98. She always thought that, one day, she would return, she says, but after the festival moved to head up Impressions Gallery, where she remains director today. Photoworks could have disappeared at this point, but Liz Kent, who had previously worked with McNeill, kept it going. Then David Chandler was appointed director – and stayed for 13 years, the longest of any Photoworks director to date.

"What can I say? It was just a bit of a brilliant time," he chuckles over the phone, "Though Anne deserves huge credit for plucking the organisation out of almost nothing." He adds that Photoworks was still a "fledgling organisation" in 1997 when he was asked to apply for the role. A Brighton resident, he had served on the Photoworks board and had previously been head of exhibitions at The Photographers' Gallery. He was working at the Institute of International Visual Art (Iniva), in London, when he was approached, alongside Gilane Tawadros, now director of Whitechapel Gallery.

Having got the job, Chandler set about establishing a network of contacts "and a more secure support from the Arts Council England for a more distinct identity for the organisation based around commissioning".

"I was interested in developing the commissions, trying to get more experienced people in to do more important commissions," he continues. "And Photoworks also had a magazine called *Insight*, which they had occasionally published, a folded black-and-white sheet. So I saw an opportunity there."

He "just put in a lot of energy", he says, driving 400 miles a week around the southeast; the journey from Brighton to Maidstone alone took two hours, and he went to the office four days a week. Within a couple of years, he was able to put together a small team, employing Gordon MacDonald in 1999 as head of projects and curator – shortly after his stint on the 1998 Shoreditch Biennale with Val Williams – and Rebecca Drew as deputy director in 2000. "Rebecca was very much on fundraising and overseeing the organisation, and she was extraordinarily good at that," says MacDonald. "I was brought in for a more creative role.

"I started expanding on what programme was already there, making bigger exhibitions and working in a more expansive way with other institutions," he continues. "So that was incredibly exciting. But at points we were working with village halls in Kent – the southeast was our remit, so we worked in little halls, putting up theatre flats [mobile screen scenery] and screwing works into them.

"Then, at other times, we were working with bigger institutions, for example the Towner Gallery, where I curated *The House in the Middle – Photographs of Interior Design in a Nuclear Age*, including Anne Hardy, Richard Billingham and Los Alamos National Laboratory (US), among many others."

Chandler describes a "beautiful" public gallery in Folkestone in which Photoworks exhibited images of Dungeness Power Station, commissioned from local photographer Nigel Green; this work was published as a book in 2003. Other interesting projects from this early period include Helen Sear's year-long residency at Maidstone's museum and library, published as a book, *The Whole Story*, in 2000. Meanwhile, Tony Glanville was commissioned to make work in rural Kent from 1997 to 2000; exhibited at the V&A, this work was also published as a book in 2000, titled *Actual Life*.

Chandler wanted to commission more national and international image-makers and, feeling stymied by the lack of an art and photography scene in Maidstone, "decided we couldn't really grow the organisation there". Spurred on by Brighton & Hove's designation as a city in 2000 – and by the fact that he, MacDonald and Drew were all based there – he moved the Photoworks office at the turn of the century. "We found this amazing office – it was huge and we got it for a reasonable rent," he says. "And the whole thing changed."

SCALING UP

At this point, Photoworks was able to scale up its commissioning and publishing activities, he says, including founding *Photoworks* magazine in 2003. But the organisation lacked an exhibition space, which meant its shows were always held in partnership with others; setting up the magazine and a more concerted publishing programme ensured the organisation had a discrete public face, visible across the whole country and beyond. MacDonald headed up the publishing wing and became founding editor of *Photoworks* magazine, which published two issues per year and gained national and international distribution and recognition.

The excitement and drive was infectious, and Photoworks was able to take on more members of staff, partly because of its large office and partly because Chandler raised extra funding. Ben Burbridge joined in 2003, initially as an intern, but soon in a more permanent role across the whole programme. "We had a sort of purple patch – we all got on very well, and we were all playing at the top of our game as a team," says Chandler. "It was a hotbed of activity."

Burbridge, for his part, says Chandler was "extraordinary".

"I mean, he had an extraordinary vision, and he was an extraordinary boss," he explains. "He saw an opportunity to turn a relatively small thing into something. It was his baby, although he is very, very modest."

The first issue of *Photoworks* magazine also testifies to a wider excitement around photography at that time. It features a survey of *The Summer of Photography* in London, including reviews of exhibitions by Cindy Sherman, Thomas Ruff, Philip-Lorca DiCorcia and Wolfgang Tillmans, who had won the Turner Prize in 2000. It also includes a discussion around *Cruel and Tender* – Tate Modern's first ever photography show – between Chandler and curators Charlotte Cotton, David Mellor and Frances Morris, centred around the question, what is the place of documentary photography in art?

Photoworks commissions at this time include *Falling* by Neeta Madahar, a co-commission with Fabrica and Iniva, and *A Picture Book of Britain* by Henna Nadeem; Madahar's work was published in the book *Nature Studies* by Photoworks in 2005, and Nadeem's in a photobook of the same name in 2006. Photoworks also secured funding from Arts Council England to start a publishing initiative with Steidl in the mid-2000s, working with Michael Mack (who later left Steidl to set up Mack Books). Image-makers such as Nigel Shafran, Sophy Rickett, Gareth McConnell and Dan Holdsworth all published books with this imprint, which were edited by Celia Davies, head of exhibitions at the De La Warr Pavilion. In 2007, Photoworks co-published Fig, by Adam Broomberg and Oliver Chanarin with Steidl, which it commissioned; the accompanying exhibition, in partnership with John Hansard, then toured. It was, says MacDonald, "the Photoworks model at its peak".

Like photography exhibitions, and the shift of documentary photography into art galleries, Photoworks' publishing activities speak of a wider zeitgeist. Martin Parr and Gerry Badger published the first volume of The Photobook in 2003, a testament to the wave of interest in photobooks. But Photoworks also published other kinds of book about photography, partnering with Photoforum in 2006 to publish *Stillness and Time: Photography and the Moving Image*. A theory book edited by David Green and Joanna Lowry, it included essays by writers such as Victor Burgin, Laura Mulvey and David Campany.

Photoworks' publishing programme also produced books such as *Murmuration* by Rinko Kawauchi (2010) and *Memory of Fire: Images of War and the War of Images* by Julian Stallabrass (2013), both of which point to another huge shift – the start of the Brighton Photo Biennial in 2003. Though run separately to Photoworks until 2011, BPB was intimately entwined with the organisation. Kawauchi's work, shown at BPB in 2010, was a new commission by Photoworks, for example, overseen by Celia Davies, who had had a long association with the organisation and joined in 2009. Stallabrass curated the 2008 BPB, also called *Memory of Fire*, and drew on it for his later publication.

BRIGHTON PHOTO BIENNIAL

"The Biennial was an idea that we had, in collaboration with Brighton University and various other partners in the Arts Council," explains Chandler. "I wrote the initial proposal, partly again around giving Photoworks a physical presence and a space to work in a concentrated way. It started as a germ of an idea really, limited by the fact that there aren't many flagship spaces in the southeast. But we did have some really key ones – Towner Art Gallery [now Towner Eastbourne], the De La Warr Pavilion, Pallant House [in Chichester]. Initially the Biennial was administered from the Photoworks office, before the BPB team moved into a space at Brighton University."

The first BPB, curated by Jeremy Millar, included image-makers such as Boris Mikhailov, commissioned to make new work in Brighton; the second, in 2006, was curated by Gilane Tawadros. In 2008, Stallabrass's *Memory of Fire* took an in-depth look at images of war, five years into Britain's military invasion of Iraq. In 2010, Martin Parr curated the festival and, rather than being split across disparate sites, it focused on Brighton that year. The key venue was an abandoned department store, featuring exhibitions organised by both Photoworks and the Brighton Fringe; the fringe had sprung up alongside BPB in 2003, spearheaded by MacDonald and Danny Wilson, who were passionate that BPB should also be an opportunity to platform local and emerging artists.

"It was an amazing building," says MacDonald, "although there was so much water running through it, we had to add sandbags. Brighton Photo Fringe, which I was chairperson of for over a decade, and which was fronted by the magnificent co-directors Woodrow Kernohan and Helen Cammock, managed to secure it, and in conversation with the Biennial held the space so they had some of the bigger shows of Martin's curation in it. Upstairs, we had multiple exhibitions including Lisa Barnard's *Maggie* [as part of the Fringe]. We worked very closely together, and all these things fed off each other."

These sandbags also marked a metaphorical high water point, because Photoworks' purple patch was coming to an end. In 2007, amid a worldwide economic downturn, the Arts Council England had announced the biggest cuts in its history; in 2008 the credit crunch struck, compounding the financial woes. In 2009, the Borders chain of bookshops went bust, leaving a hole in Photoworks' magazine distribution and speaking of a wider malaise for publishing. In 2010, the Conservatives took power (initially in a coalition with the Lib Dems), with a programme of austerity cuts to government spending.

"There's only a certain amount of energy you can put into things when the returns aren't great, and I guess the atmosphere generally was tightening," says Chandler. In 2010, he left to become professor of photography at Plymouth University and Emma Morris, deputy director of the De La Warr Pavilion, took over as director of Photoworks. She faced some difficult choices. BPB was in peril, because the Arts Council project funding it received was under threat, and Photoworks needed to boost audience figures, to protect its own public funding support. Morris had to merge the two organisations, including the two small teams that ran them. "It was a stressful time," she says. "Everyone, including myself, came out of it feeling bruised."

Some jobs were made redundant, while other employees decided to leave. MacDonald and Drew both departed in 2011; MacDonald went on to co-found GOST Books then *HAPAX* Magazine, while Drew moved to management positions with Fabrica, Brighton Photo Fringe and Hastings Contemporary. Burbridge continued part-time while working on his PhD – he's now professor of visual culture at Sussex University – while Celia Davies became head of programme. Juliette Buss, who had previously been at the BPB, joined Photoworks to lead its learning and education, a role she still holds today. In fact, Buss's work is so important – and so underestimated – that it has its own article (see pages 17–23).

POST-NOUGHTIES

In 2012, Arts Council England launched its National Portfolio Organisations and Photoworks became one of them, winning multi-year funding. It was a success but the funding was at a standstill, and BPB had lost its project funding altogether. "There wasn't a lot to go around," says Morris, so other changes had to be made. Over the next couple of years, the book publishing programme wound down, the curation of the Biennial went in-house, and Photoworks left its large central office, moving to the University of Brighton.

The Biennial kept going, though; in fact, the 2012 edition was the largest yet and was, wrote *The Independent*'s Peter Popham, "edgier than ever". Curated by Davies and Burbridge and themed *Agents of Change: Photography and the Politics of Space*, it included 14 exhibitions by artists such as Edmund Clark, Omer Fast and No Olho Da Rua. The latter project comprised Julian Germain, Patricia Azevedo and Murilo Godoy giving cameras to 50 young Brazilians who were living on the streets, helping them to document their lives. This edition also included exhibitions on squatting in Brighton and images from the archives of *The Argus*, the local newspaper.

Morris describes it as "a nice mix of some really big names, and then some very grassroots projects", adding that she found its approach to curating and photography refreshing, and even inspiring. "It wasn't just about the aesthetics of the image, it was about how those images can be used, socially, politically, and about grassroots archives," she points out. "It was more about the power of the image."

Some of this work was newly commissioned, and Photoworks commissions continued beyond the festival. For example, Ori Gersht created an exhibition titled *This Storm Is What We Call Progress*, in collaboration with London's Imperial War Museum, curated by Davies and shown in 2012. Morris flags this as a project that she was particularly happy with, but, having "done what needed to be done, in terms of seeing through the merger, securing NPO funding", she decided to leave Photoworks. Davies took over and, with tight staffing constraints – about half as many people as previously ran Photoworks and BPB – also had to make changes.

In 2013, she relaunched the twice-yearly magazine as an annual; the first iteration, issue 20 of the magazine, had *Family Politics* as its theme and was co-edited by Davies and Burbridge. Burbridge, who was only working one day a week at Photoworks by then, laughs that, as an early-career academic,

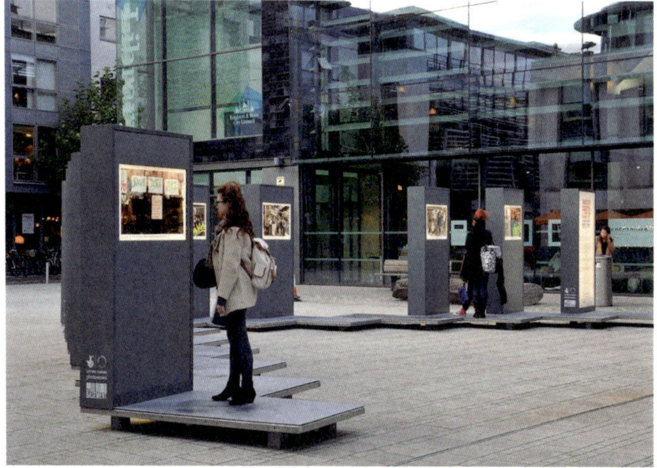

The 2012 edition was themed 'Agents of Change: Photography and the Politics of Space', and included an exhibition devoted to the archives of *The Argus*, Brighton's local newspaper.

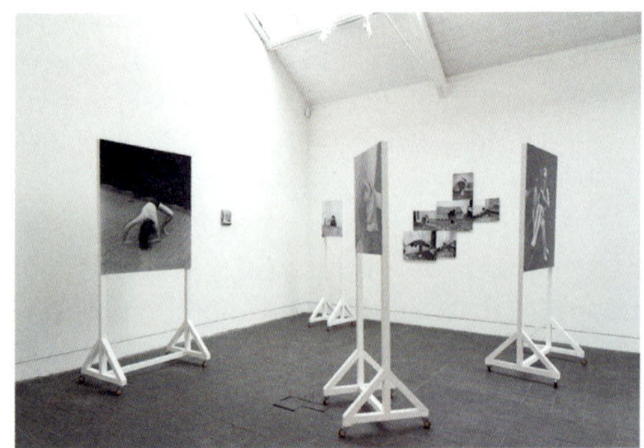

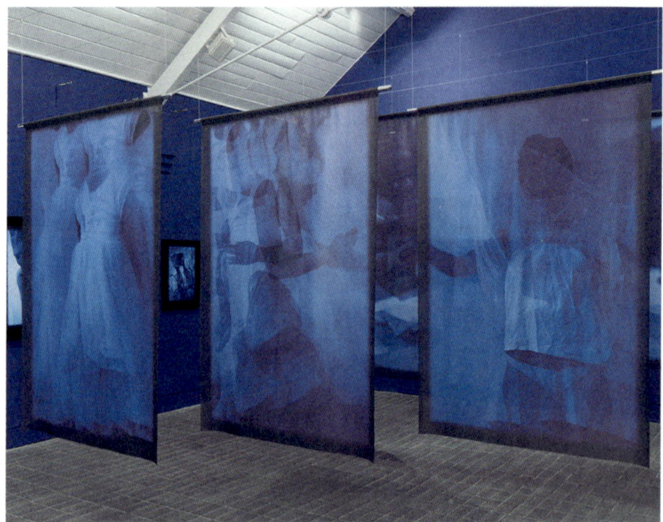

he included too many words in the publication, but the list of newly commissioned writers included influential theorists such as Terry Dennett and Geoffrey Batchen. The featured artists included practitioners such as Wendy Ewald and Anthony Luvera, whose community-focused approach has since become more prominent.

The *Family Politics* annual supported an exhibition of the same name curated by Photoworks at the Jerwood Space in London, a collaboration that led to the Jerwood/Photoworks Awards. Co-founded in 2015 by Davies with Shonagh Manson, then director of the Jerwood Charitable Foundation, these awards are still running today, and provide artists with the support to make and show a new body of work. The Jerwood partnership is also of note because Jerwood is a charity based on a private foundation, making the award a public/private initiative – an increasingly prevalent funding model, promoted by Arts Council England.

"The intention was to provide photographers who had been working less than five years with an award to support their time, access to mentors, resources, a production fund and an exhibition tour to profile new work," says Davies. "I am proud of this project and what it has gone on to achieve. It demonstrated how Photoworks operated as a national development agency, and I feel proud of what this has done and continues to do for photographers."

ARTIST SUPPORT

The first edition of the Jerwood/Photoworks Awards supported Tereza Zelenkova, Joanna Piotrowska and Matthew Finn; after exhibiting at the Jerwood Space, it travelled to Impressions Gallery (Bradford), Belfast Exposed and Open Eye Gallery (Liverpool). The second edition, in 2018, went to Alejandra Carles-Tolra, Sam Laughlin and Lúa Ribeira, with the exhibition travelling from Jerwood to Impressions and Belfast Exposed. All six artists are still practising today: Piotrowska has gone on to exhibit at the V&A and Le Bal in Paris, while Ribeira has joined Magnum Photos.

The projects made via Jerwood/Photoworks Awards were (and are) also shown on Photoworks' website and social media; during her tenure, Davies introduced an online programme aimed at increasing public access, and examining how digital platforms are impacting photography. Photoworks' programme of artist-Instagram takeovers started in this period, while *A Return to Elsewhere* by UK photographer Kalpesh Lathigra and South African artist Thabiso Sekgala, a co-commission by Photoworks and the Market Photo Workshop shown at BPB in 2014, was also presented as an online project supported by British Council, the BBC and The Space.

The 2014 BPB was themed *Communities, Collectives and Collaboration*, and the 2016 edition themed *Beyond the Bias – Reshaping Image*; the biennials were curated collaboratively, with a team that included Mariama Attah, who joined as programme curator in 2014. These biennials were also accompanied with annuals expanding and exploring the same themes, edited by Davies and Burbridge in 2014, and by Attah in 2016. Even though Photoworks was working with national and international artists, it was still committed to bringing photography to southeast England, and embracing local communities.

"I always approached the biennial as wanting to overwhelm the city with photography, wanting to be everywhere, and to be really partnering with people within the city and bringing people in as well," says Attah. "Finding venues to work in was tricky, and that made it difficult in terms of being visible in a space or using pre-existing space," she continues, adding that Photoworks also used external spaces and billboards to display images. "The flip side is that this led into my later work around socially engaged photography and practice, working in partnership with people."

Attah left for *Foam Magazine* in 2017, and the same year Davies exited to become a garden and landscape historian and designer; Burbridge, who had dropped days over the years,

The Jerwood/Photoworks Award were founded in 2015 to support artists making a new body of work and showing it in London and beyond.
Joanna Piotrowska (left) was one of the first winners; Heather Agyepong (right) won an award in 2022.

left altogether in 2018. Shoair Mavlian was appointed director in 2018, after working across photography and international art at Tate; Julia Bunnemann joined Photoworks as curator the same year. Working after the UK's Brexit vote, and amid rising nationalism – and drawing on Photoworks' roots in a collaboration between two countries – they created a festival and annual themed *A New Europe*.

The festival included an exhibition on The Cross Channel Photographic Commission, featuring work by nine photographers who had documented the French people and landscape; the BPB that year also included work by emerging artists such as Tereza Červeňová, Ronan McKenzie and Harley Weir. Similarly, the annual included newly commissioned texts by both established and emerging writers, such as Urs Stahel and Jamila Prowse. Europe also became the theme of the first *Photography+* issue, Photoworks' ongoing online magazine, signalling the start of a comprehensive digital reboot.

DIGITAL REALM

"In 2019, we started working on a rebrand which included refreshing the organisation's mission, vision and values, and a full branding and website redesign," explains Mavlian. "Our digital presence was a key part of Photoworks' strategic plan. Our website and social media were very important because, as an organisation without a physical venue, our digital platforms are the primary connection point with our audiences.

"During this time, we spoke a lot about being a platform for photography that existed online and in real life, and that these two things were equally important," she adds. "Photoworks was already publishing a lot of online content, including interviews, articles and videos, so I didn't invent anything new. I just changed how it was packaged... *P+* was also there to enhance things Photoworks did IRL; for example, we often did issues linked to the festival or exhibitions that would drop at the same time, driving online and IRL engagement."

Issue 2 of *P+*, themed *Dance*, coincided with a group show curated by Prowse and Claire Wearn, Photoworks curator (maternity cover), in a large warehouse space at Peckham24 photo festival, and alongside contributions from Webber Gallery and Der Greif. Including live performances and video installations as well as photography, this south London event was dynamic and youth-orientated, and made a virtue of the fact that Photoworks has no permanent space. "Part of my strategic plan while leading Photoworks was embracing the fact that we didn't have a physical venue," says Mavlian.

"I felt like this had always been seen as a negative in the past, but I wanted to own it and embrace it as a positive. What this meant was that, instead of audiences coming to us, we could go to them and meet them where they were already gathered, like at Peckham 24. We focused on building great partnerships, which meant we could show up at places that already had a physical audience and physical infrastructure."

This thinking proved especially valuable in 2020, when the pandemic hit and real-life events fell victim to lockdowns and social distancing. Without a physical venue, Photoworks' overheads remained low, and with a new website, launched in spring 2020, the organisation could still reach audiences. Photoworks also left its office at the University of Brighton, moving into a much smaller space that remains its base today; it primarily serves as an archive and storage room, while the staff work remotely. Photoworks' remit was national by this point and disengaging from an office meant its staff could be based all over the UK – as well as continuing to work through Covid.

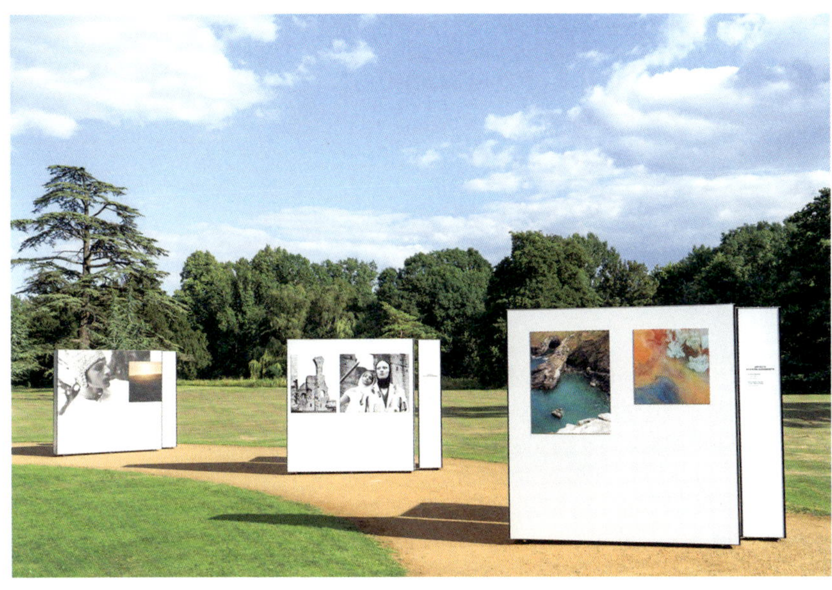

A partnership for young artists with English Heritage and Shout Out Loud, England's New Lenses launched in 2018 and was so successful it went on to be exhibited at Wrest Park, Bedfordshire.

COVID YEARS

Photoworks kept operating throughout the pandemic in fact, none of the staff were put on furlough and all programming continued, albeit sometimes in adapted forms. Prowse edited a new issue of the annual in 2020 to mark its 25th anniversary, and the organisation launched an accessible version of the festival the same year, utilising outdoor spaces and billboards in Brighton. Themed *Propositions for Alternative Narratives*, and rebranded Photoworks Festival, it featured a truly international cohort of artists including Farah Al Qasimi, Sethembile Msezane and Guanyu Xu.

The artists' work was also made available as a set of broadsheet-style prints, which users could curate as they chose; the so-called *Festival in a Box* was Covid-proof and accessible, and a challenge to traditional hierarchies. "We were already questioning the traditional festival model prior to the pandemic, and Covid made us push the idea further," says Mavlian. "We were interested in deconstructing the festival model, to think about accessibility, freedom of movement and environmental sustainability. It was also about rethinking power structures and handing over power, so the audience became the curator."

Mavlian adds that commissioning and supporting artists remained key to Photoworks, both in the pandemic and beyond. Expanding decisively beyond the southeast, Photoworks set up partnerships with organisations with national reach and infrastructure, and reached out to artists who might otherwise go underrepresented. *England's New Lenses* was a project with four young artists initiated by Juliette Buss in 2018 with English Heritage and Shout Out Loud. Originally planned for online dissemination only, the work by Kemka Ajoku, Abena Appiah, Megan Mechelle Dalton and Mia Parker-Tang was so strong that it culminated in an exhibition at Wrest Park, Bedfordshire, and a publication. Buss, head of L&E at Photoworks, describes this project in detail in her interview (see pages 17-23).

In 2021, Photoworks launched a new award, the Ampersand/Photoworks Fellowship. Aimed at mid-career artists, this award went to Johny Pitts in the first year, who created new work titled *Home Is Not a Place*, which went on to be shown at Graves Gallery, Sheffield, Stills Gallery, Edinburgh, and The Photographers' Gallery, London. The 2023 winner, Felicity Hammond, is working on an ambitious, evolving set of *Variations*, large-scale installations exploring digital imaging, artificial intelligence, mining, and surveillance; she is being supported by Photoworks curator Danit Ariel and assistant curator Amin Yousefi.

Mavlian departed Photoworks in late 2022 to head up The Photographers' Gallery; programming such as the Ampersand/Photoworks Fellowship and the Jerwood/Photoworks Award continued, as did the annual. Issues 30 and 31, titled *The Thing* and *Multi Multi* and published in 2023 and 2024, questioned the medium of photography and the ideology embodied in it, gathering work by international artists who are subverting how images frame and reproduce reality. *Multi Multi* was launched with events in London, Brighton and Paris, the latter a symposium on photographic technology arranged with The Photographers' Gallery, Der Greif and *Foam Magazine*.

Louise Fedotov-Clements joined Photoworks as director in winter 2023, having previously led QUAD's artistic direction for 20 years (among other roles including co-founding and directing Format International Photography festival). Like Mavlian, Fedotov-Clements is clear that Photoworks' major contribution is in "supporting the living, breathing ecosystem" of photography, commissioning and assisting people who are making and writing about images, across the whole of the UK – and, increasingly, beyond. "I describe Photoworks as the UK's leading development agency for photography, working nationally, internationally, and also very locally," she says.

"That includes all ages, from early years to more established, and also includes

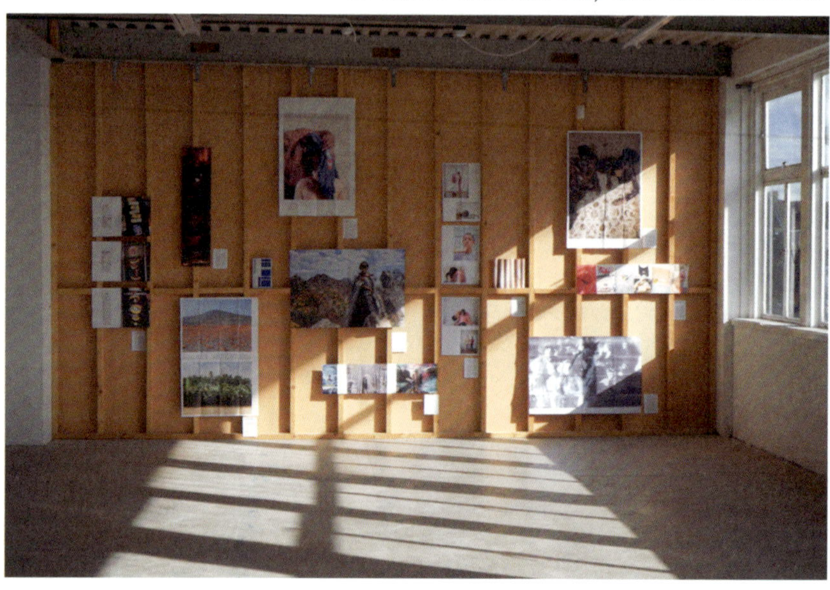

As Covid hit in 2020, Photoworks launched the *Festival in a Box*, a collection of artists' images that users could curate as they chose.

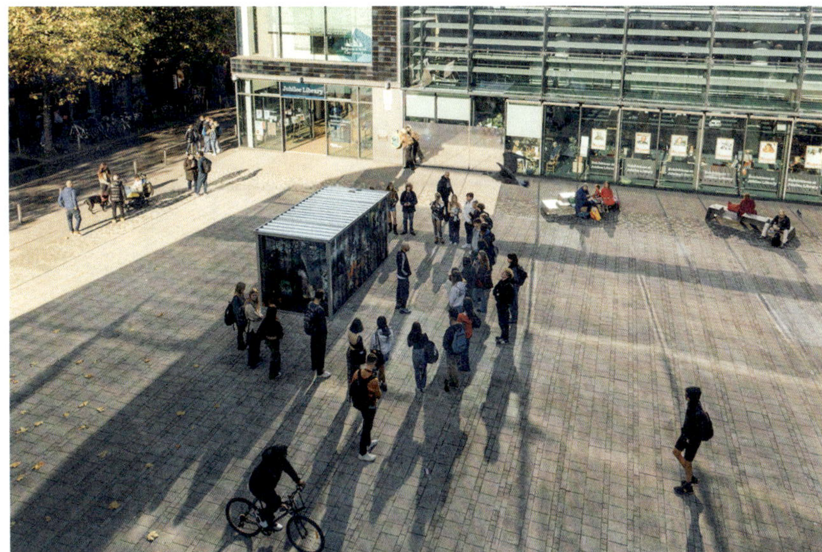

developmental intent around photography," she continues. "So we now have seed grants [launched with MPB in 2025] to help people develop momentum around going to see something, or having a conversation with somebody, or asking someone to write a text for them, or facilitating their network."

CONTEMPORARY WORK

Fedotov-Clements sees the potential of online networks – "Our digital programme is enormous, charting the digital territories" – but is also keen to create in-person opportunities to create or expand networks. She spearheaded events such as the Photoworks Summit in spring 2024, and the Photoworks Weekender in autumn 2024; both were held in Brighton and the latter involved close partnerships with local institutions such as Brighton University, Dreamy Place and Photoworks artist-led development programme Peer Matters. The first iteration of Hammond's *Variations, VI: Content Aware,* also opened during the Photoworks Weekender, before moving on to Format Festival, QUAD, The Photographers' Gallery, London, and Stills Gallery, Edinburgh.

Fedotov-Clements adds that Photoworks' definition of photography is broad and understood in terms of the familiar still image but also expanded media, cross-sector collaboration, society and social change; she emphasises the importance of Buss's work in Learning & Engagement, and its integration into the wider programme. Buss is creating a network of Photography Champions, for example, who support photography in their area, however that manifests. "We want to develop those legacy programmes on the ground, and support and facilitate the growth of photography as a medium, but also as a creative career – and support audience engagement – and best practice as well," says Fedotov-Clements. "Through our equality, diversity and inclusion work, and our understanding of best practice for access for neuro-spicy, neuro-divergent, diverse, disabled and other perspectives, we want to ensure our thought leadership – in the way that we do things and support others to learn through that process, but also how we learn from them too."

In 2024, Photoworks partnered with Project Art Works and Aspex Gallery, Portsmouth, as part of the *Explorers* programme, to show new work by Lauren Joy Kennett exploring her experience of living with undiagnosed autism, *Sorry I'm Not Sorry*; Photoworks also partnered with Jane & Jeremy to co-publish this work as a photobook. Fedotov-Clements points to the latest iteration of Photoworks' English Heritage x Shout Out Loud collaboration too, which allowed emerging artists Sally Barton, Serena Burgis and Yuxi Hou to develop new work around stone circles and display it in Stonehenge visitor centre.

Meanwhile, Photoworks is also developing its international contacts, mentoring the Bakashimika International Photography Festival in Zambia and collaborating with partners in Brazil, Hong Kong, Singapore, Japan, South Korea, Lagos and Uganda. Photoworks joined forces with PhEST in Italy and the Italian Cultural Institute to commission Piero Percoco to make new work in Brighton, shown at PhEST and in this annual. Fedotov-Clements also plans to reintroduce a physical photography festival to Brighton in 2026, though she says Photoworks now has an opportunity to consider what a festival is, why it happens, and what its long-term impact can be. The organisation has a duty of care, she adds, "of being good ancestors really".

"You know, with a 30-year legacy, at Photoworks, we are obviously custodians of an organisation that's changed hands many times," she reflects. "But we are fortunate to be an Arts Council NPO and to have programmes that are proving to be vital for us and our partners. It's important to value that, and to continue to adapt, innovate and develop."

Felicity Hammond, the 2023 Ampersand/Photoworks Fellowship winner, launched her ambitious *Variations* project at the Photoworks Weekender event in 2024 in Brighton.

ART OF ENGAGEMENT

JULIETTE BUSS INTERVIEW

ART OF ENGAGEMENT

The longest-standing Photoworks staff member – and working at Brighton Photo Biennial prior to that – Juliette Buss has created an award-winning Learning and Engagement programme that has made key differences to audiences and artists alike, finds Diane Smyth.

Photoworks is well known for its exhibitions, commissions, festivals and publishing, work that has a public face (as well as great efforts behind the scenes). But alongside these events lies a rich Learning and Engagement (L&E) programme, working at grass roots to support schoolchildren, young adults, individuals with additional needs and members of marginalised communities in engaging with and learning about photography. Often invisible to a wider audience, this programme provides critical input in helping people access and question the power of images.

It's masterminded by Juliette Buss, whose involvement with Photoworks dates back to 2011 – and before that to 2001 with Brighton Photo Festival – making her by far the longest-standing staff member. Buss is a leader in her field, who won the Marsh Award for Excellence in Gallery Education in 2017, but she emphasises the importance of collaboration in her efforts. She points out that she works with an L&E team, and notes she really found her feet when she found the confidence to develop longer-term programmes with communities, "to be more ambitious with the partnerships that were being developed".

PEOPLE'S ART

Buss has been involved with art all her life, having grown up in the rambling Nicholas Treadwell Gallery near Canterbury, which championed the Superhumanist 'people's art movement' ["Just Google 'Nicholas Treadwell' and all the craziness will come up!"]. She studied fine art at De Montfort University, Leicester, then moved to Brighton. Volunteering at the Fabrica Gallery, she realised she wanted to make a career out of opening access to, and dismantling, the hierarchies around art and galleries. Deciding she needed to know more about L&E and gallery education, she trained as an art teacher at the University of Brighton, "though I said from the start I didn't want to be an art teacher".

She then freelanced for three years until Jeremy Millar got in touch, explaining he was curator of the first Brighton Photo Biennial, to be held in 2003, and asking if she would like to head up the L&E. "He was, like, 'We're setting up this festival, do you want to come and give it a go?'" says Buss. "There was nothing [in place], it was literally from the ground up."

Buss says she was inexperienced, and particularly with photography because she hadn't studied the medium; she has come to see the latter as a strength, as it means she brings other perspectives, but at the time felt awkward about her lack of knowledge. Drawing on her teacher training, she created a project in which local primary school kids were given cameras and talked through the festival themes, and their resulting portraits and collages were put on display. "I remember I'd never hung an exhibition before, and all of a sudden, I had these schools' work and I had to put it on a gallery wall," she says. "But Jeremy was great. He taught me how! He taught me everything at that point really, but it opened into letting me shape things into how I thought they should be."

Buss adds that this project emulated the way a teacher might run a project in a school, and was 'tacked on' at the end of the festival programming. But she quickly realised she could take a different approach, capitalising on the fact that Brighton Photo Biennial (and later Photoworks) was run by a small team whose members worked well together, and developing close relationships with artists such as Helen Cammock and Annis Joslin – who placed participation at the heart of their work. Choosing to let artists run the projects became central, she says, ensuring children who might otherwise never meet an artist "get to see that they are a real thing, a real person, and that art is a real career". She also quickly shifted to working with secondary schools, where her input could have the most impact.

Getting involved with the organisation Engage, the National Association for Gallery Education, Buss became an area representative for the southeast "during those whole early days, thinking about visual literacy and community engagement"; she says this deeply influenced the way she approaches developing projects. She adds that the 2000s were an optimistic time in the UK, with institutions such as the Baltic Centre for Contemporary Art, Walsall Gallery and, later, Turner Contemporary all opening, and putting community at the heart of their programmes. Sir Ken Robinson was also instrumental in the development of Arts Council England's Creative Partnerships programme at that time, an educationalist passionate about fostering children's creativity. Funding was more generous and, with the biennial happening every two years, Buss had time to "try to figure out where the learning sat, and how and why it was connected to the festival".

Then, in 2010, Martin Parr curated Brighton Photo Biennial and commissioned new work from Molly Landreth and Zoe

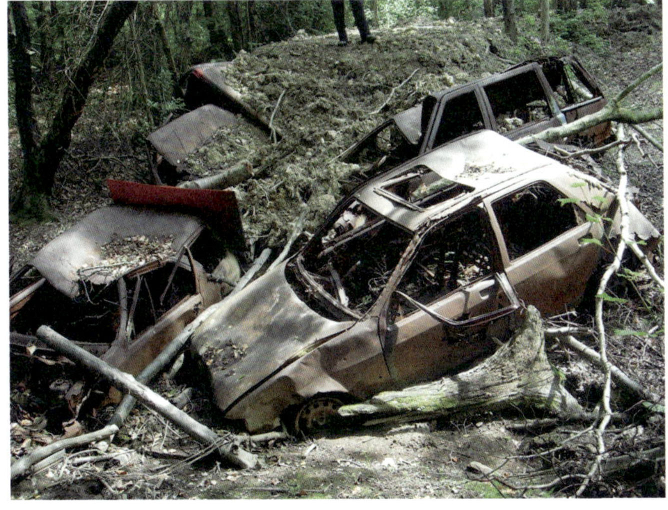

Coghurst Wood, Kez from the Hillcrest School Project with the late Danny Wilson; 2006.

Strauss, who created an exhibition named *Queer Brighton* exploring everyday LGBTQ+ life in the city. Buss was asked to support engagement with local communities, and for the first time saw how L&E could help artists create, not just draw on their activities. "It's not a criticism because it's how things worked then, things were brought into the city," says Buss. "Brighton Photo Fringe worked at grassroots with locals, but we were very different. It was the first time I had been asked to engage with communities as part of the exhibition development, and I realised that this was a different way of working. I realised my work could feed into the shaping of an exhibition."

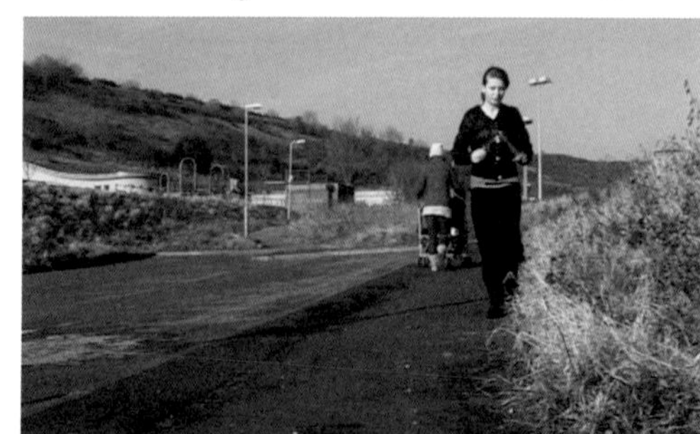

PHOTOWORKS YEARS

Brighton Photo Biennial and Photoworks merged in 2011 and Buss was absorbed into the wider Photoworks team; Celia Davies, as acting director then director, encouraged her to form a closer partnership with Photoworks' in-house curators, and invited her to be part of the programming team for the annual. "I was feeding into these conversations at a curatorial level, which meant I could have a much more integrated approach to programming, learning, engagement with curatorial vision, and those outputs could be shared," Buss says.

The 2014 festival included an outdoor exhibition on large light boxes in central Brighton titled *Looking into the Family Album*, for example, a project created with many pupils across two large Brighton secondary schools for Art at Work – a two-year Arts Council England-funded programme, led by Photoworks and Lighthouse in partnership with the Aldridge Foundation. Year 10 and 11 students from the Brighton and Portslade Aldridge Community Academies collaborated with artist James Casey in facilitated workshops to create their own staged family albums, inspired by artists such as Cindy Sherman and Thomas Demand. Producing giant backdrops and costumes, the kids constructed fantasy group portraits, which made a lively addition to the festival.

For the 2016 festival, Photoworks teamed up with Fabrica to commission Ewen Spencer, meanwhile, who is known for his work with young people and youth culture. Spencer collaborated with youngsters to create large portraits, which were installed at large scale in the space; the kids also got involved with

Whitehawk Walk, Film Still from *Together Alone* with young people and artists Helen Cammock, Denis Doran, Rosie Holmes; 2009.

the exhibition, with Buss and her team taking over for an afternoon to create a fun event for them. Bringing popcorn, ice cream, DJs and artist-led workshops, they attracted more than 1,000 youngsters into the gallery in just a few hours – the first time many had visited.

BEYOND SCHOOLS

By this point, Buss was thinking more widely around L&E, and setting up partnerships outside educational settings with local community groups. Identifying a need, she developed programmes for youngsters facing disadvantage or struggling with mental health; Photoworks runs Queer youth programmes, for example, in which "vulnerable young people can use photography to unpick what they can't express with words". "Photography is such a powerful tool in helping people through mental health challenges," Buss adds.

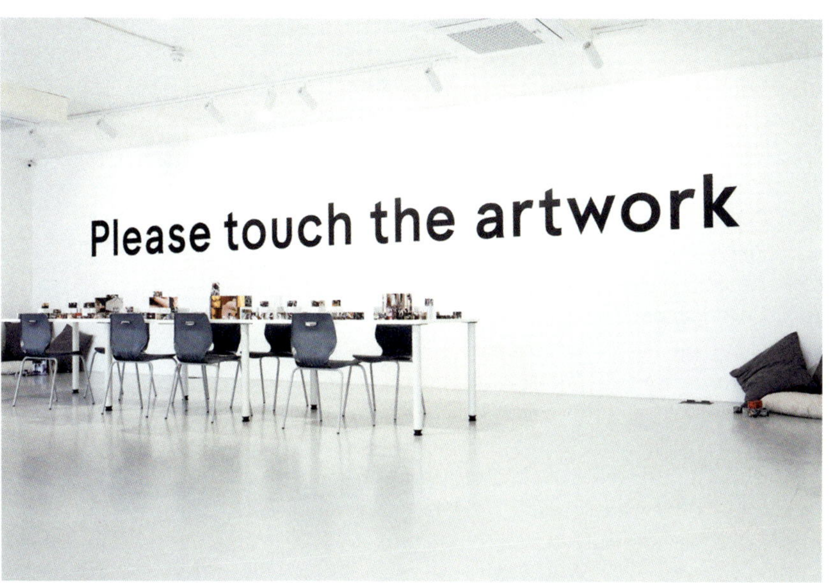

In 2016, with Davies, Buss started working with Project Art Works on the major, multi-partner Arts Council partnership for the national Explorers programme, which facilitates and commissions work by neurodivergent artists. It's a project with a personal dimension for Buss, because her sister has Down's Syndrome; when the first pilot was announced she jumped at the opportunity, she says, recognising that it was an opportunity to learn how better to engage and support neurodiverse adults and children.

But doing so was a complex process, with Photoworks taking time at the start to consult and reflect before realising that what was needed was a new, inclusive model for commissioning work, and practical help. Researching and developing new opportunities in photography for adults with high levels of complex support needs, Buss developed partnerships with adult social care providers, such as the day centres who work with them. She then set up an action research training programme, led by Annis Joslin, which paired experienced artist facilitators with support workers at the centres, so they could together explore working creatively with photography in these settings.

In 2019, Photoworks and Project Art Works co-commissioned new work that shifted the parameters of how a commission might usually work. Claire Wearn, Photoworks curator (maternity cover) and Buss created a different type of brief on how to apply for the opportunity, and held open forums to help advise potential applicants; they also created PDFs with easy-to-read and speech functionalities, and included a neurodiverse panel in the decision-making and commissioning process. Anna Farley, who describes herself as an autistic artist, was selected to undertake the commission, supported by Buss, Wearn and artist Becky Warnock, Farley's support worker at that time.

Photoworks exhibited Farley's work at the Phoenix in Brighton, alongside the resulting images from the action research programme with neurodiverse adults, artist facilitators and support workers. Explorers is now an ongoing project, with learning from the first iteration brought to bear on the second, and shared with others in conferences around rights and representation. "Key to a lot of this way of working is recognising when you're not part of a community, you don't have that lived experience," notes Buss. "So what gives you the right to come in and say how it should be? There is tentative partnership building, and then agendas are shared so we can come up with a common ambition."

This gives you a score of 0, Anna Farley, installation view, Syl Ojalla, part of the Explorers Project; 2019.

Buss also set up a partnership with English Heritage, which was using its long-term National Lottery Heritage Fund support to research, develop and pilot youth engagement work, with national partners such as the National Youth Theatre and Council for British Archaeology. This partnership featured photography clubs and an online mass participatory project; eventually, these initiatives led to more ambitious commissions, in which photographers aged 18–25 were offered fees and mentoring to make new work, in English Heritage sites across the UK. The resulting images by Kemka Ajoku, Abena Appiah, Megan Mechelle Dalton and Mia Parker-Tang were exhibited as a major outdoor exhibition at Wrest Park and published in 2019 as *England's New Lenses*.

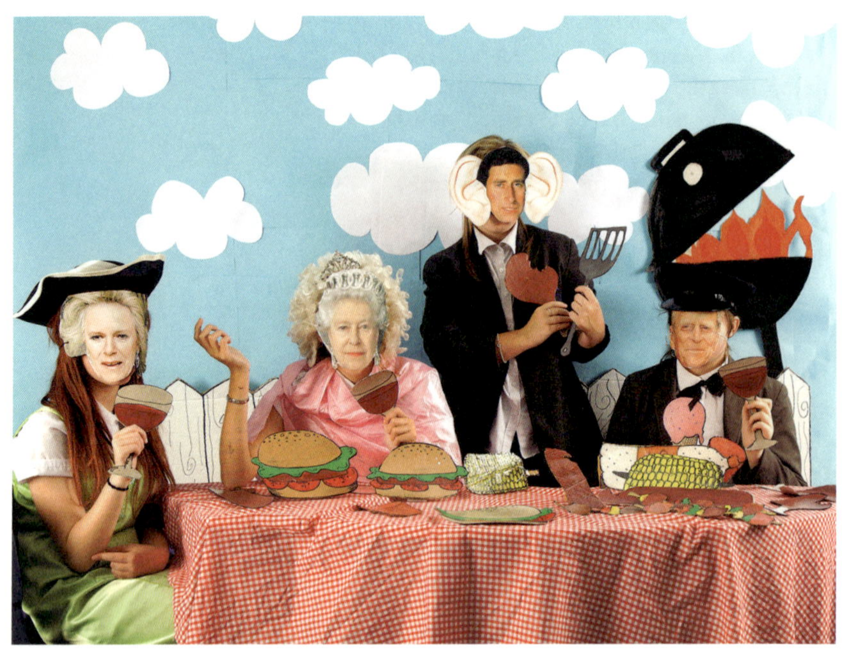

This project was created in close collaboration with Photoworks' curatorial programme, and in particular Photoworks curator Julia Bunnemann. "It was approached like a curatorial commission," says Buss. "Julia and I worked closely together, tackling it as a commissioning model but building in mentoring and training, looking at what support we'd need to add to enable a young person to be commissioned. There was a certain tension, in that Photoworks and English Heritage wanted something that could stand up in a public space with an audience. But one of the things I've learnt over the years is that young people rarely let you down on that front. The quality of the work and the ideas are never a problem.

"The problem can be your expectation, because if you invite them [to make images] you have to give them the freedom to respond how they want to respond. Quite often, that's totally different to your expectation."

NATIONAL REMIT

Explorers and *England's New Lenses* stretched across the UK, rather than being based in Brighton or the southeast; working nationally is now part of Buss's remit, after Covid, a change in director (Shoair Mavlian took over in 2018) and new funding commitments. Buss resisted this at first, she says, wary of "parachuting in" and working short-term, but was happier to do so after devising a partnership-centred approach. The key is to establish "where you can support what's already happening, and meet a need that someone else has identified", she says, ensuring everything is bespoke and (as with *England's New Lenses*) relinquishing some control.

Photoworks now runs a Photography Champions network, with hubs in five locations – Portsmouth, Barnsley, Dudley, Blackpool, and Medway. The idea is that there is a representative in each area, who has seed funding and is responsible for making things happen, but within an existing framework. "Their work is embedded in what's already happening in that place, so it's different in each location because they all have different cultural ecosystems," says Buss. In Portsmouth, Photoworks has supported a community darkroom to secure significant Arts Council funding for a space and a three-

The Royal BBQ, part of *Looking into the Family Album*, with artist Marysa Dowling and students from Portslade Aldridge Community Academy; 2014.

year programme, for example. In Barnsley, it has facilitated a research project with the University of Leeds exploring barriers that students face to entering the photography sector, as well as portfolio reviews and supporting artists' careers.

"They're not necessarily young people [in Barnsley]," explains Buss. "There the question of access to arts is more a class issue. It's thinking about community and photography in broadest terms and access, so it's not just about people who have been to university and trained as photographers."

With Photoworks now headed up by Louise Fedotov-Clements and given an increasingly international scope, the L&E programme is expanding beyond the UK. Again, partnerships are key, as is a close connection with the Photoworks curatorial team. Photoworks recently worked with the Chennai Photo Biennale on its exhibition of children's photography, *What Makes Me Click!*, which included the Photoworks/The National Gallery/ Brighton & Hove Museums project Hey, Rembrandt!, facilitated by Alejandra Carles-Tolra. The tie-up with Chennai Photo also included a darkroom residency in the city, supported by the British Council and open to residents in Chennai and the UK.

Buss is also thinking beyond galleries and darkrooms towards photography as a wider cultural practice. Photoworks L&E has partnered with the Marine Conservation Society on beach cleans, she says, which weren't photo-led but instead engaged with "photography as a tool for social change, as much as it is an art form". She says visual literacy is increasingly important, particularly for young people, as we are exposed to an ever-increasing flow of images via commercial and media sources and social media. "As a parent of a young person, I feel that giving support on navigating that world has become part of the learning programme's responsibility," she says.

"Young people are struggling and suffering through that whole currency of images, and helping them gain more agency and control over how they are seen and how others see them has become important in a way that it wasn't 20-odd years ago. It's massive in a way we can't get our heads around."

She wants to go full circle and re-engage with schools, "because the climate has shifted, and the exposure that young people get to photography and art in school is rapidly diminishing"; either way, she says making and talking about images is essential, helping individuals to engage with – and understand – the power of photography. "I've seen it even with small children," she smiles. "They've made cyanotypes, they've put objects on paper, and that's great. They've learnt how sunlight works and how light-sensitive paper works. And then they have also learnt about mark-making, the camera, their place and how they interpret it, and how they have agency over all of that.

"How do you read and understand images, how do you make images?" she adds. "The two go together. I don't like to do one without the other."

PAST PERFECT

25

THE VILLAGE
1993

In 1993, Anna Fox was commissioned to document life in a rural village in south England by the Photoworks predecessor, The Cross Channel Photography Mission. Shooting in the community that her mother grew up in, Fox recorded rural events such as Halloween celebrations, weddings and fetes, picking out sinister elements lurking within a seemingly bucolic way of life. She drew inspiration from images made around the UK by Sir Benjamin Stone in the 1900s, but with a contemporary twist; when exhibiting The Village at Worthing Museum, East Sussex, in 1993, she collaborated with curator Val Williams to create innovative installations of photographs, projections and sound recordings.

Born in 1961 in Alton, Hampshire, Fox graduated in audiovisual studies from the West Surrey College of Art & Design, in Farnham. Her early *Work Stations* project, a look at office culture in the Thatcher years, was published by and exhibited at Camerawork, in London, in 1988. Fox has had solo shows at institutions such as The Photographers' Gallery, in London, and the Shanghai Center of Photography, and been included in group shows at the Barbican Art Gallery and Tate Britain, both in London, and Les Rencontres de la Photographie, in Arles, France. Fox is professor of photography at the University for the Creative Arts in Farnham and leads the Fast Forward: Women in Photography research project.

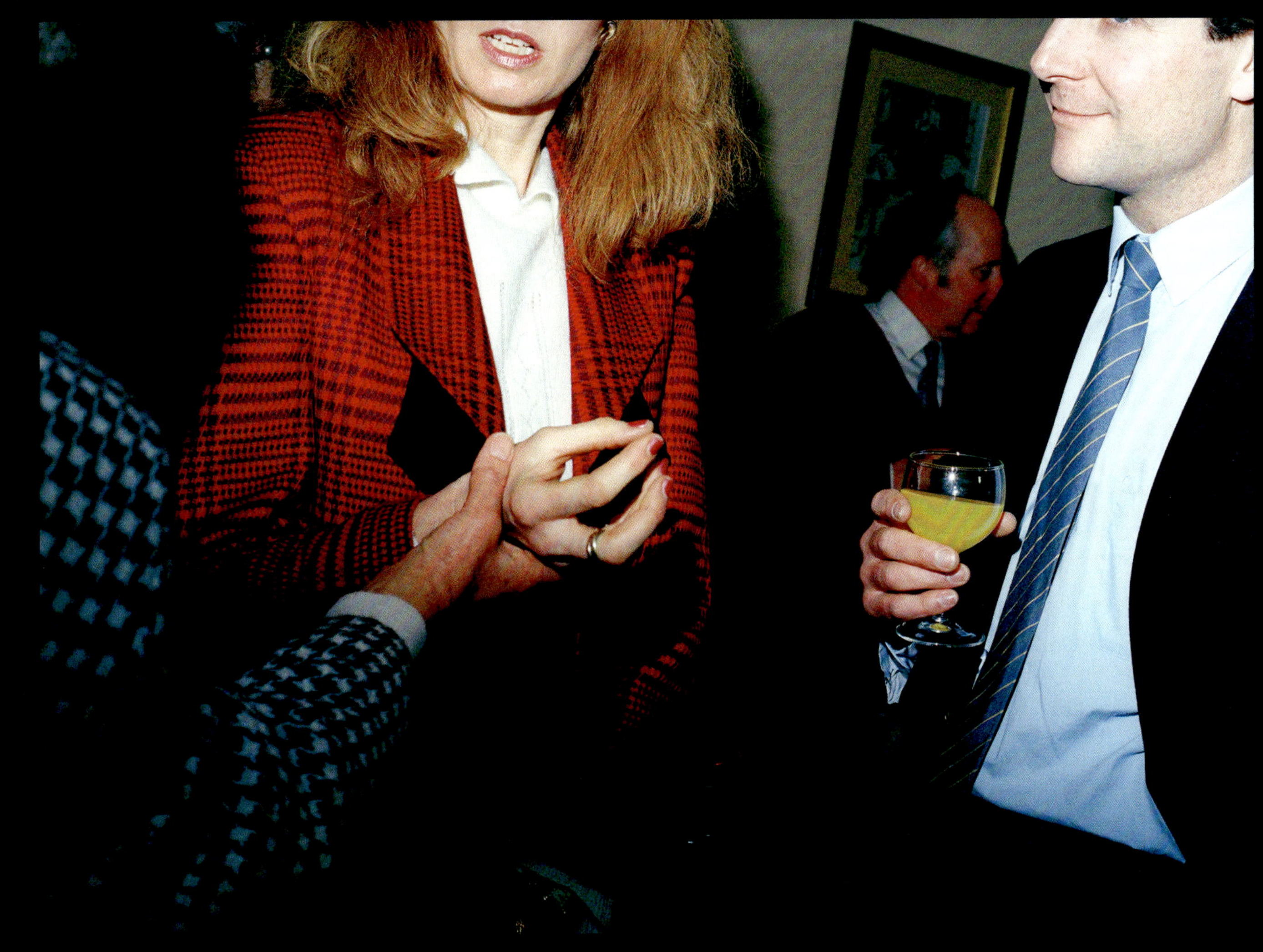

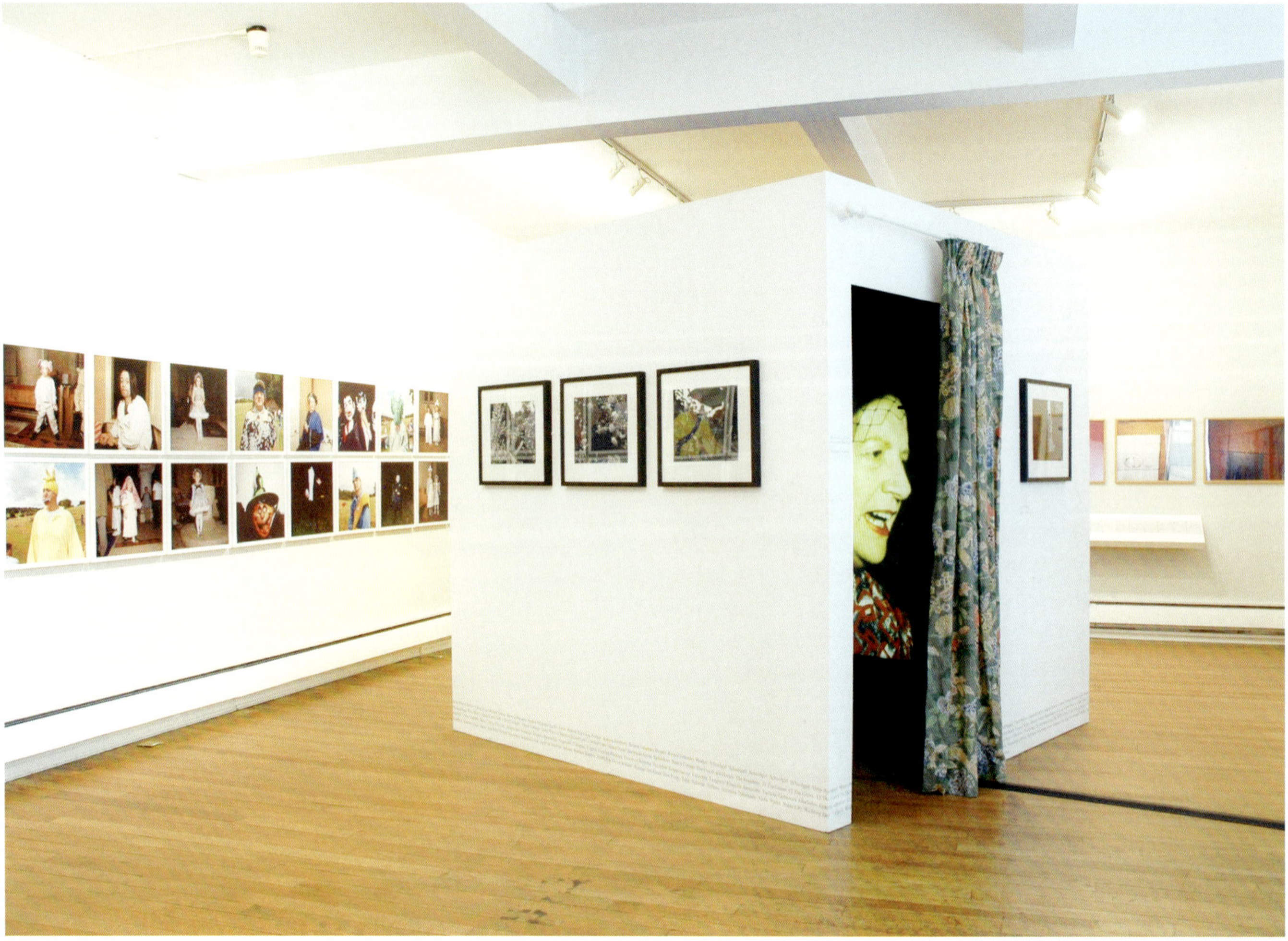

Access the sound recordings via this QR Code.

Anna Fox collaborated with curator Val Williams when exhibiting *The Village* at Worthing Museum, East Sussex, creating innovative installations of photographs, projections and sound recordings. Image courtesy Anna Fox.

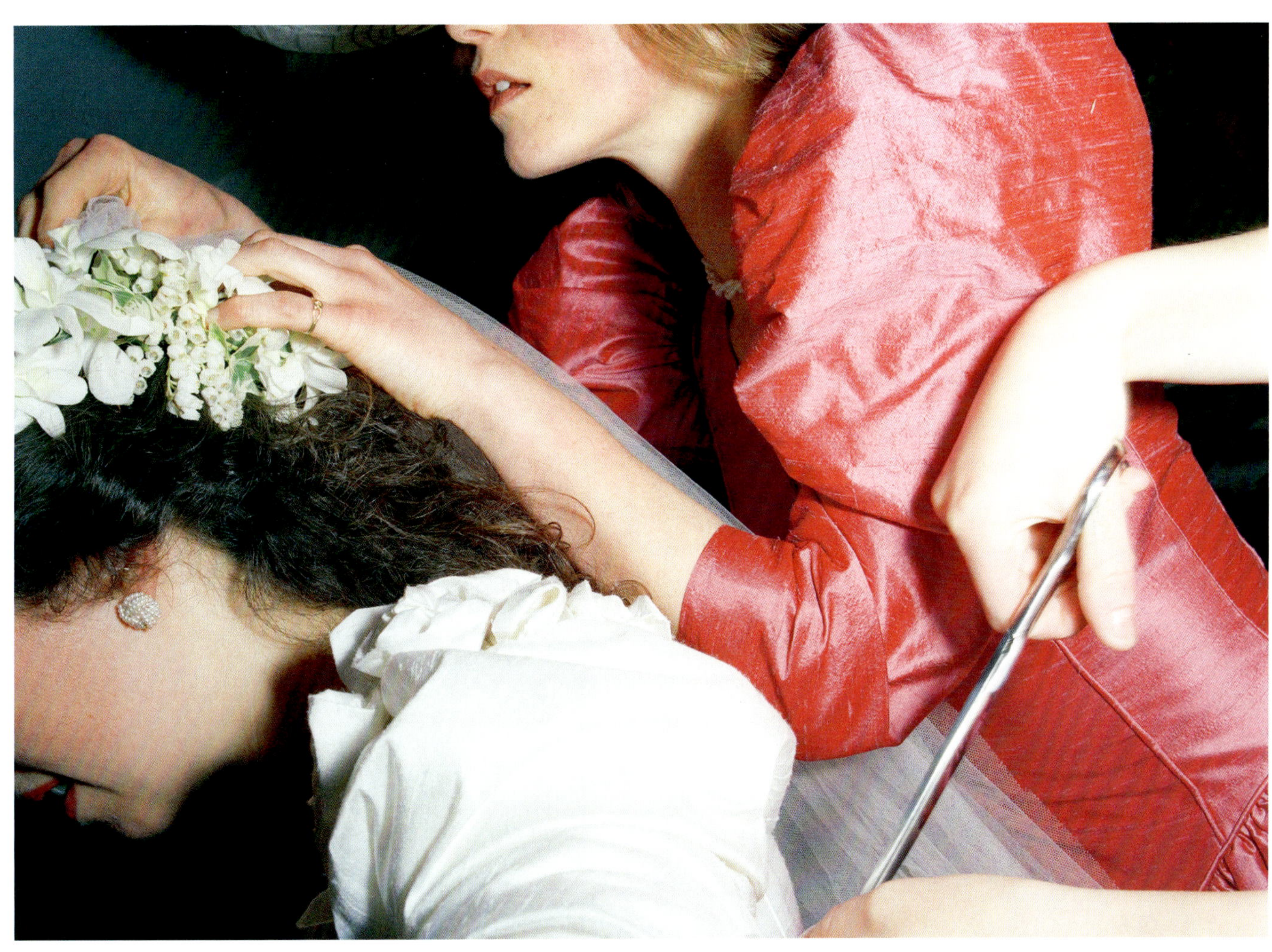

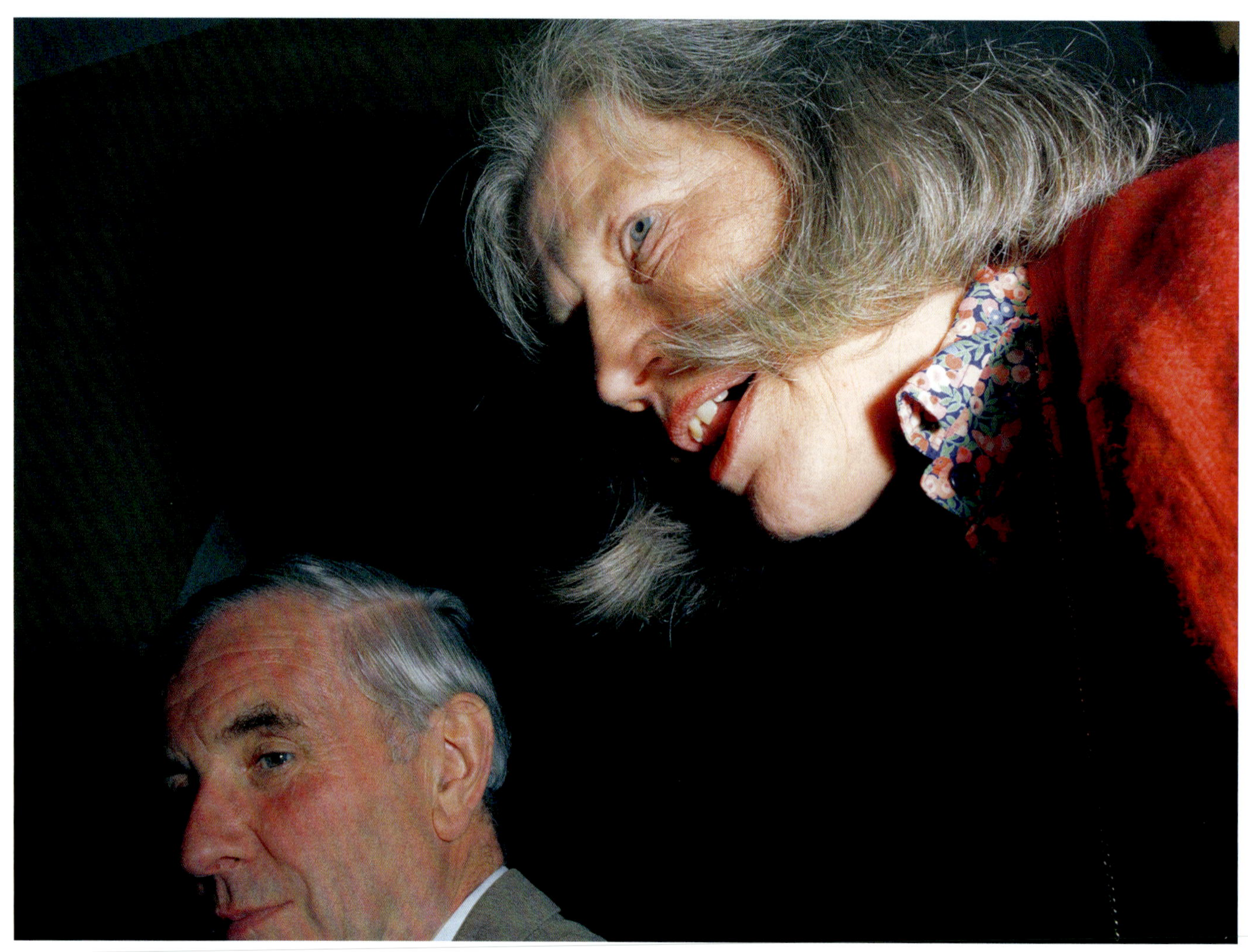

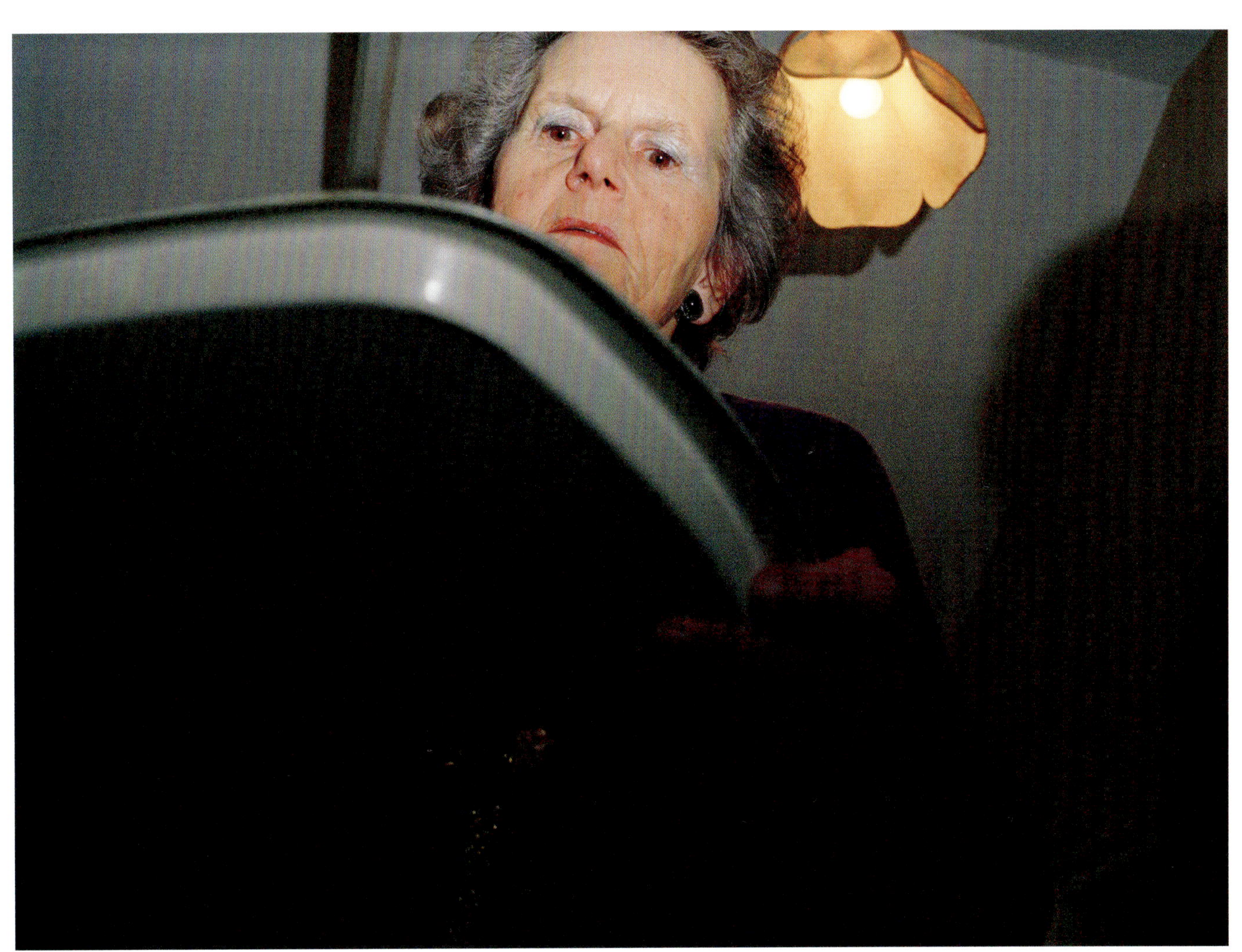

THE WHOLE STORY 2000

In 1999, Photoworks commissioned Helen Sear to undertake a year-long residency at Maidstone museum and library, two separate institutions located next to each other. Conscious of her position as an outsider, Sear questioned the narratives on show, making images that blurred the boundaries between public and private. Opting to work in the museum's storerooms, she documented usually-hidden pieces and curators' neat notes; on exhibiting this work, she drew further attention to this behind-the-scenes labour, re-cataloguing her images as large, numbered composites, stuck directly onto the wall. In the library, she asked visitors to read aloud from their books and recorded them, subverting both the act of reading to oneself and the convention of silence in the space. When showing the resulting videos she gave viewers the same benches as her subjects, confusing the border between observer and observed.

Helen Sear graduated in fine art in 1979 and went on to take postgraduate studies at the Slade, University College London; in 2015 she became the first woman to represent Wales with a solo show at the Venice Biennale. Sear was awarded a PhD by publication in 2009, and worked with Photoworks again from 2017 to 2020 on the Connect - 3Ts Hospital Redevelopment Commission.

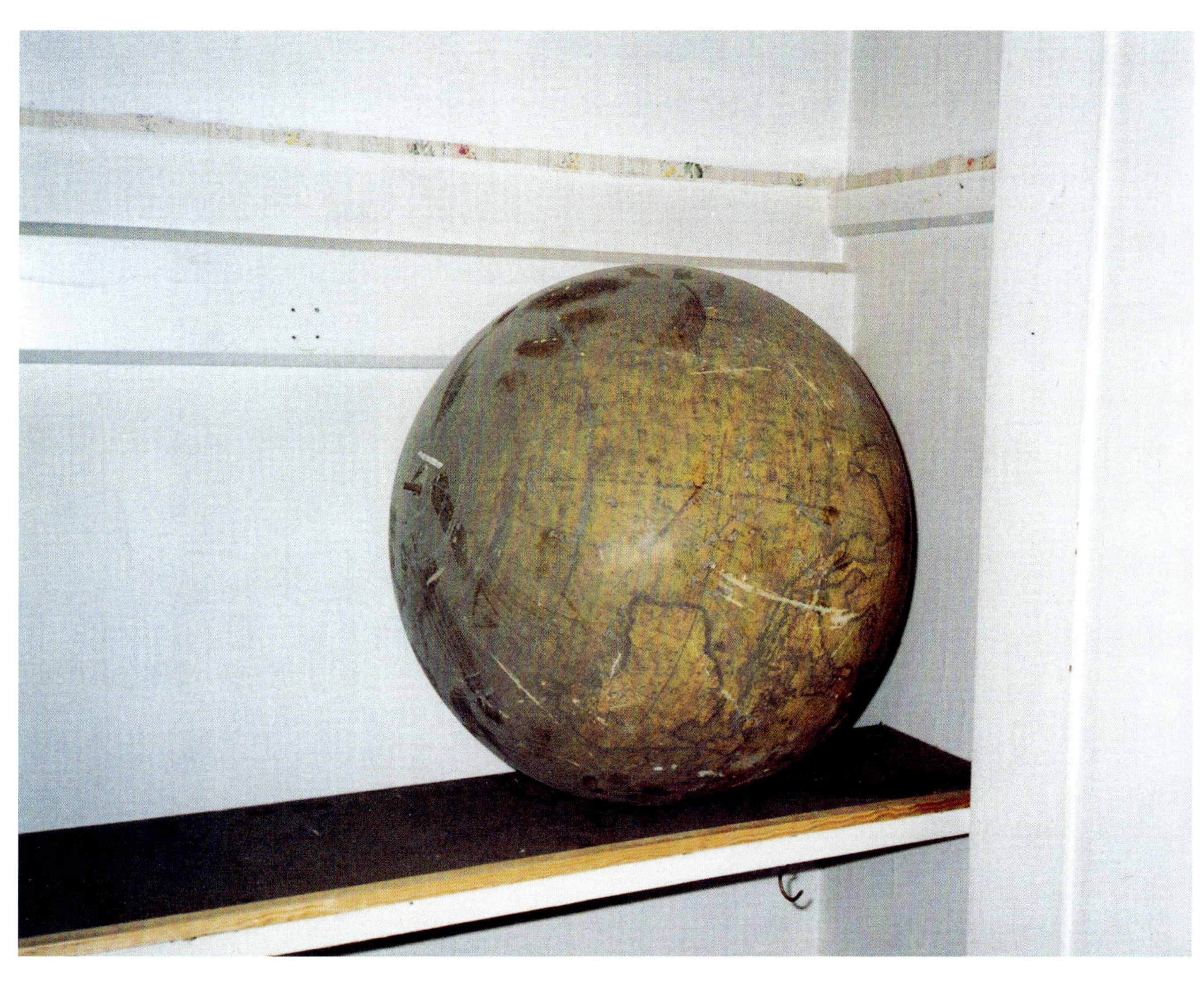

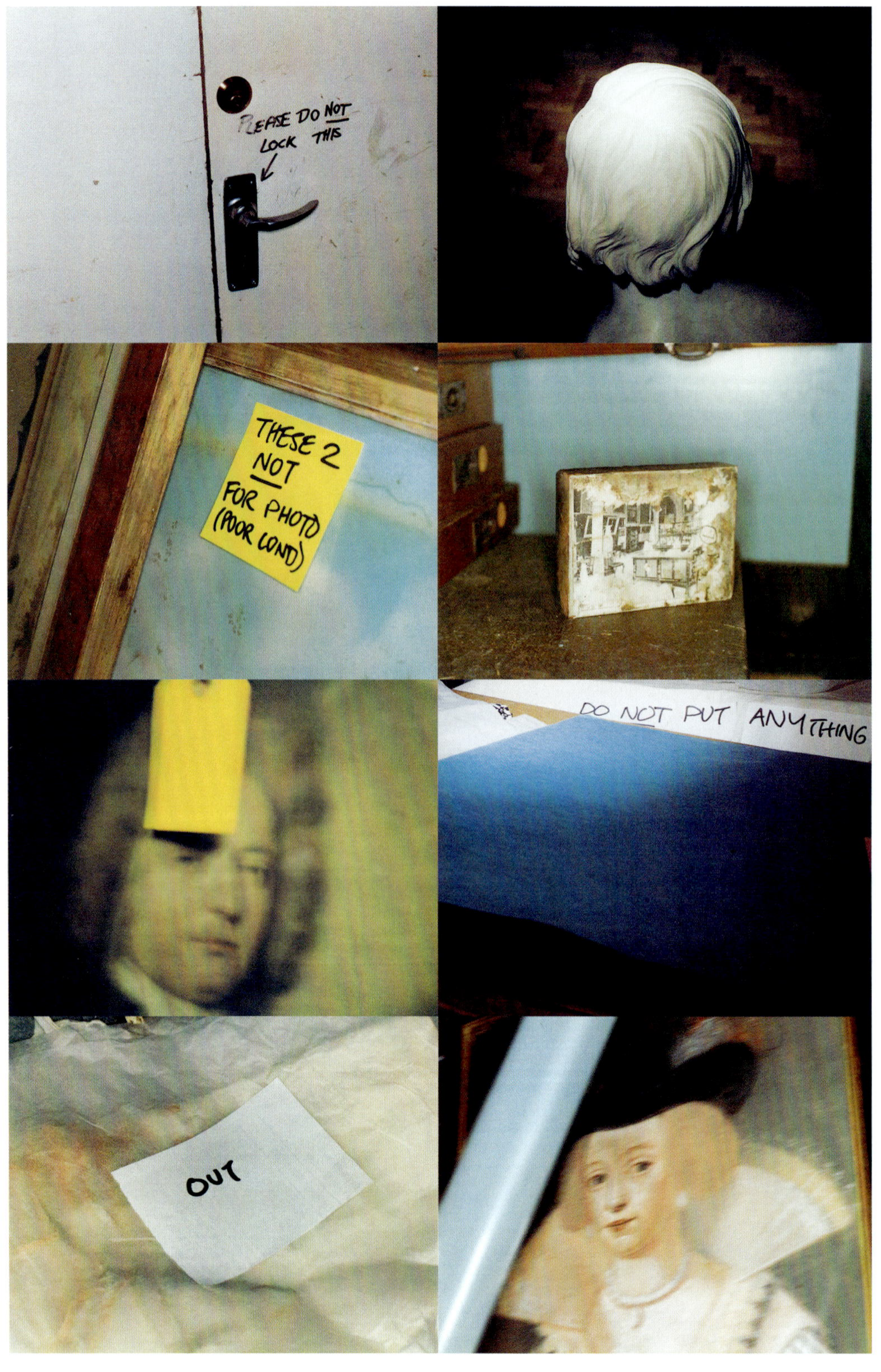
PLEASE DO NOT
LOCK THIS
THESE 2
NOT
FOR PHOTO
(POOR COND)
DO NOT PUT ANYTHING
OUT

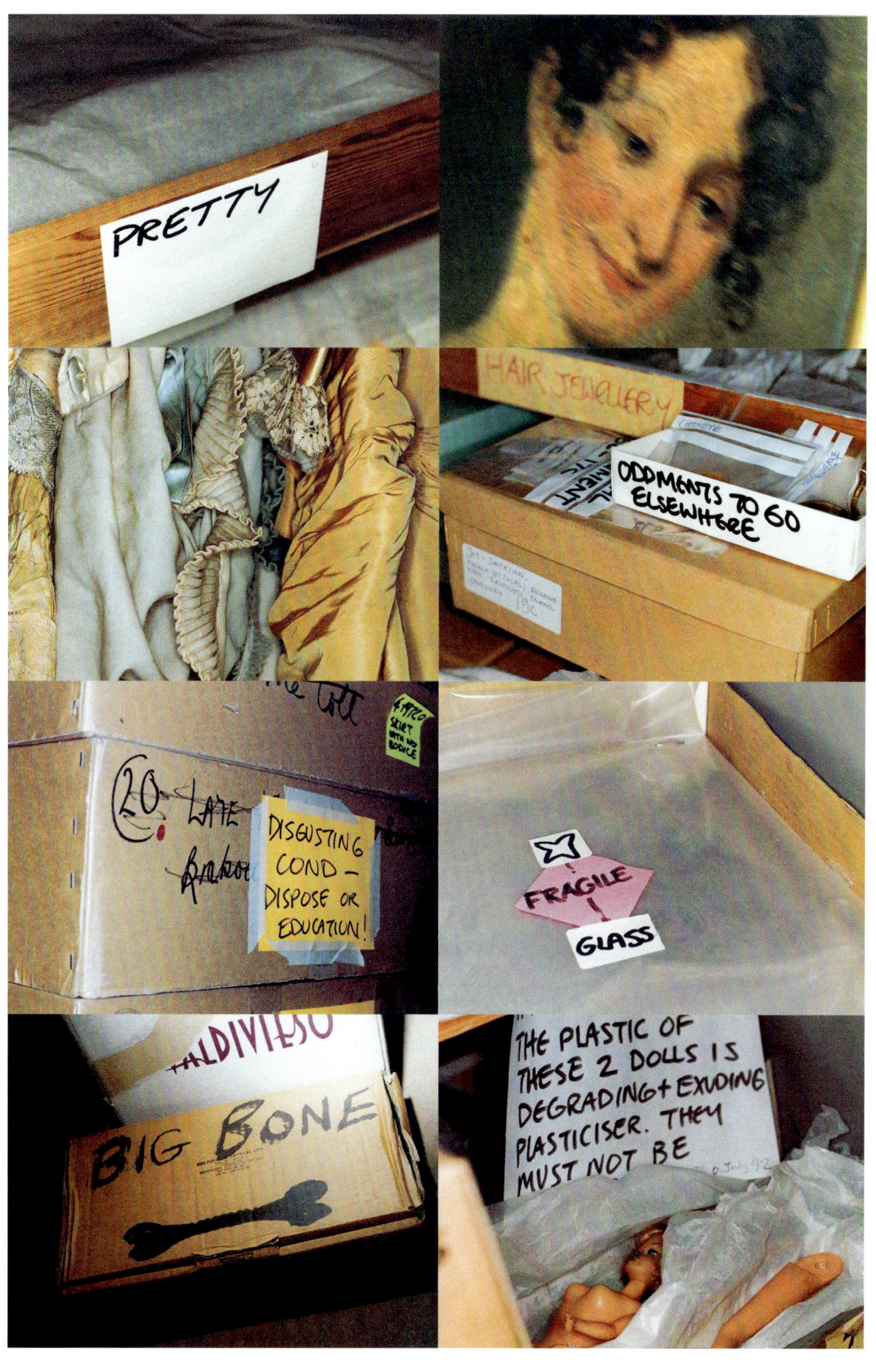
PRETTY
HAIR JEWELLERY
ODDMENTS TO GO ELSEWHERE
DISGUSTING COND – DISPOSE OR EDUCATION!
FRAGILE
GLASS
BIG BONE
THE PLASTIC OF THESE 2 DOLLS IS DEGRADING + EXUDING PLASTICISER. THEY MUST NOT BE

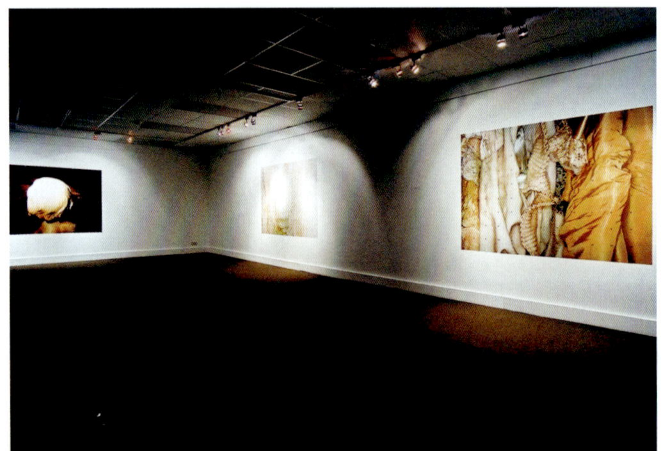

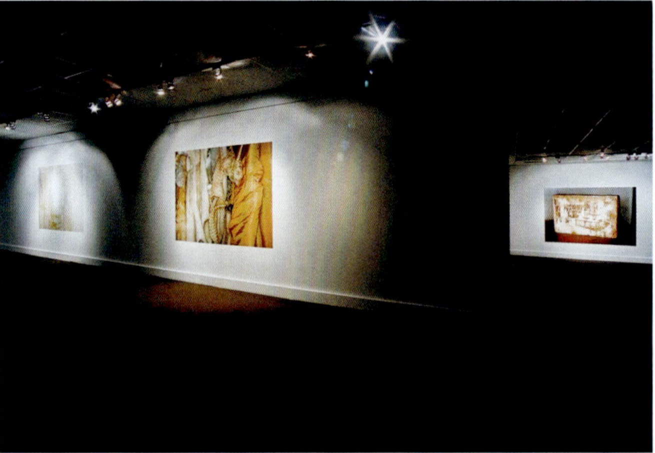

36 Sear's work in the Maidstone museum and library.
37 Composite pictures from the museum store room stuck directly onto the wall. Images courtesy Helen Sear.

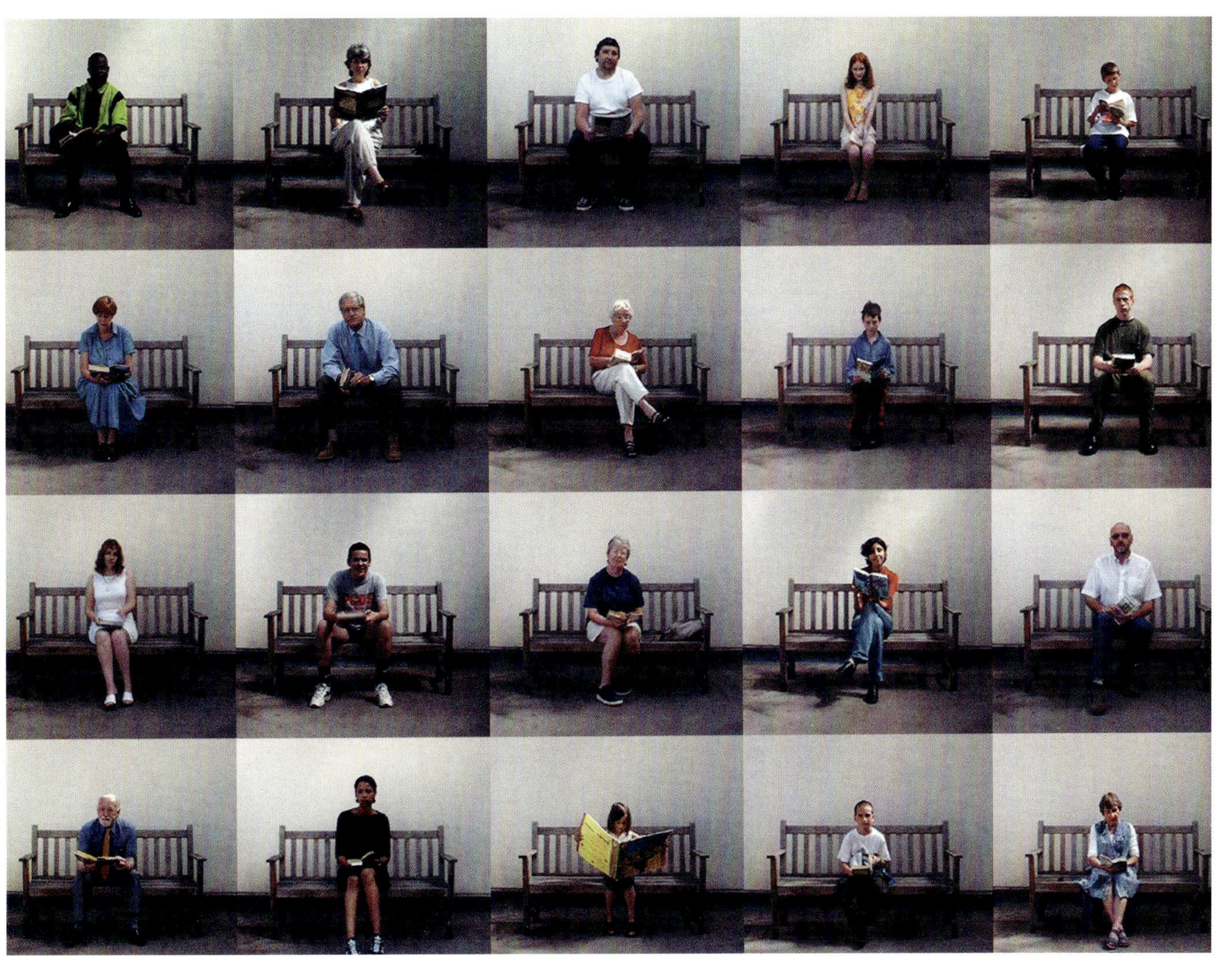

VERY MISCELLANEOUS 2000

The Country Life series, curated by Val Williams for Photoworks, invited artists to respond to the George Garland Collection archived at the West Sussex County Records Office. Garland made thousands of photographs from his studio in Petworth, from the early 1920s until his death in 1978, recording the rural England that he knew would soon disappear. The second commission in the series, German artist Joachim Schmid's *Very Miscellaneous*, combined portraits by Garland with fragments of newspaper articles held by the West Sussex County Records Office. Schmid's work on the nature of history and memory – and on how we understand the past through the partial narratives contained in, and created by, archives – was published in 2000.

Having studied visual communication at Fachhochschule für Gestaltung Schwäbisch Gmünd and Berlin University of the Arts (1976–81), Schmid became a freelance critic and publisher of Fotokritik. In the early 1980s, arguing against notions of art photography in favour of a wider concept of photography as a cultural practice, he started to work with found images. He has exhibited his projects around the world, and in 2007 published a comprehensive monograph with Photoworks and Steidl.

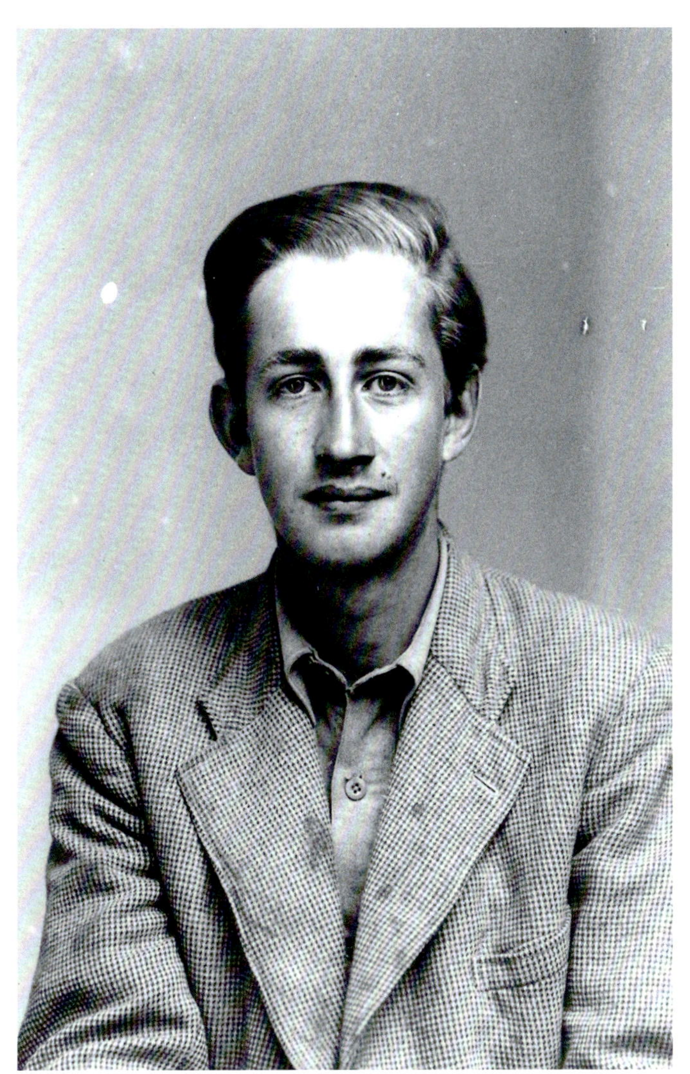

Mr B. G. Langford, representing the parents, thanked Mrs. Kent for her work during the past nine years.

"You have done your best for each individual pupil," he said, "and by your hard work brought the school to its present standard, which is as high as, or higher than any school in West Sussex."

Mrs. R. Fentiman, a past pupil, made the presentation of the dinner-service

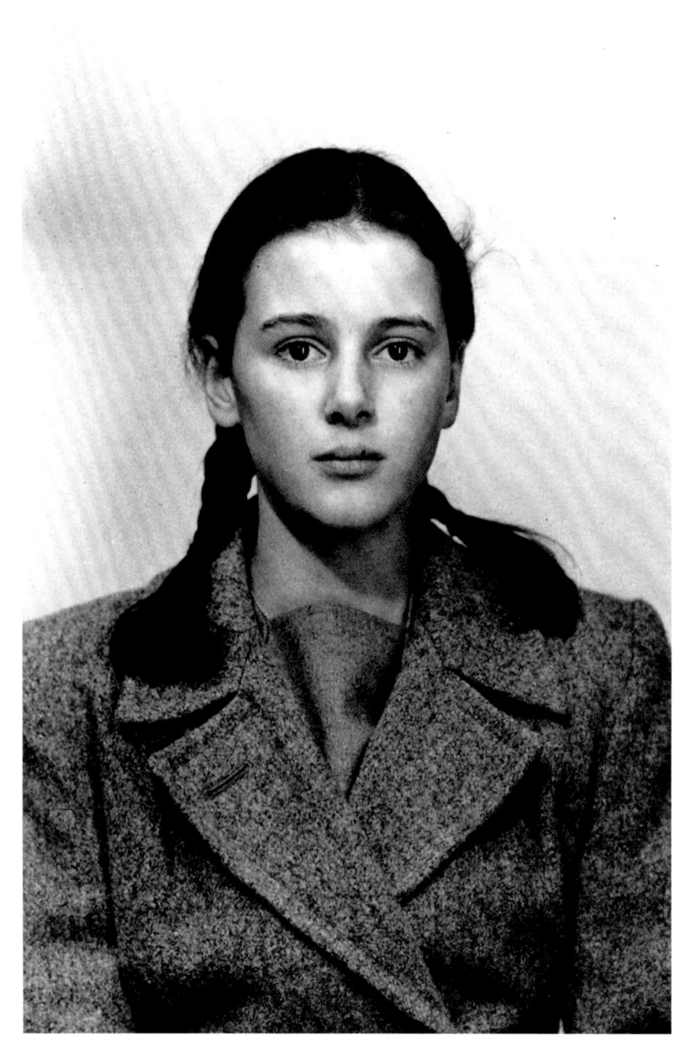

"He loves the Army, and he
signed on for five years," said Mrs.
Leggatt. "The trouble with my
amily is they are all Army mad."
She said: "My Dad was an ex-
uardsman. My brother Maurice
latthews was on the Reserve in
Coldstream Guards. He rose
the rank of Captain, was de-
obbed at the end of the war, re-

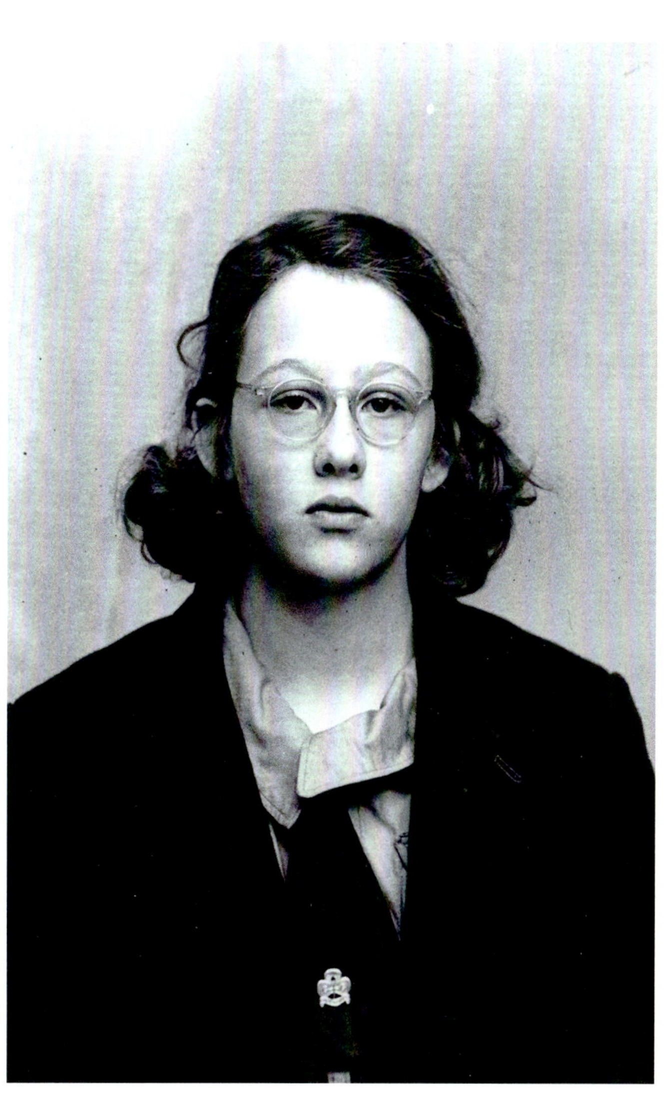

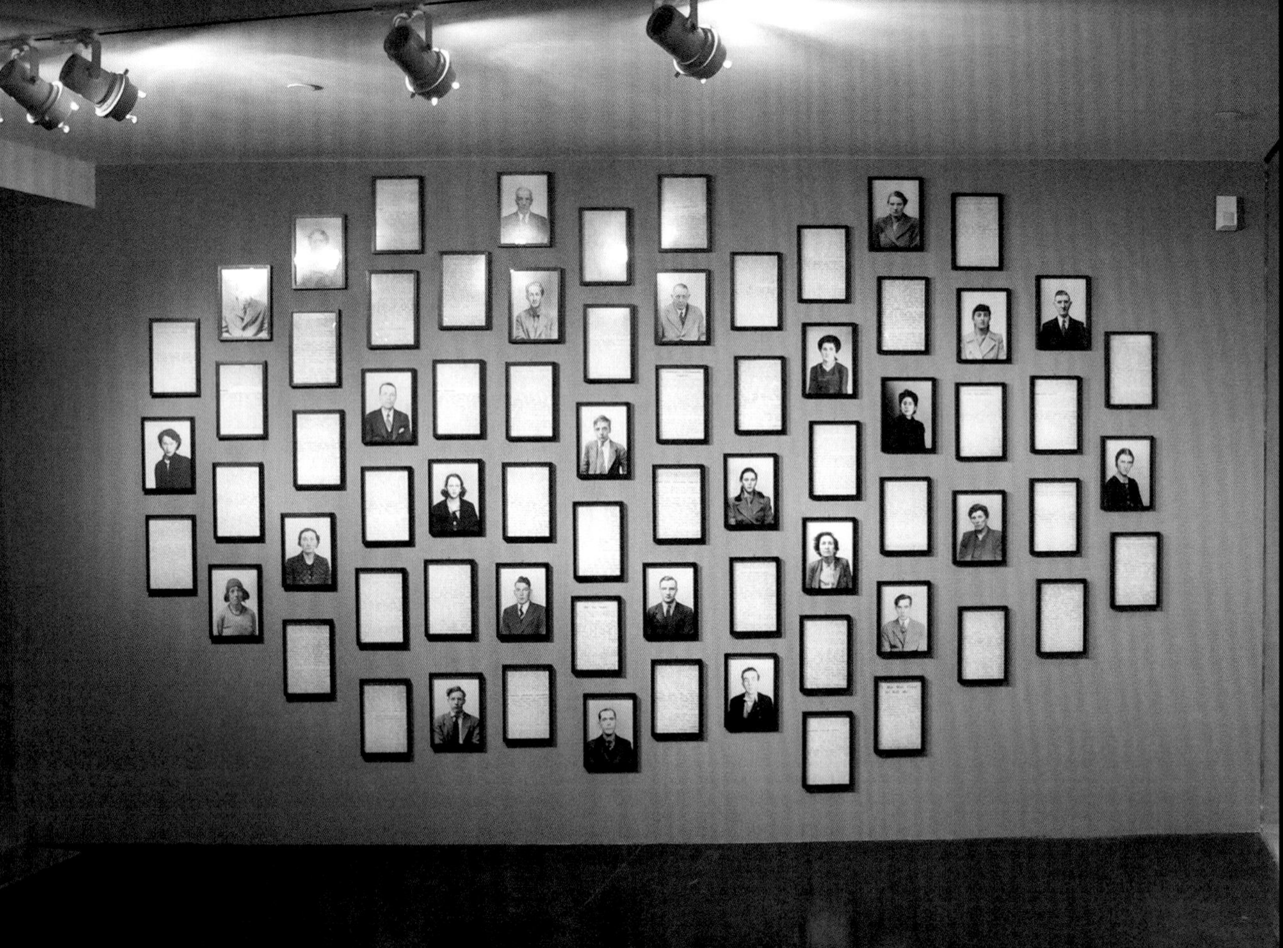

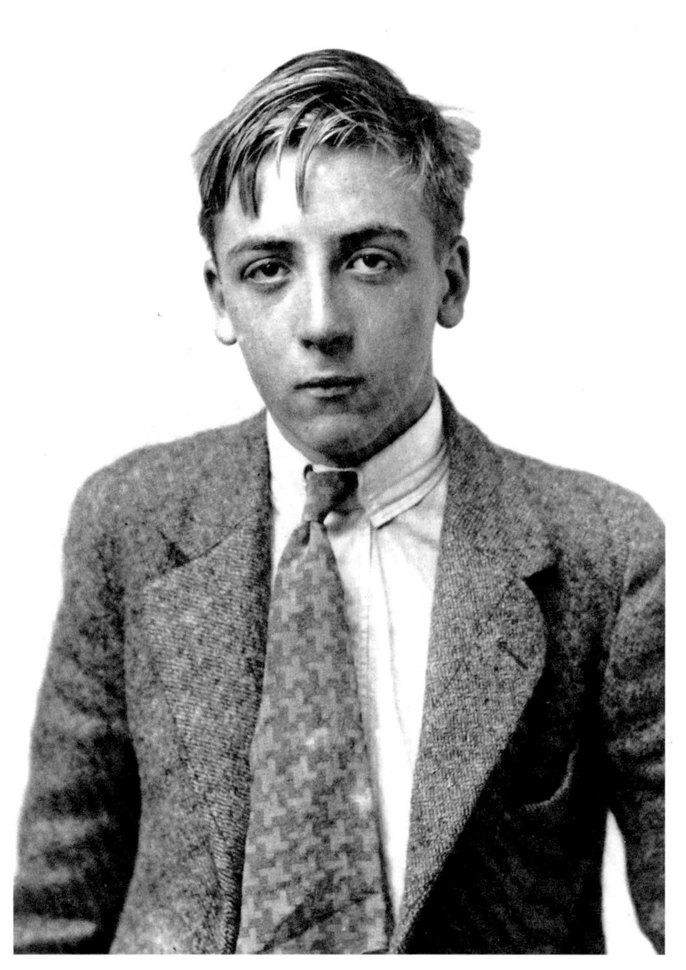

NATURE STUDIES 2005

In 2005, Neeta Madahar published a book and DVD with Photoworks, called *Nature Studies*. It combined two different projects – Sustenance, a series of colour photographs made in 2002–03, and Falling, a video animation and five still images co-commissioned by Photoworks, Fabrica and Iniva in 2005. Though different in form, these two works are conceptually related, responding to nature and our conception of the world, documenting aspects of the environment with a heightened sense that introduces a detachment element. *Nature Studies* was published by Photoworks to coincide with the first complete showing of Falling at Fabrica, Brighton, in October 2005.

Born in London in 1966, Madahar studied mathematics for her first degree. Following her passion for art via evening classes, she went on to study for a BA in fine art at Winchester School of Art and the University of Southampton, and in 2003 graduated from the School of the Museum of Fine Arts, Boston and Tufts University, USA, with an MFA in studio art. She went on to exhibit her work at Les Rencontres de la Photographie in Arles, and the National Science and Media Museum in Bradford. In 2021, exploring beyond western approaches to representation, she started training in the tradition of painting Indian miniatures with Master Ajay Sharma.

45–47 From the series Sustenance
48–49 From the series Falling

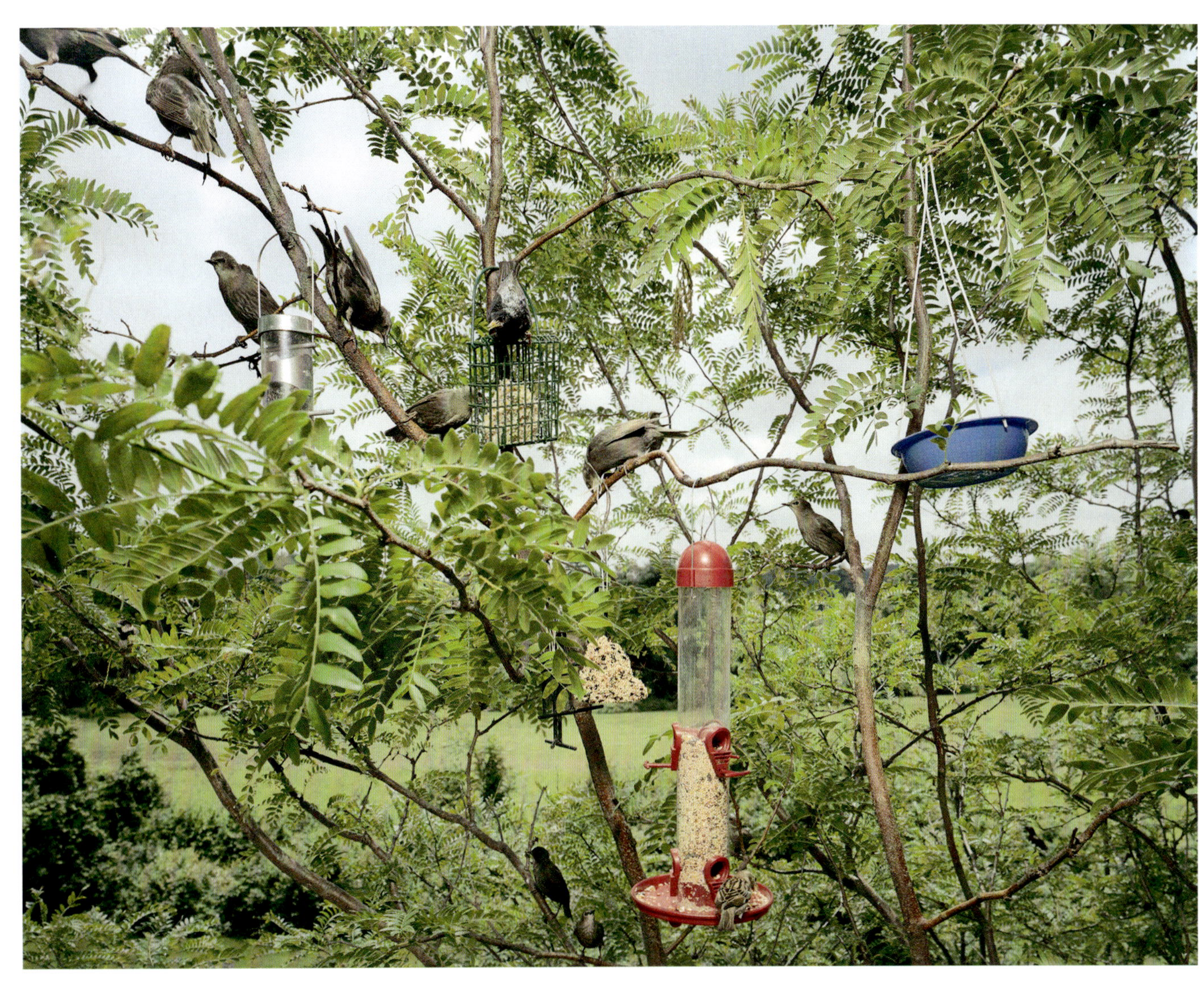

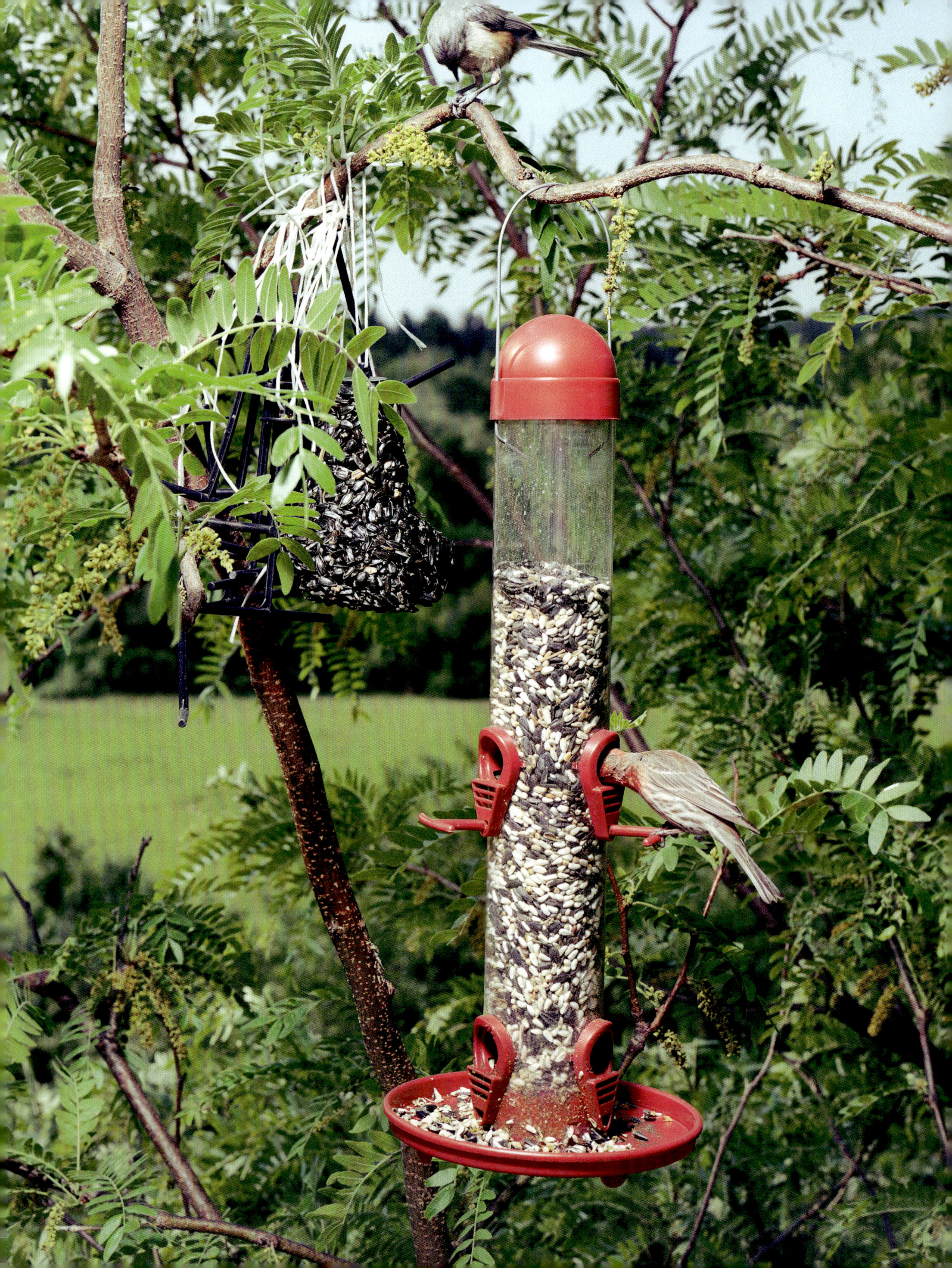

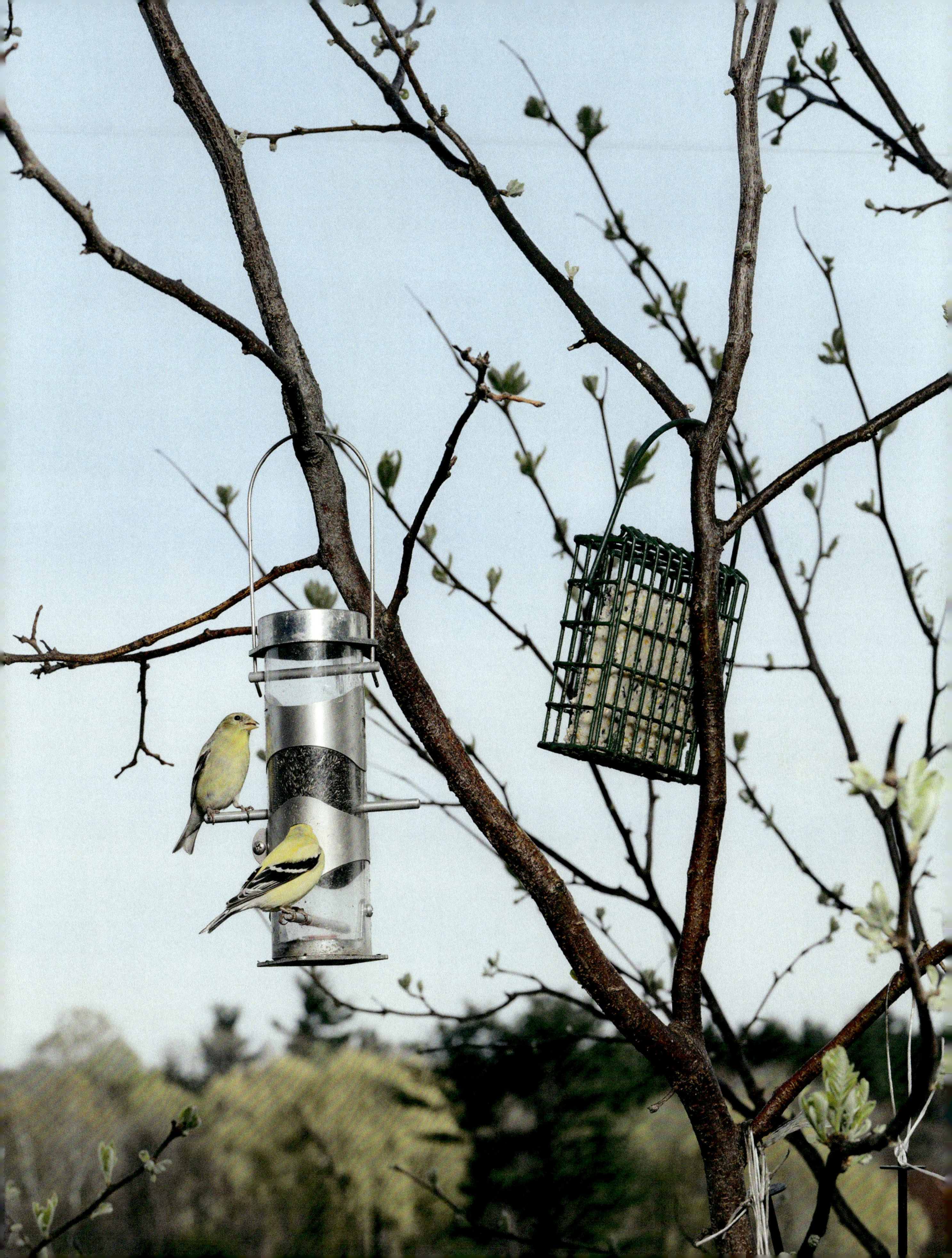

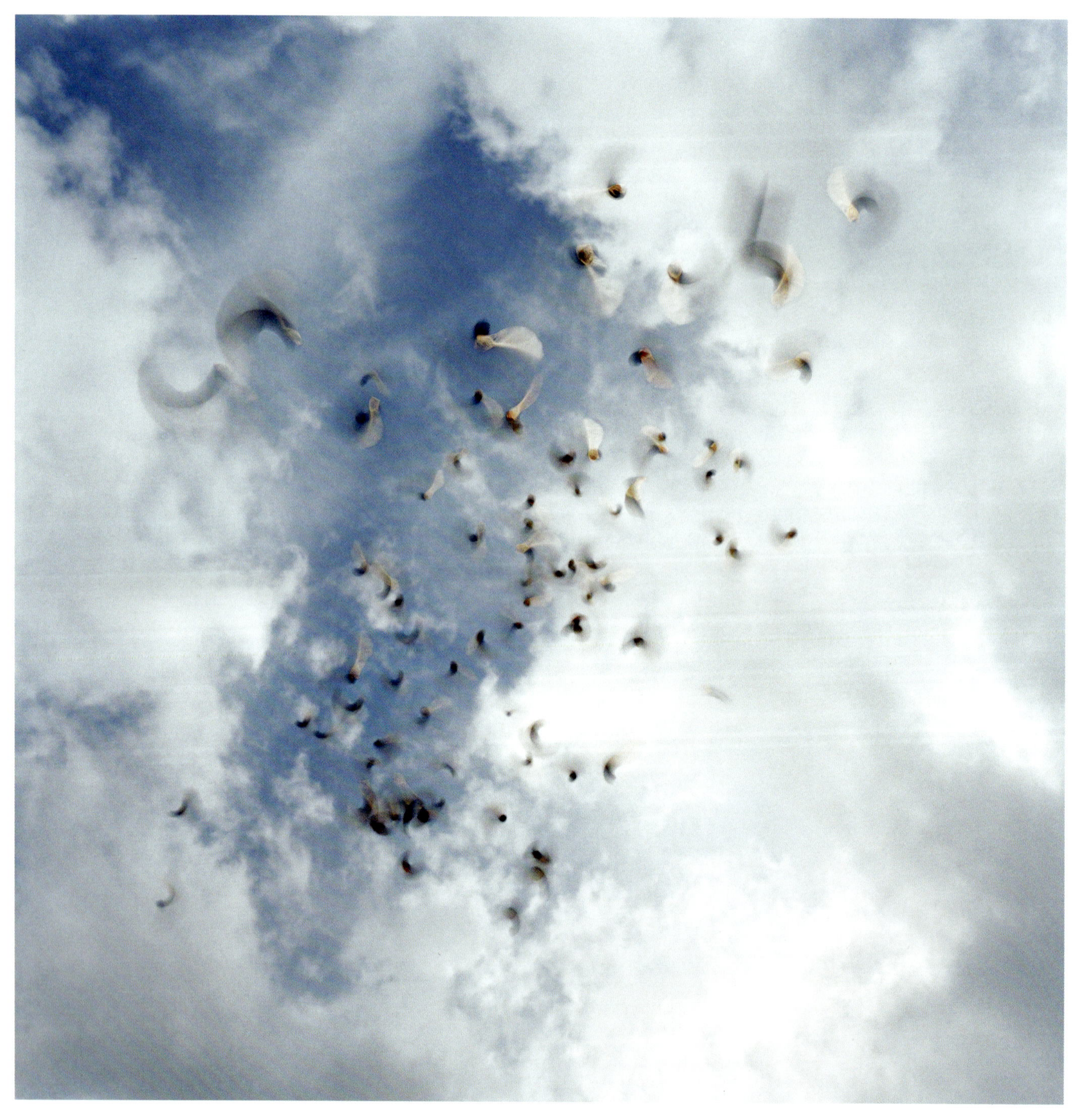

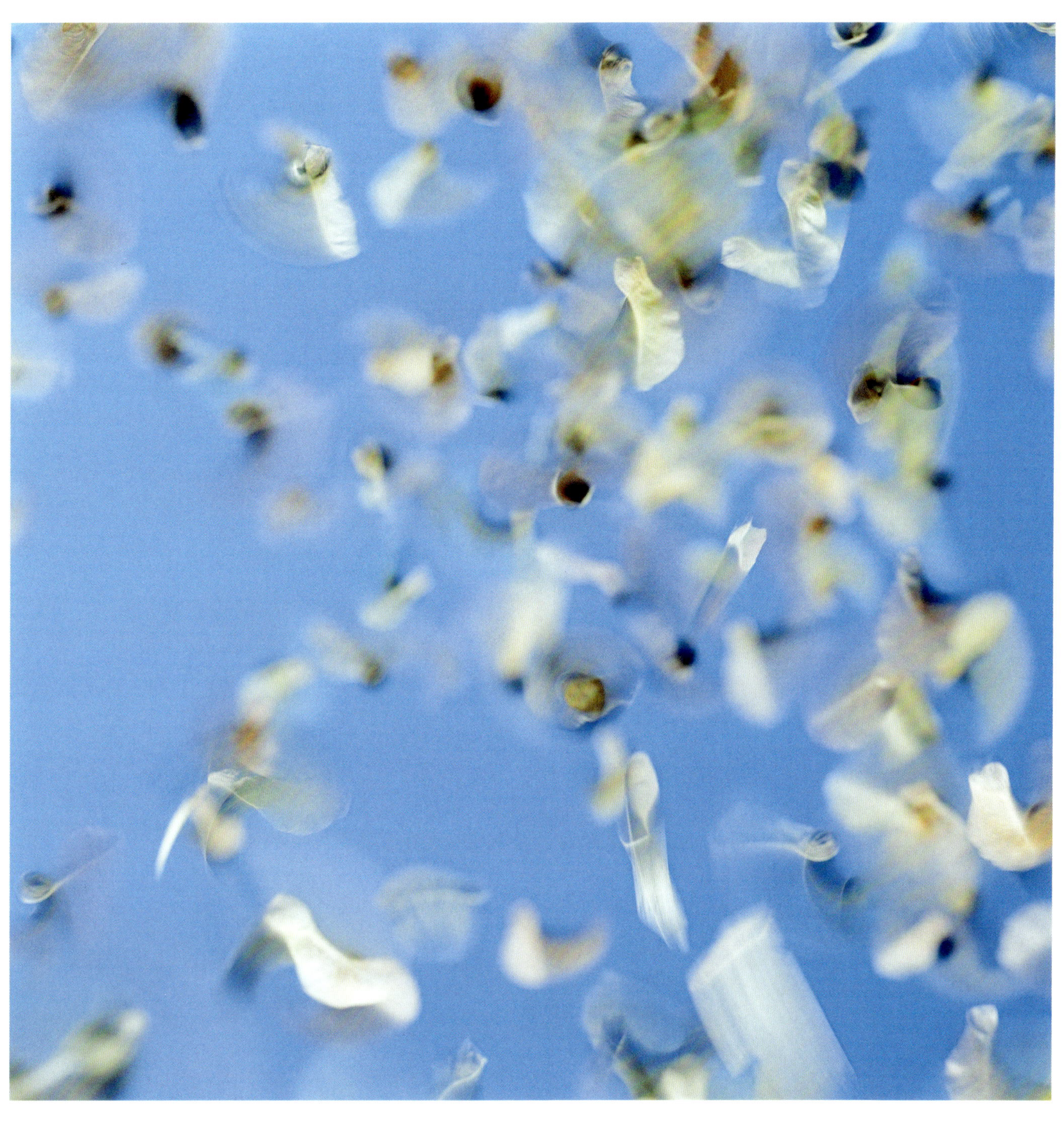

A PICTURE BOOK OF BRITAIN 2005

In 2006, Photoworks commissioned and published Henna Nadeem's monograph, *A Picture Book of Britain*. A series of delicate collages, it was created using images sourced from Country Life's *The Picture Books of Britain*, which were published from 1937 to 1975. Country Life's publications, which were popular with contemporary audiences, drew on particular pictorial traditions to present a very subjective view of Britain. Using patterns from a range of non-western sources, Nadeem grafted together multiple images to disrupt the picture-postcard effect, creating intricately layered pieces which suggest a much richer, less familiar mix.

Born in Leeds in 1966, Nadeem graduated with an MA from the Royal College of Art, in London, in 1993. Many of her works use found images, sourced from old books and a variety of magazines, cut by hand and rearranged using scissors, scalpels and tweezers. Nadeem has used this deliberately lo-fi approach to create large-scale public works, including a Platform for Art commission for Piccadilly Underground station, window manifestations for the Department for Culture, Media and Sport, and a decorative gate for a project in Brick Lane, east London. Her work has been exhibited in group and solo exhibitions at Norwich Castle Museum & Art Gallery, Tate Britain, South London Gallery and the Institute for Contemporary Arts, and acquired by the UK Government Art Collection, the British Council and Autograph.

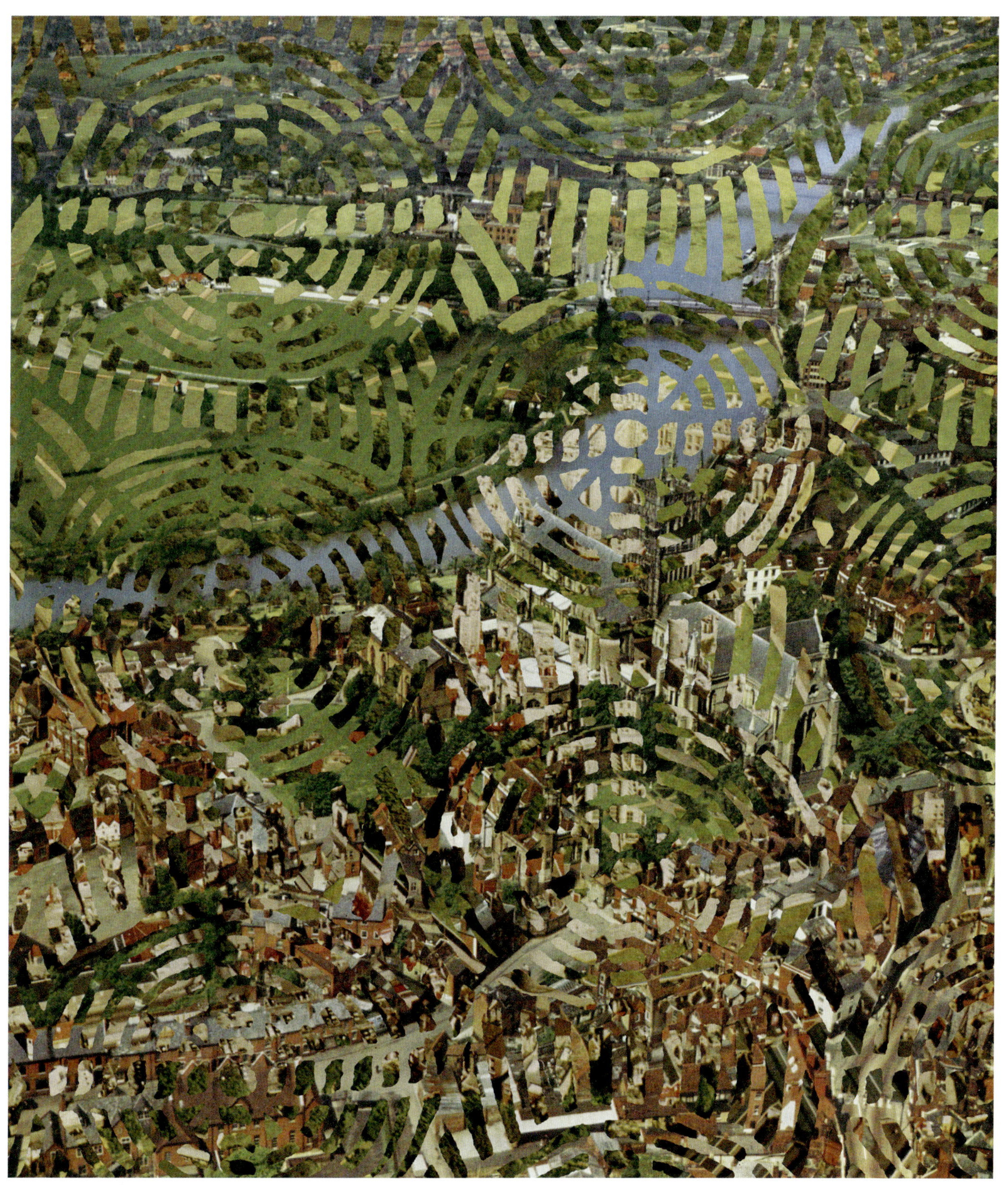

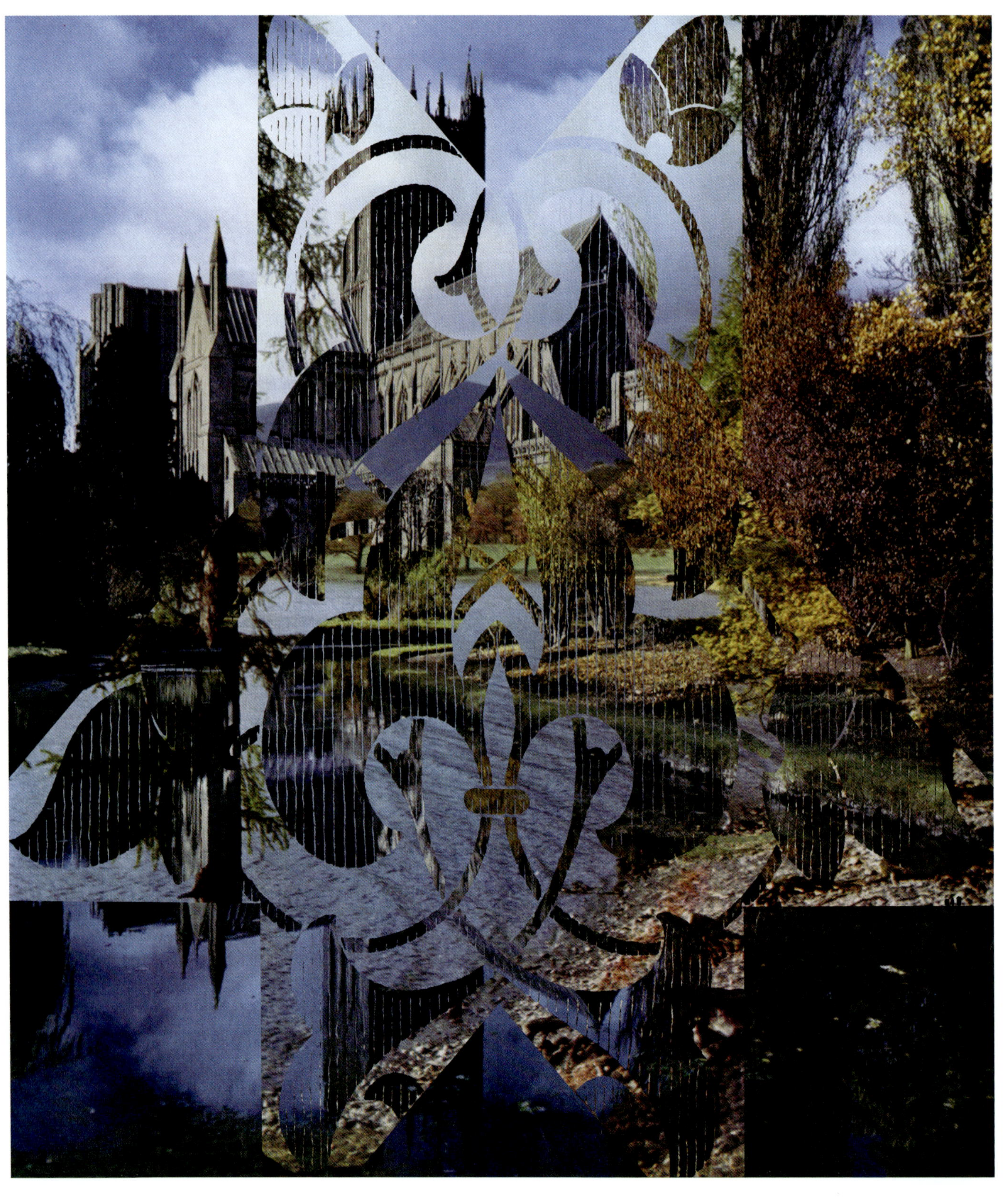

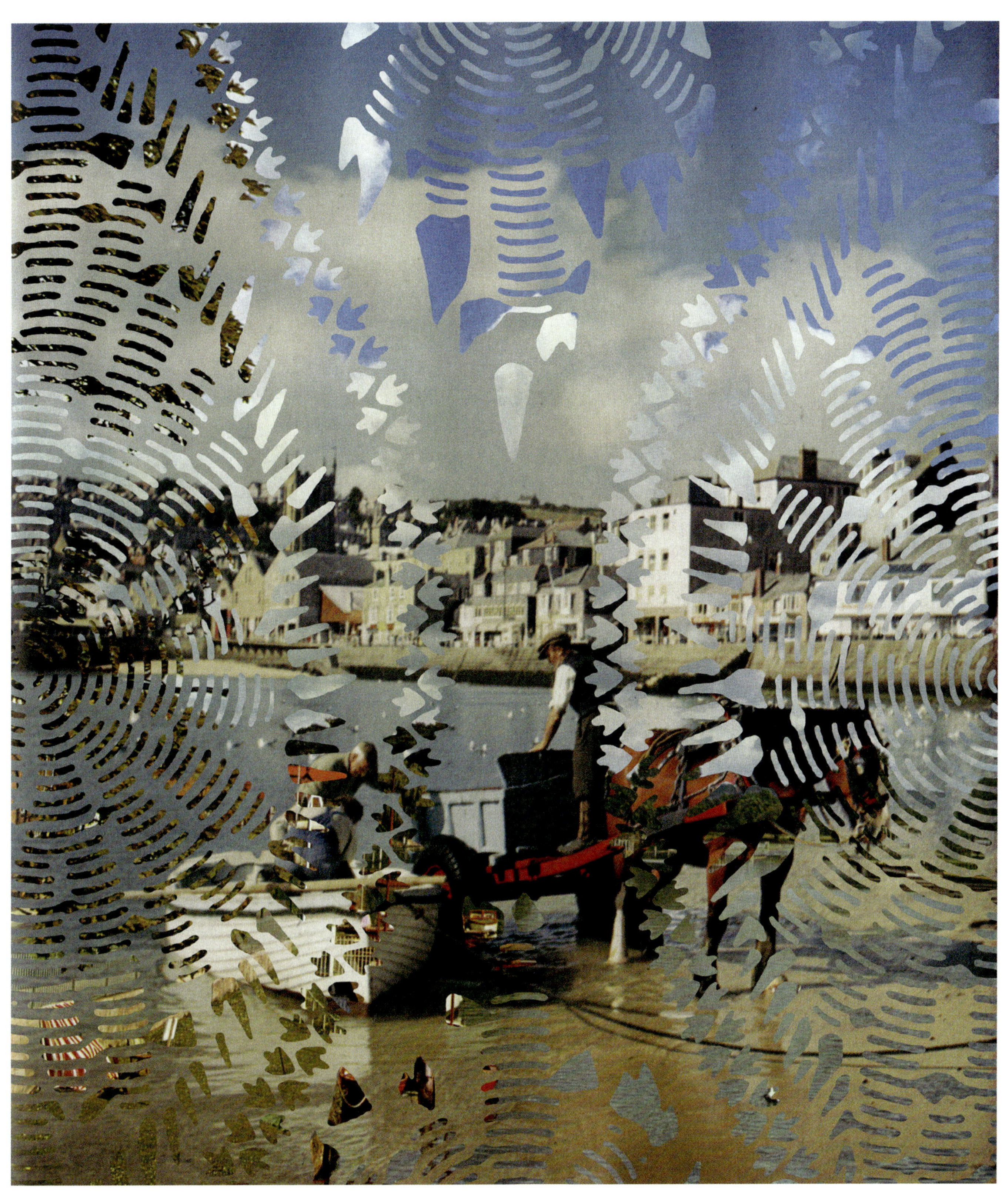

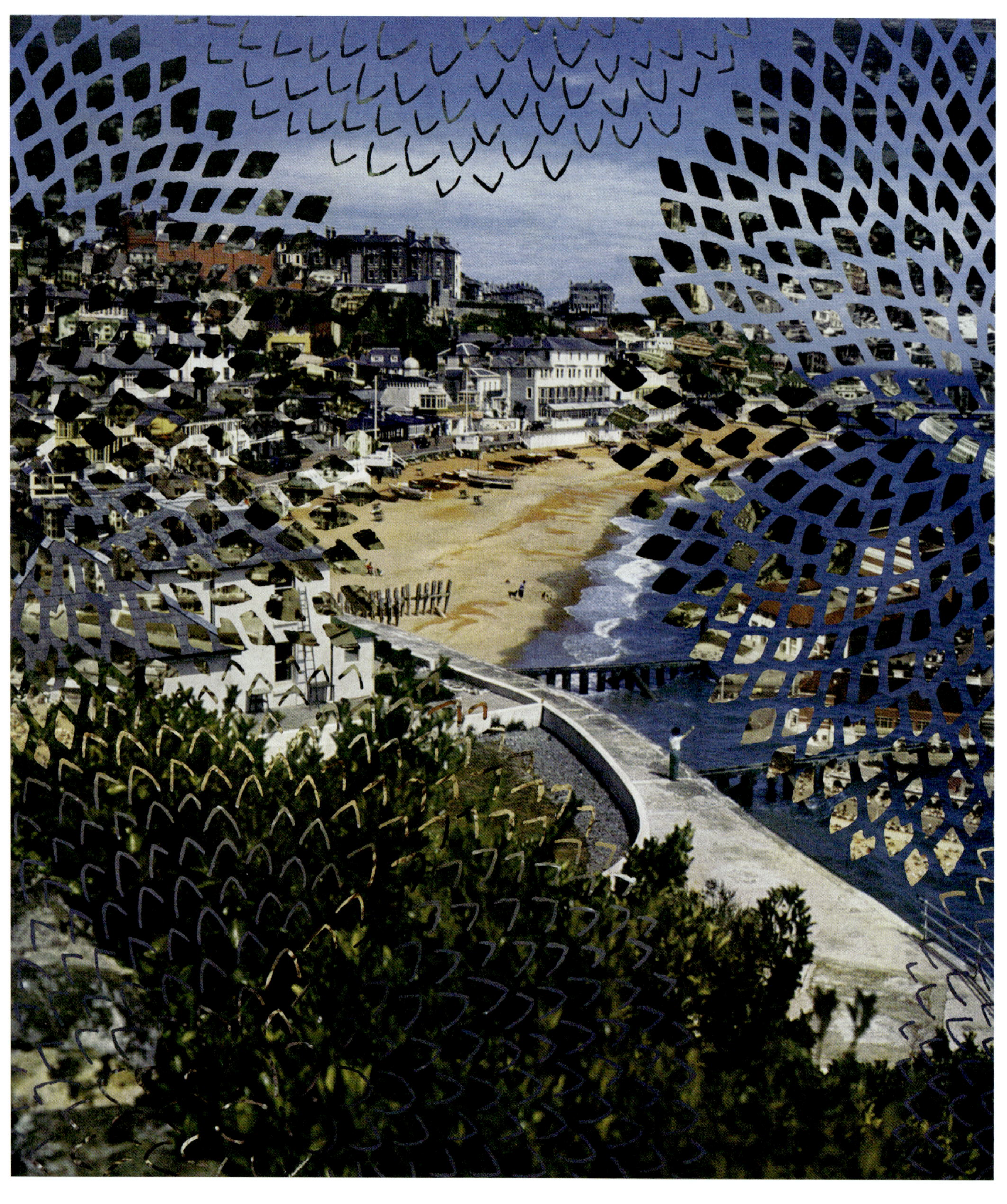

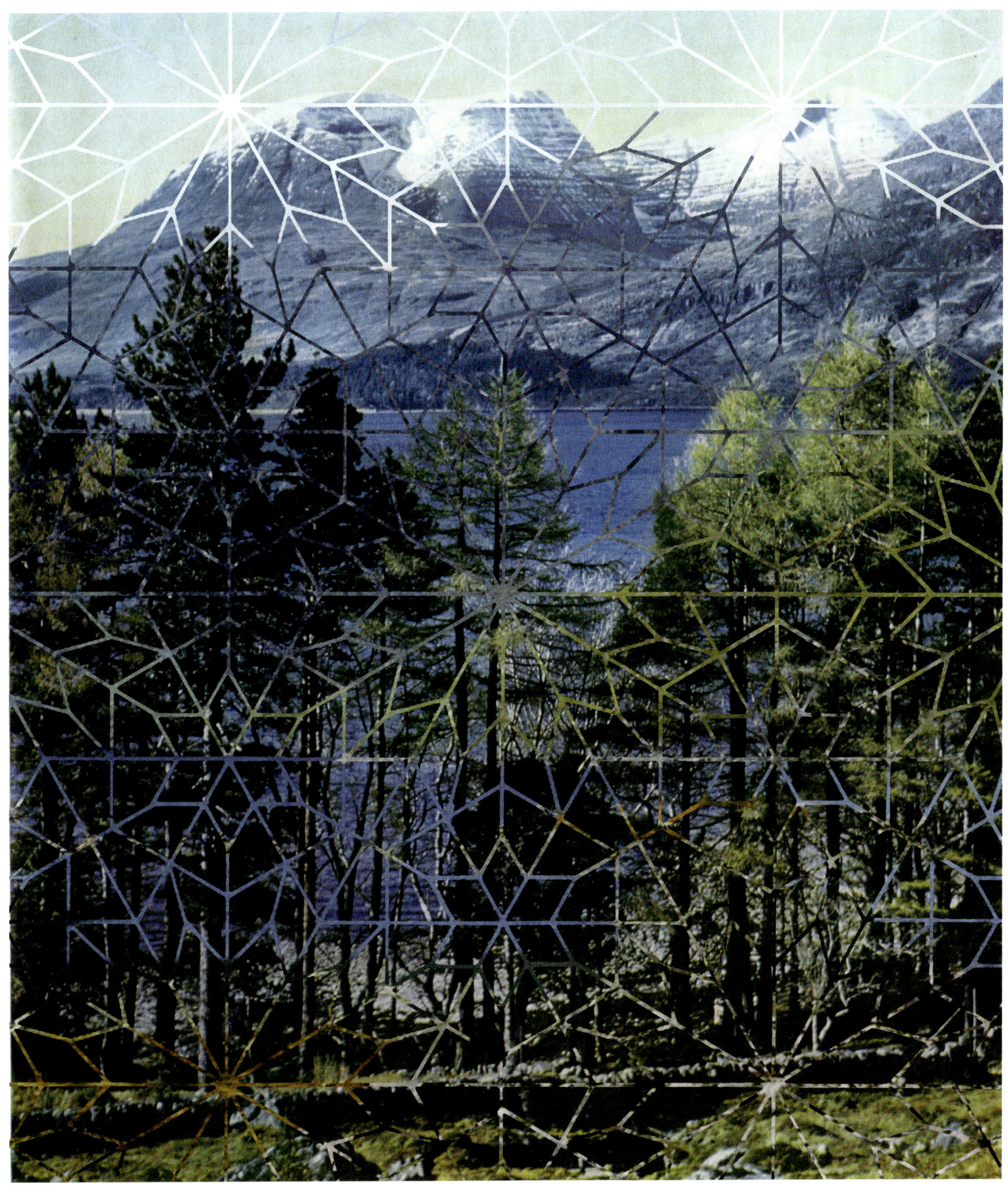

MURMURATION 2010

In 2010, Rinko Kawauchi was commissioned by Photoworks to make new work for the Brighton Photo Biennial: *New Documents*, curated by Martin Parr. Invited to work in Brighton, she was drawn to the spectacle of starlings flocking at the West Pier in winter at dusk, where they gather in wheeling clouds known as murmurations. Fascinated by the ephemerality of these movements, and by the place of the natural world in Brighton, Kawauchi started to photograph the birds, as well as groups of people in the city. The commission, her first in the UK, was supported by funding from The Japan Foundation, The Great Britain Sasakawa Foundation, and The Daiwa Anglo-Japanese Foundation. Photoworks also published a book of the project.

Born in Shiga, Japan, in 1972, Kawauchi gained international acclaim for her photobooks *Utatane*, *Hanabi* and *Hanako*, all published in 2001. She has since published more than 20 photobooks, and her work has been shown at Les Rencontres de la Photographie in Arles, Lianzhou Foto Festival, in China, the V&A Museum in London, San Francisco Museum of Modern Art, and many more. Kawauchi also works with moving image.

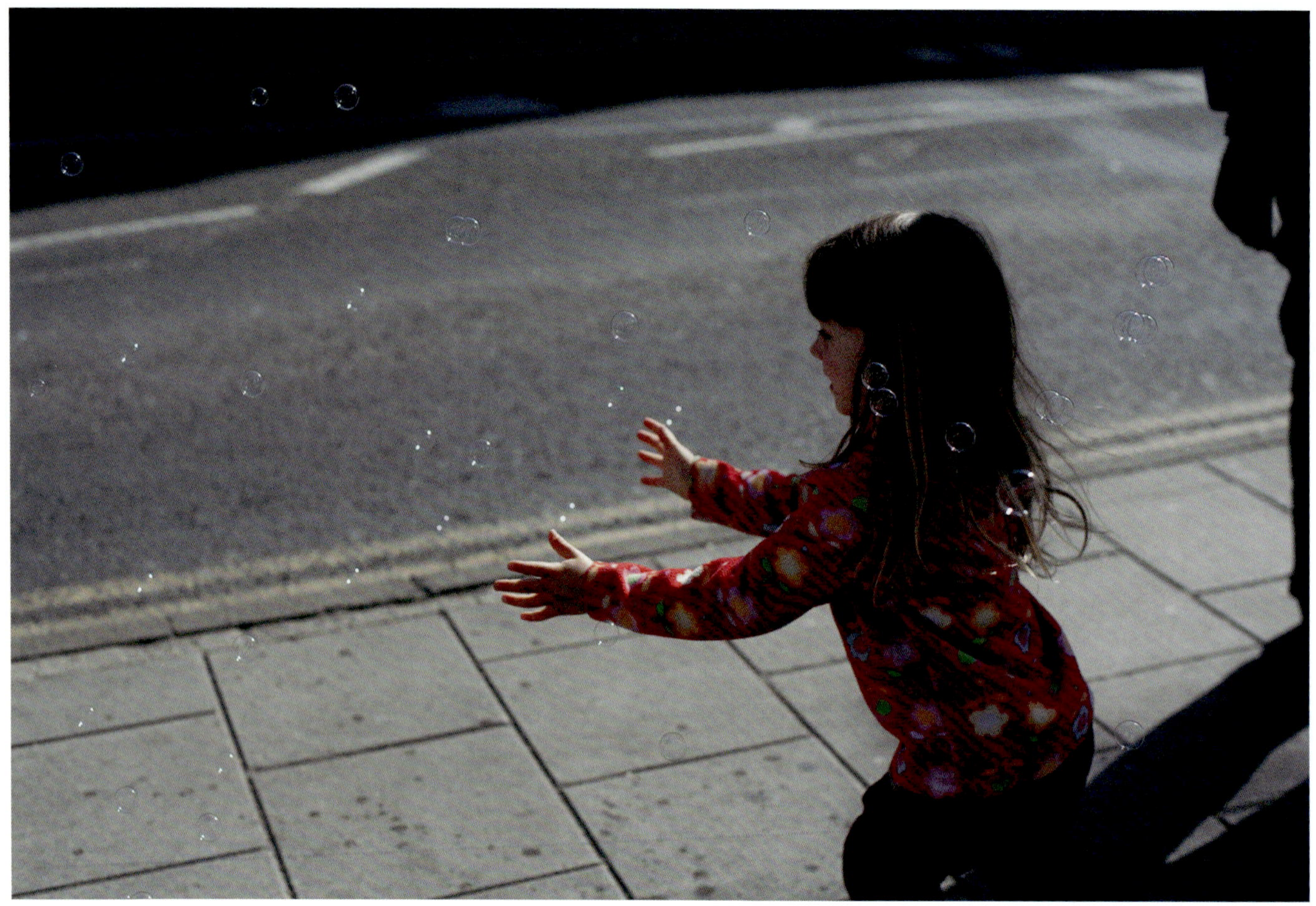

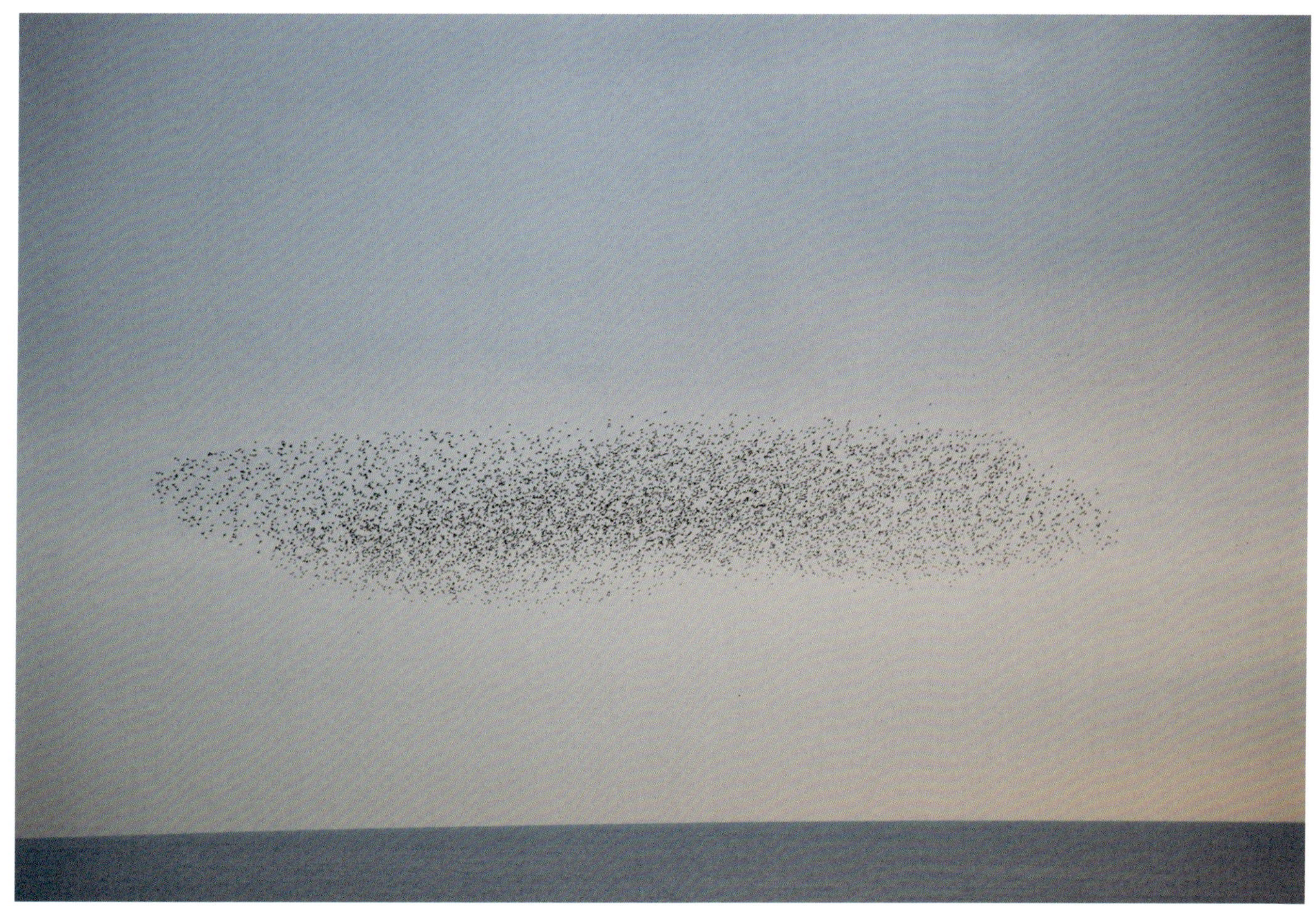

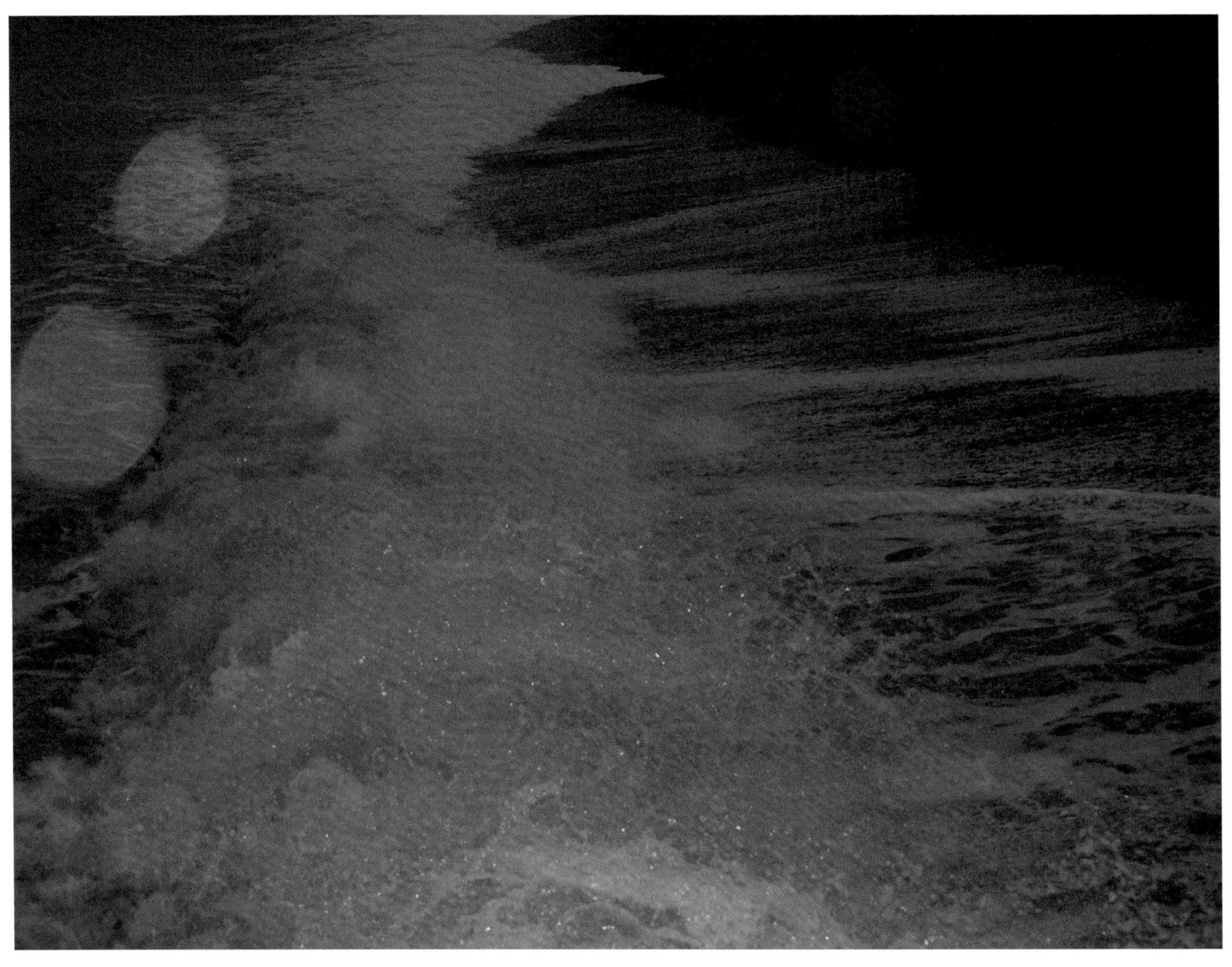

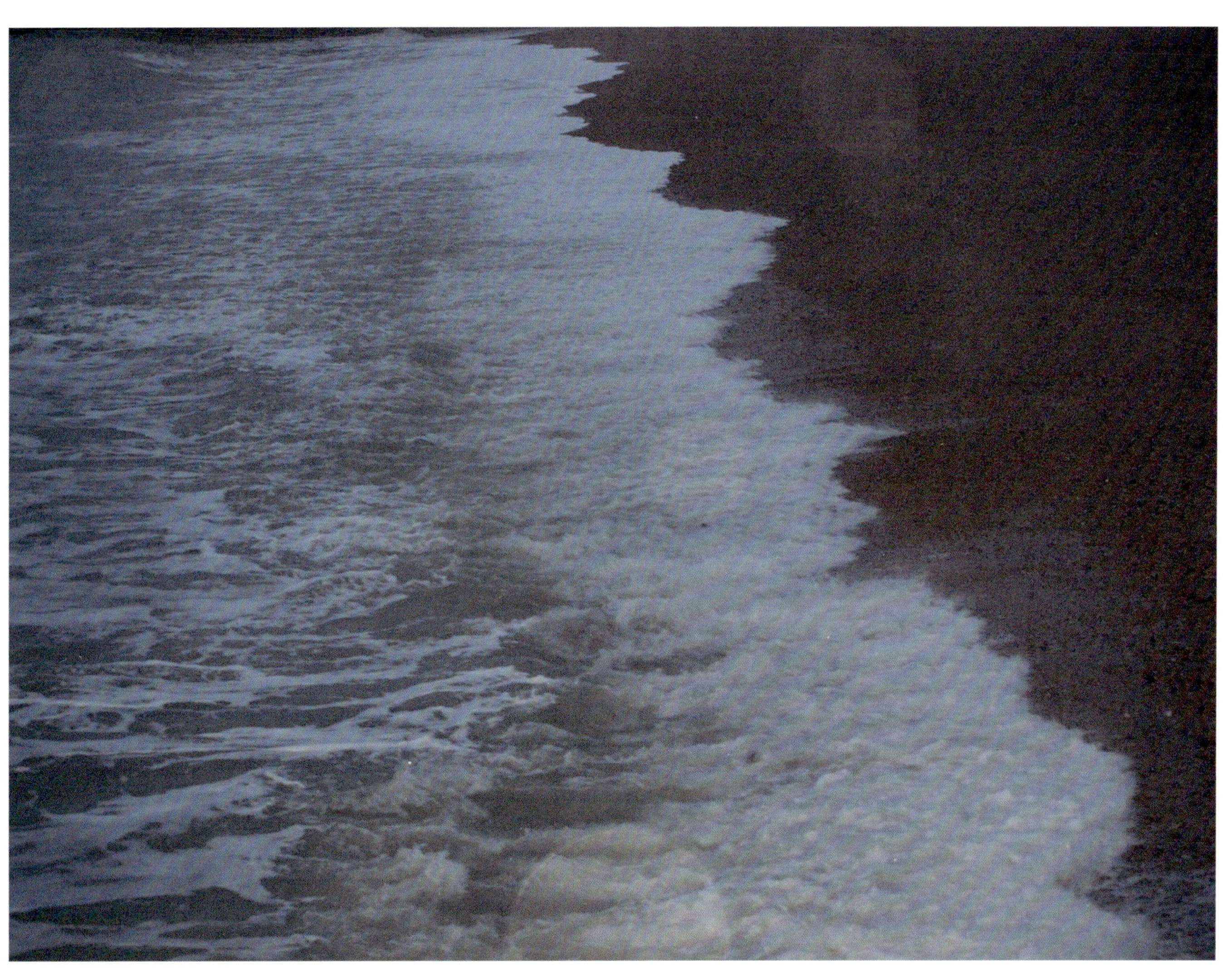

A RETURN TO ELSEWHERE 2014

A collaboration by British photographer Kalpesh Lathigra and South African photographer Thabiso Sekgala, *A Return to Elsewhere* was shot in two primary locations – Pretoria, South Africa, and Brighton, UK. Working closely, the two image-makers drew on their own experiences to create a single project, concerned with representation, community and belonging. Marabastad was a diverse area of Pretoria before forced relocation in the late 1940s, while Laudium, on the outskirts of the city, was proclaimed an Indian Township in 1961 under the Group Areas Act. Meanwhile, one of Brighton's largest ethnic minority groups is of Indian descent – a community well-established in the UK since the mid-18th century and the start of the British colonisation of India. In World War One, British Indian Army soldiers were temporarily hospitalised in the Royal Pavilion, a landmark of Brighton's landscape and identity.

Co-commissioned by the British Council Connect ZA programme with Photoworks, Market Photo Workshop and The Space for Brighton Photo Biennial 2014, *A Return to Elsewhere* was shown in Brighton and Johannesburg. Lathigra is based in London; initially a photojournalist, he moved towards documentary photography after winning a World Press Photo award in 2000, and has since published three books. Sekgala studied at the Market Photo Workshop and exhibited his work across Africa and Europe; he died in 2014.

63–64 and 66 Kalpesh Lathigra
65 and 67 Thabiso Sekgala

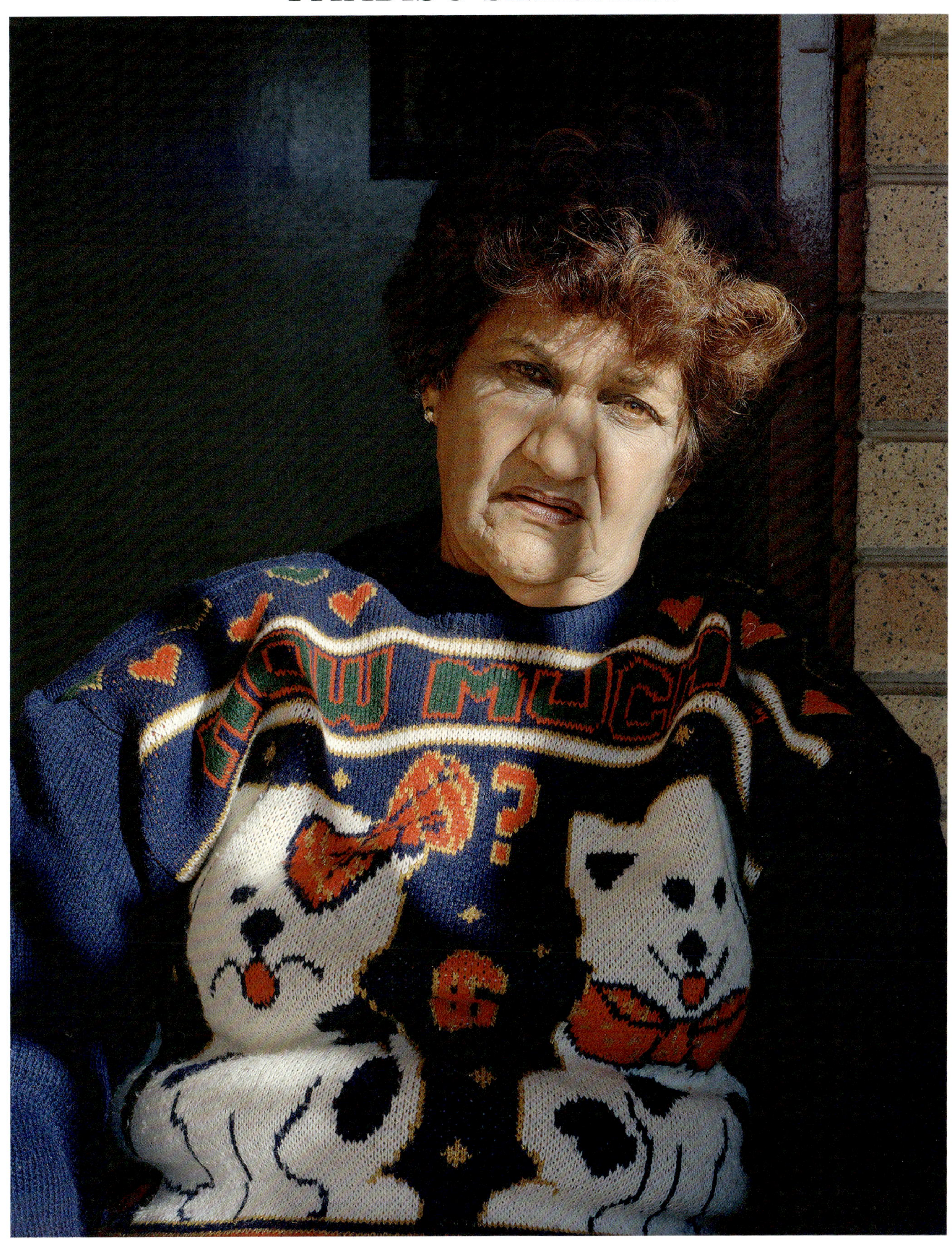

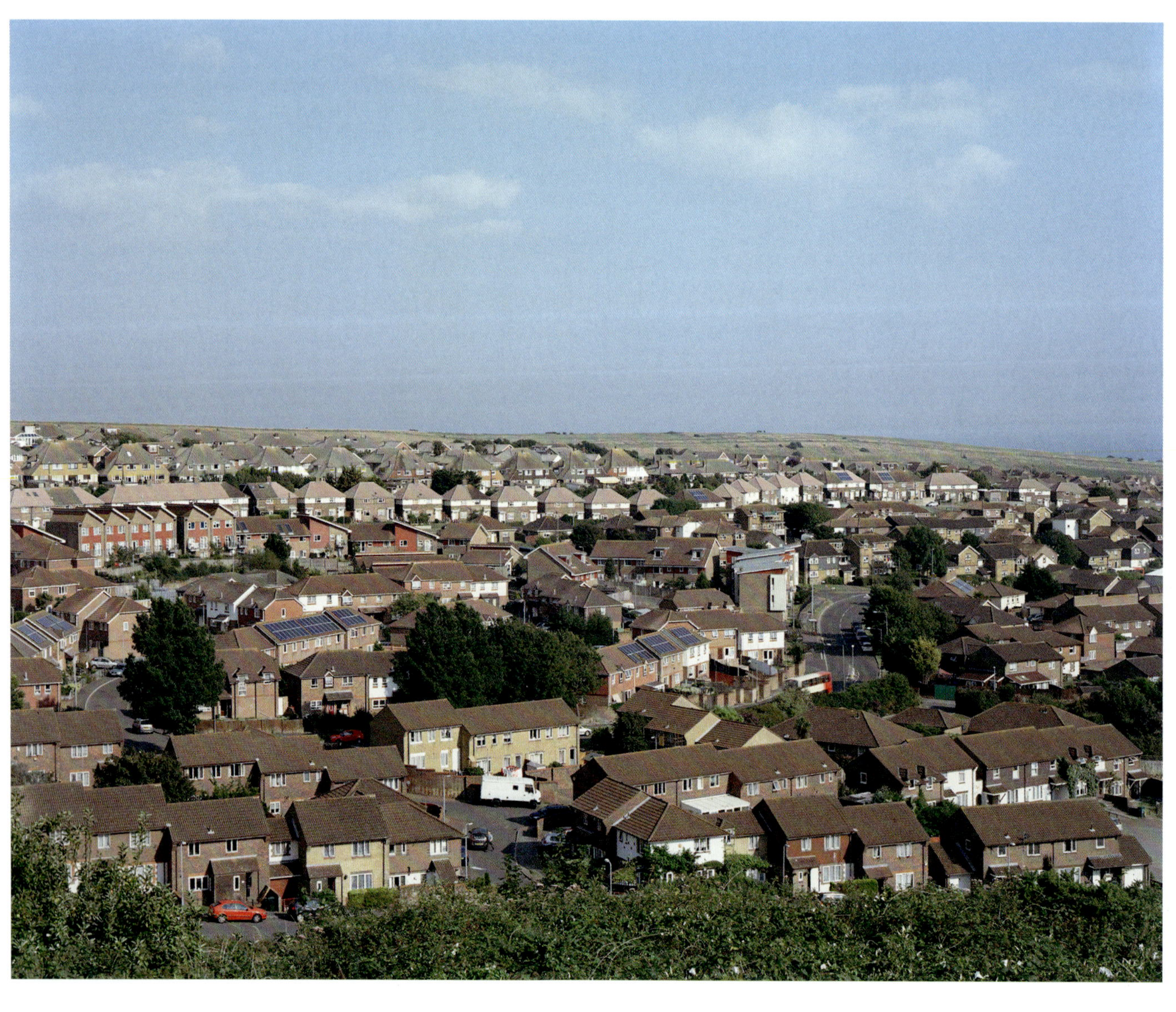

KALPESH LATHIGRA and THABISO SEKGALA

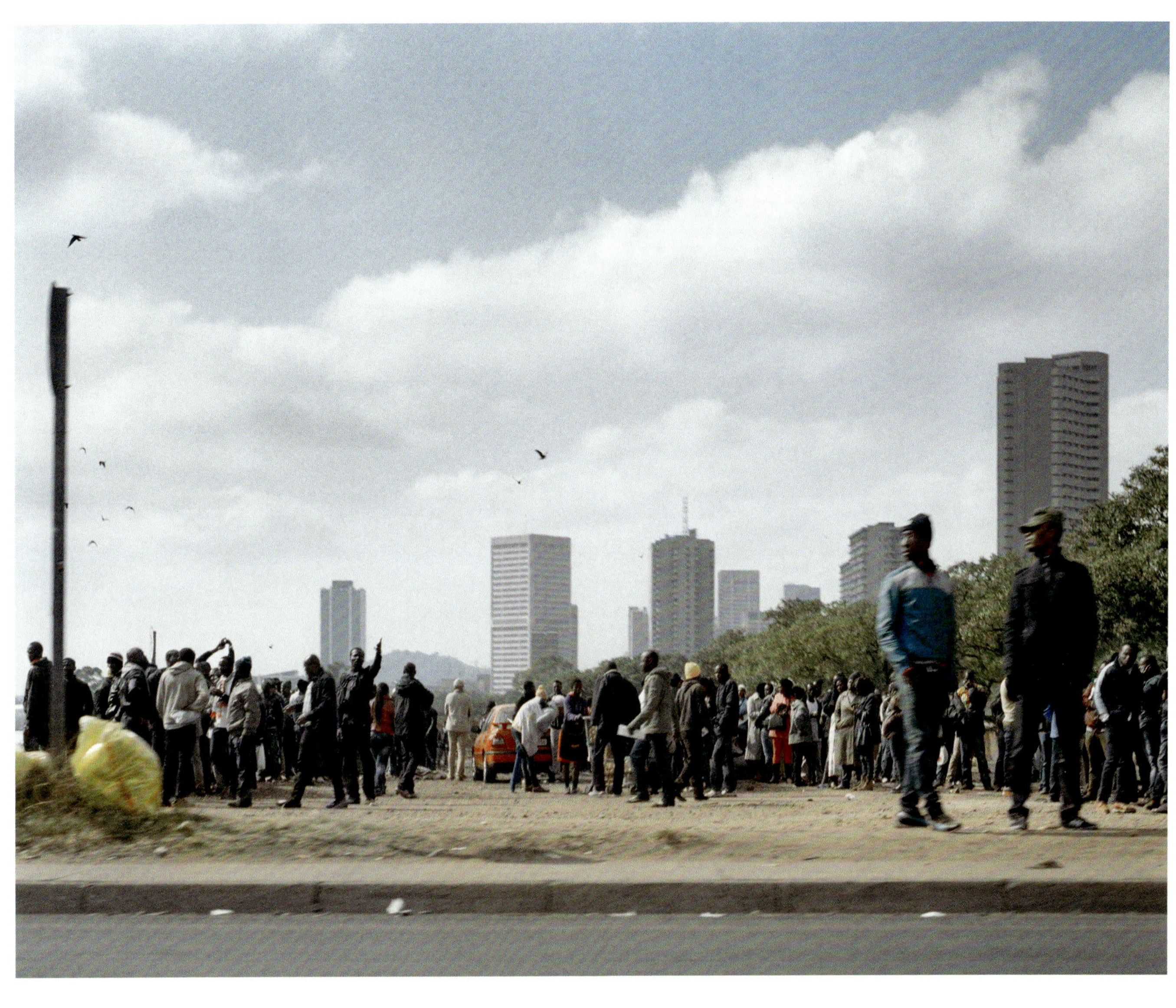

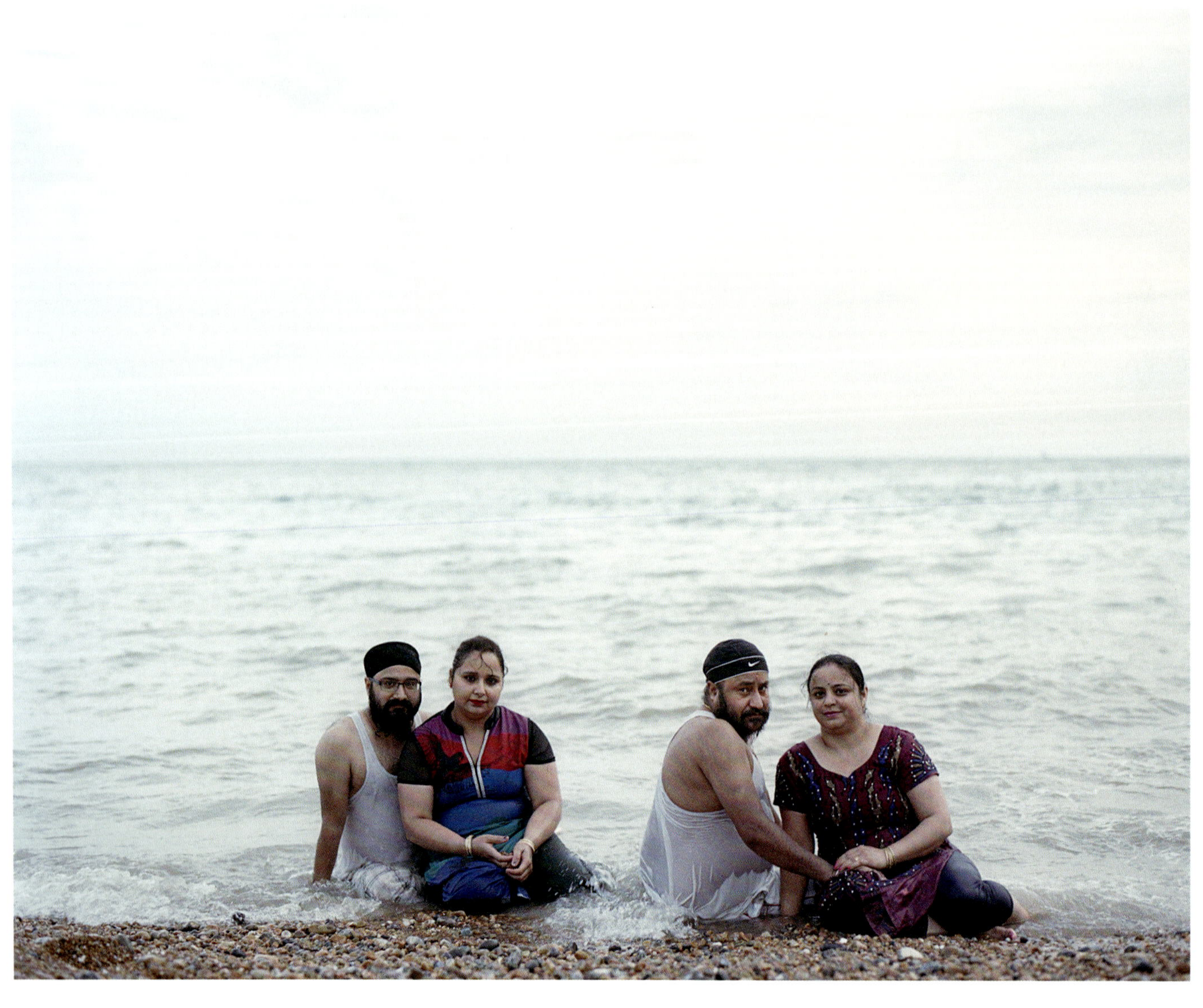

KALPESH LATHIGRA and THABISO SEKGALA

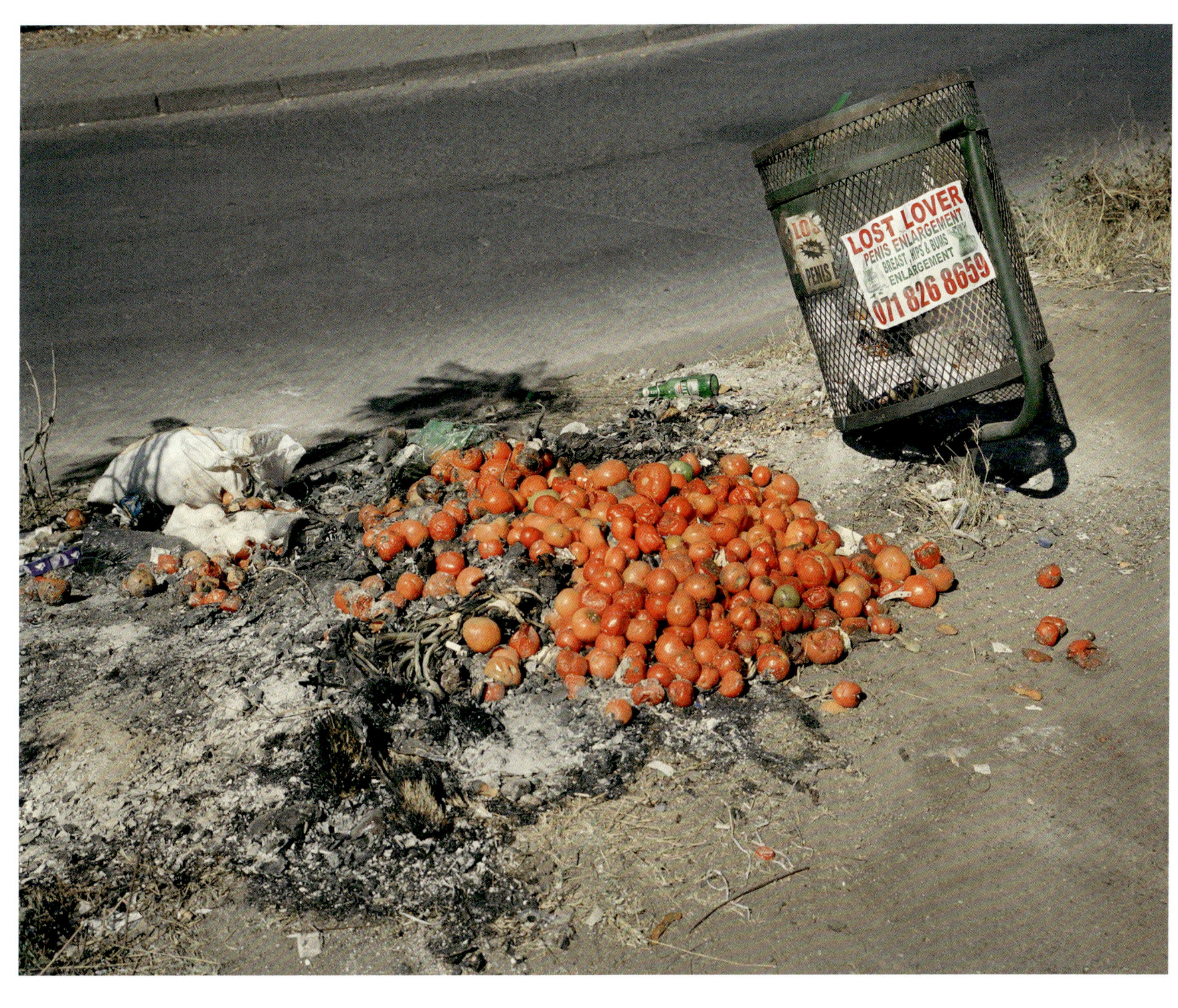

SUBIDA AL CIELO, 'HEAVENLY ASCENT' 2017 and 2020

In 2017, Lúa Ribeira was part of the second cohort of photographers to win the Jerwood/Photoworks Award, alongside Sam Laughlin and Alejandra Carles-Tolra. All three won funding to make new work, which went on show in London's Jerwood Space and Bradford's Impressions Gallery. Ribeira's series, *Subida al Cielo (Heavenly Ascent)*, was initially inspired by questioning the medium of photography and its capacity to transcend what is material. Through encounters with acquaintances and strangers, the work explores the function of mythology and religion in relation to death and the fragility of the body, while remaining rooted within the documentary tradition; it took place in Bristol in 2017 during the peak of a housing and homelessness crisis.

Ribeira continued this series after the Jerwood/Photoworks commission, and went on to add four more chapters to create a wider project titled *Subida al Cielo*, which she published with Dalpine in 2023, alongside a solo show at Tabakalera Museum in Donostia, in the Basque country. Born in Galicia in 1986, Ribeira graduated in documentary photography from the University of South Wales in 2016. In 2020 she joined Magnum Photos as an associate member and in 2023 became a full member. Her work was shown alongside 11 other female Magnum members in 2022 at the International Center for Photography, New York.

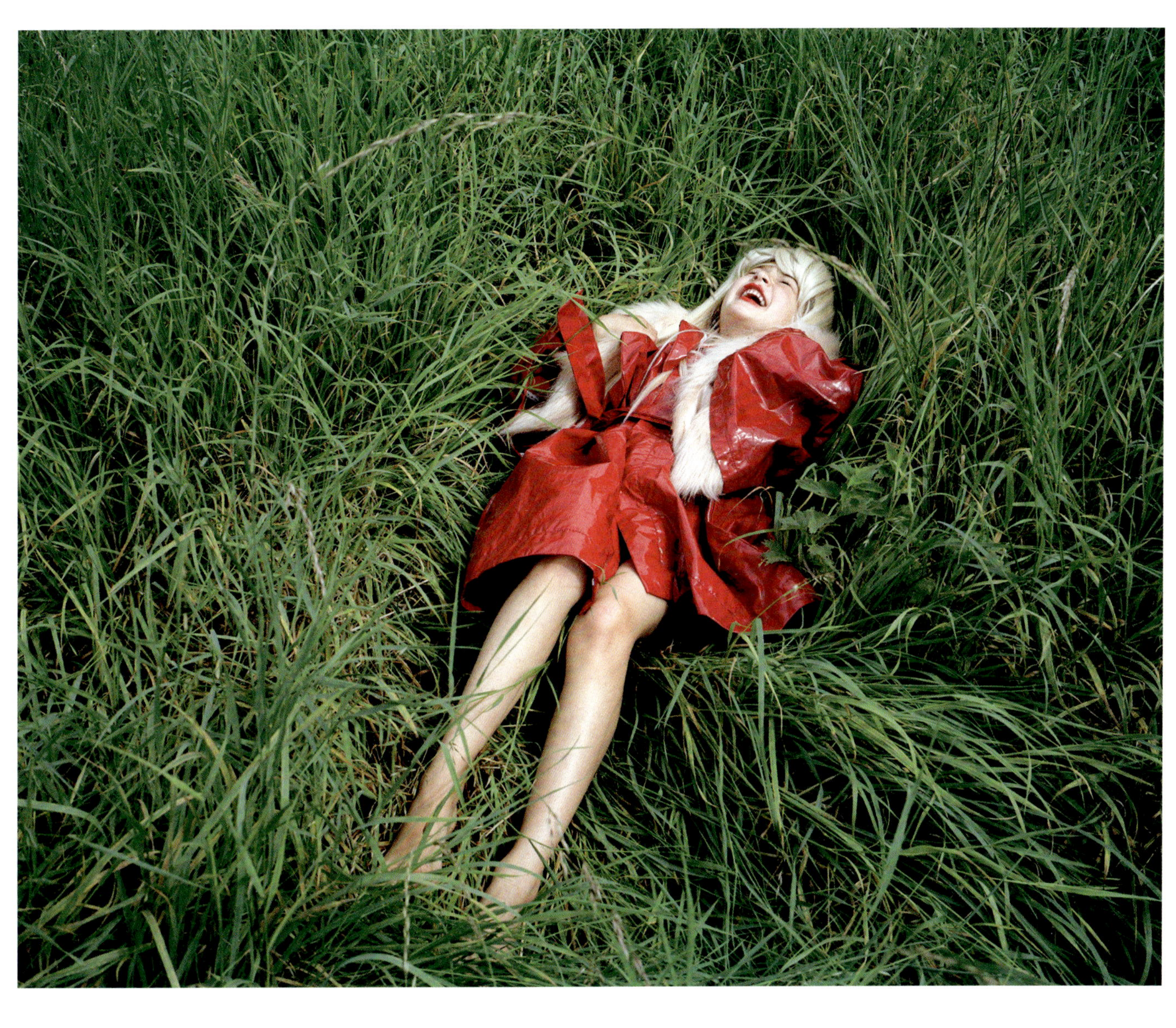

SUBIDA AL CIELO, 'HEAVENLY ASCENT'

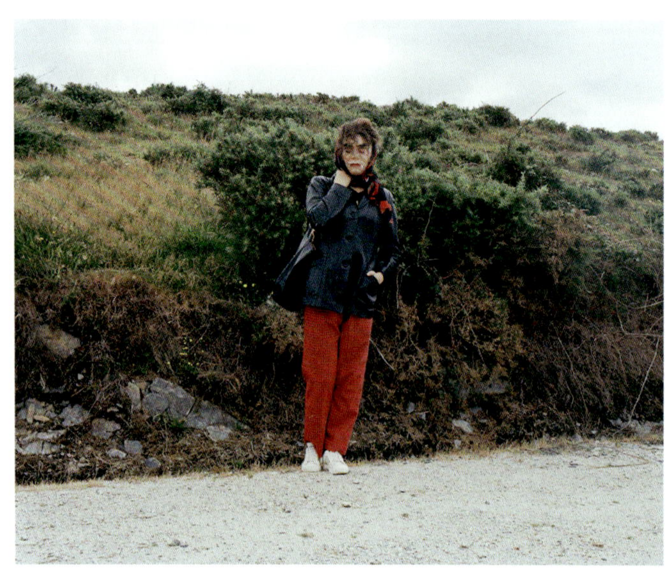

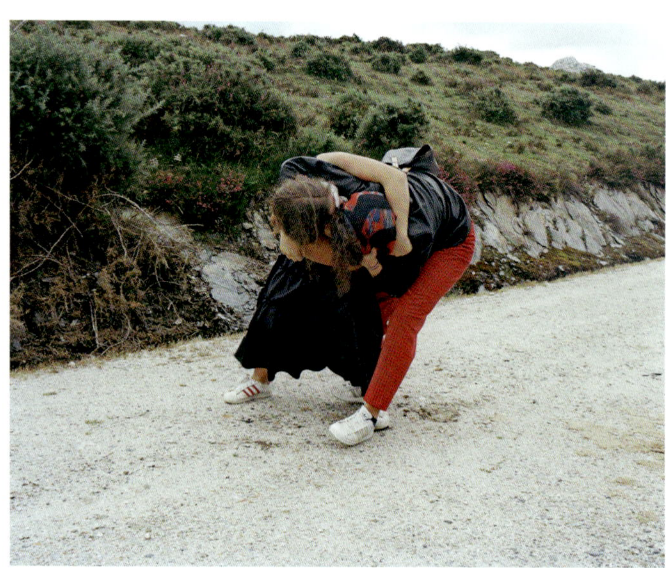

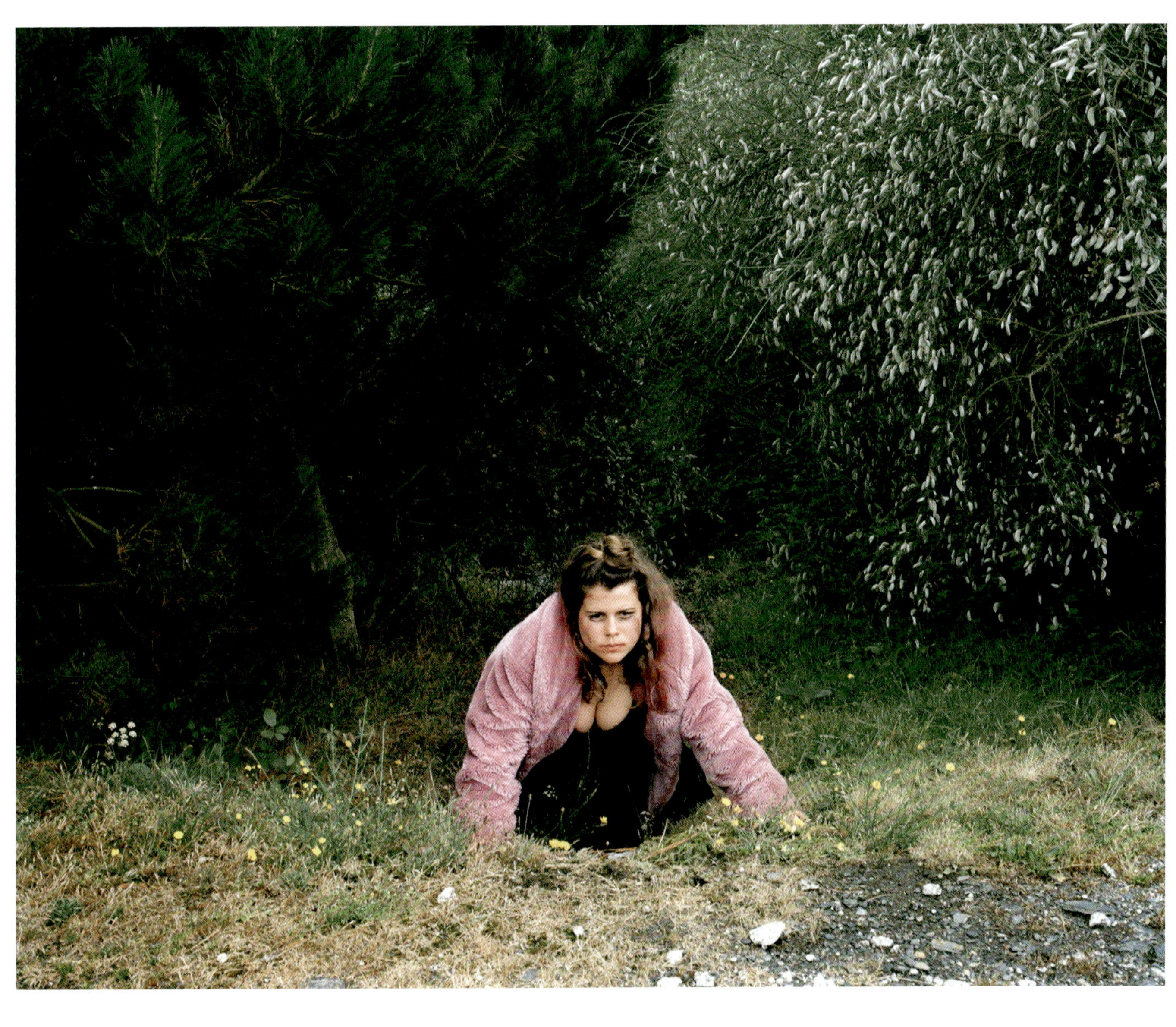

SUBIDA AL CIELO, 'HEAVENLY ASCENT'

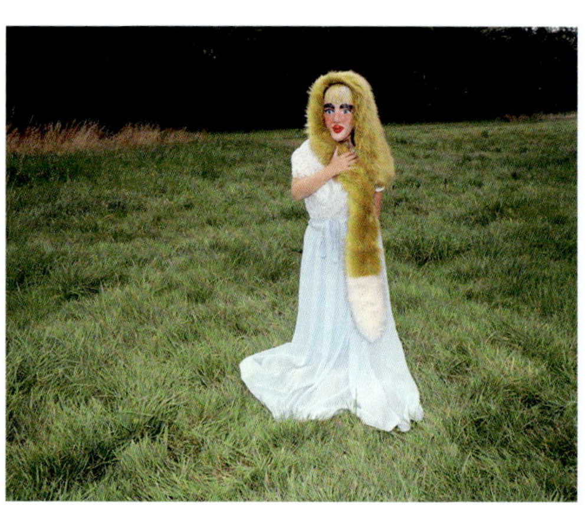

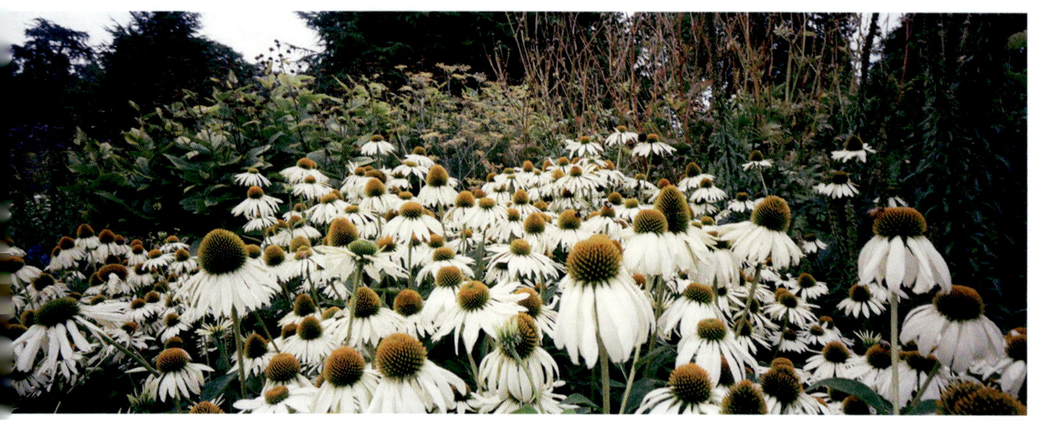

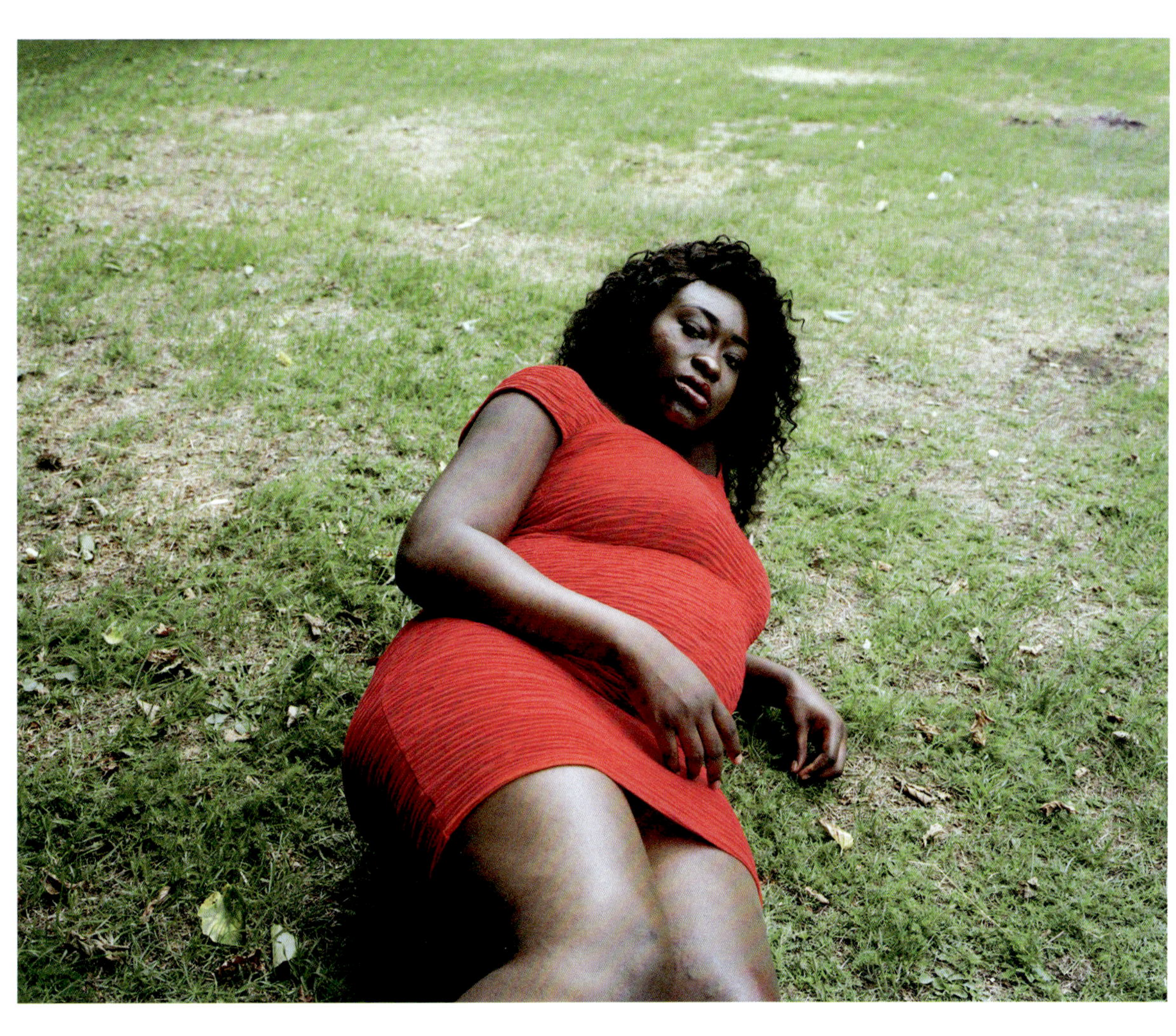

DARK INTERLUDE 2020

Theo Simpson won the Jerwood/Photoworks Award in 2019, alongside artist Silvia Rosi. Drawing on his everyday environment in northern England, Simpson made new work for the subsequent exhibition, titled *Dark Interlude*, reimagining the natural and post-industrial landscape, and traditional approaches to photography which have been so intimately involved in our collective understanding of land. Combining new images with found photography, sculpture, metalwork and printmaking, alongside common engineering and industrial techniques, his pieces were made by both hand and machine. The work was orientated and built around faultlines, strata and geometric grids, drawing upon key moments from the volatile social, political and industrial environment in 1970s and 80s Britain. Here Simpson re-presents *Dark Interlude* with new works made after 2020.

Born in Doncaster in 1986, Simpson is now based in Lincolnshire. He studied photography at Sheffield institute of Arts, and has won numerous other awards, including the Lewis Baltz Research Fund in 2021. He often makes multi-component assemblages and temporary site-specific installations that push the boundaries of the photographic medium – or avoid them entirely. His work is held by institutions such as the Victoria & Albert Museum, Arts Council Collection and Fotomuseum Winterthur.

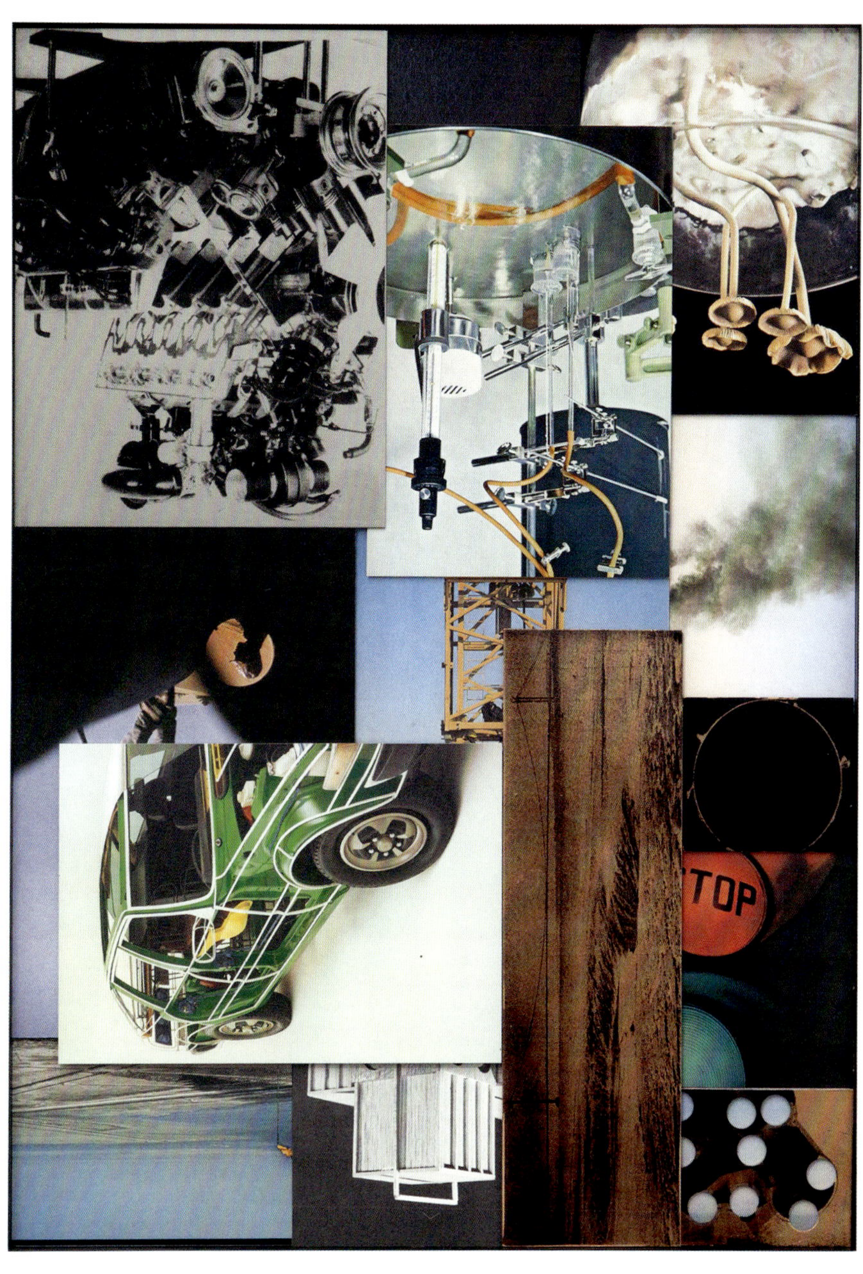
TOP

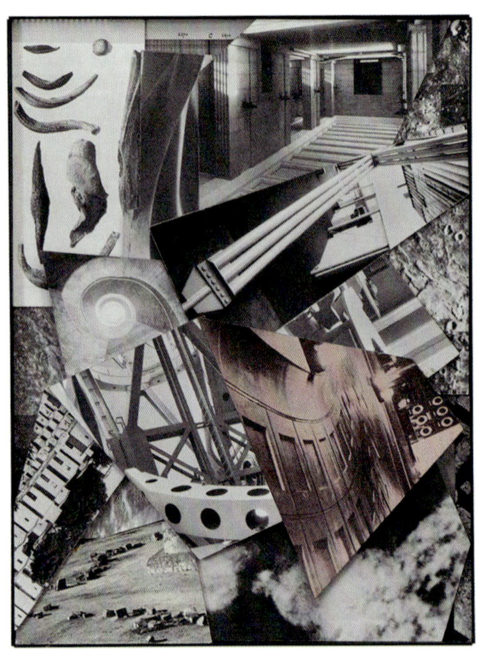

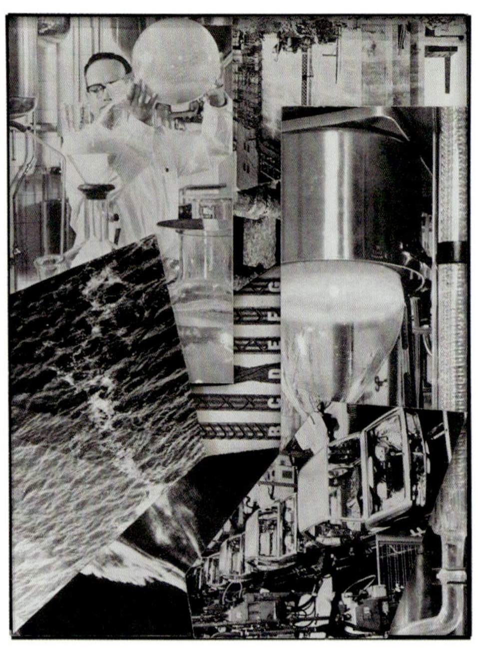

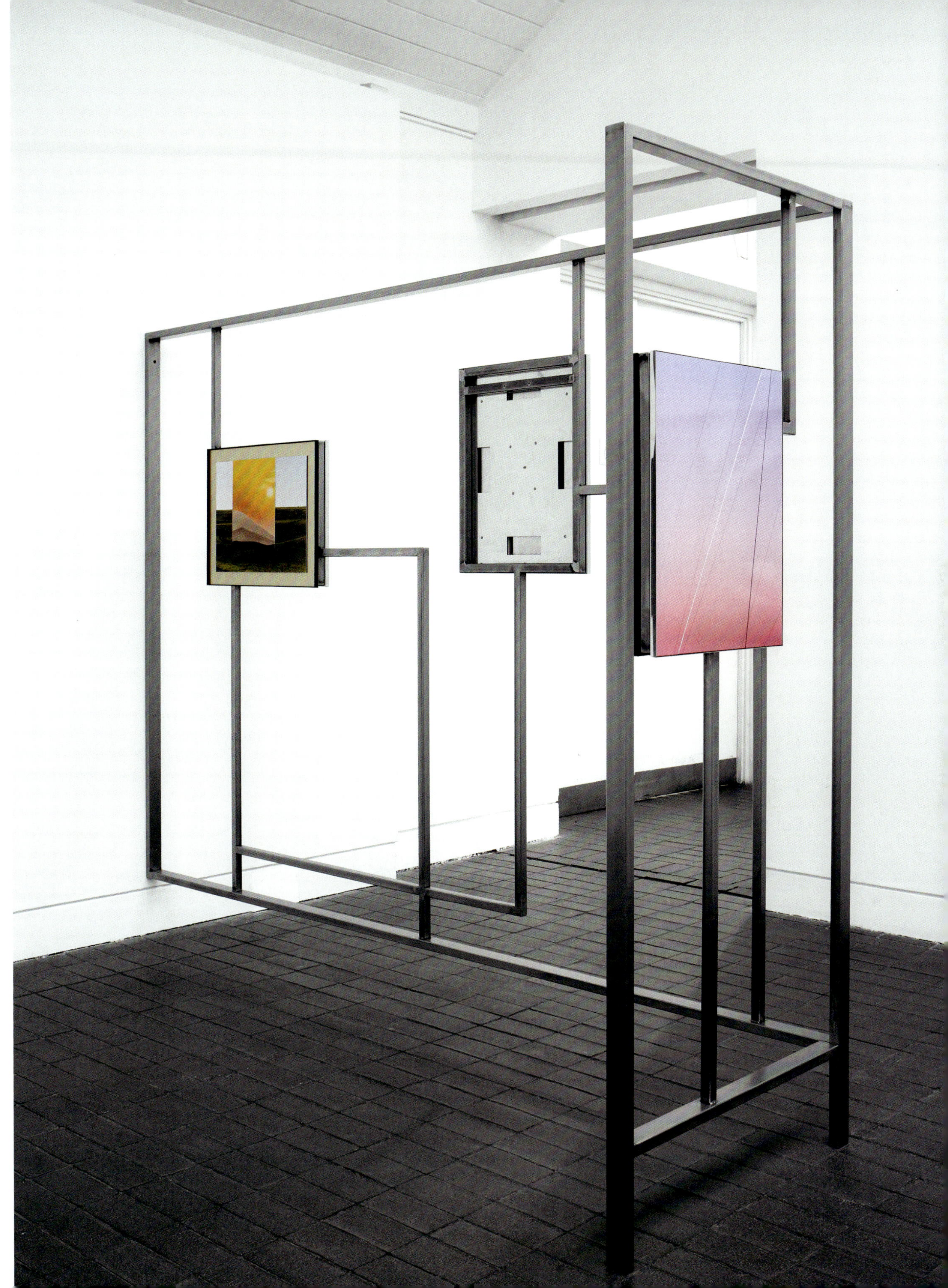

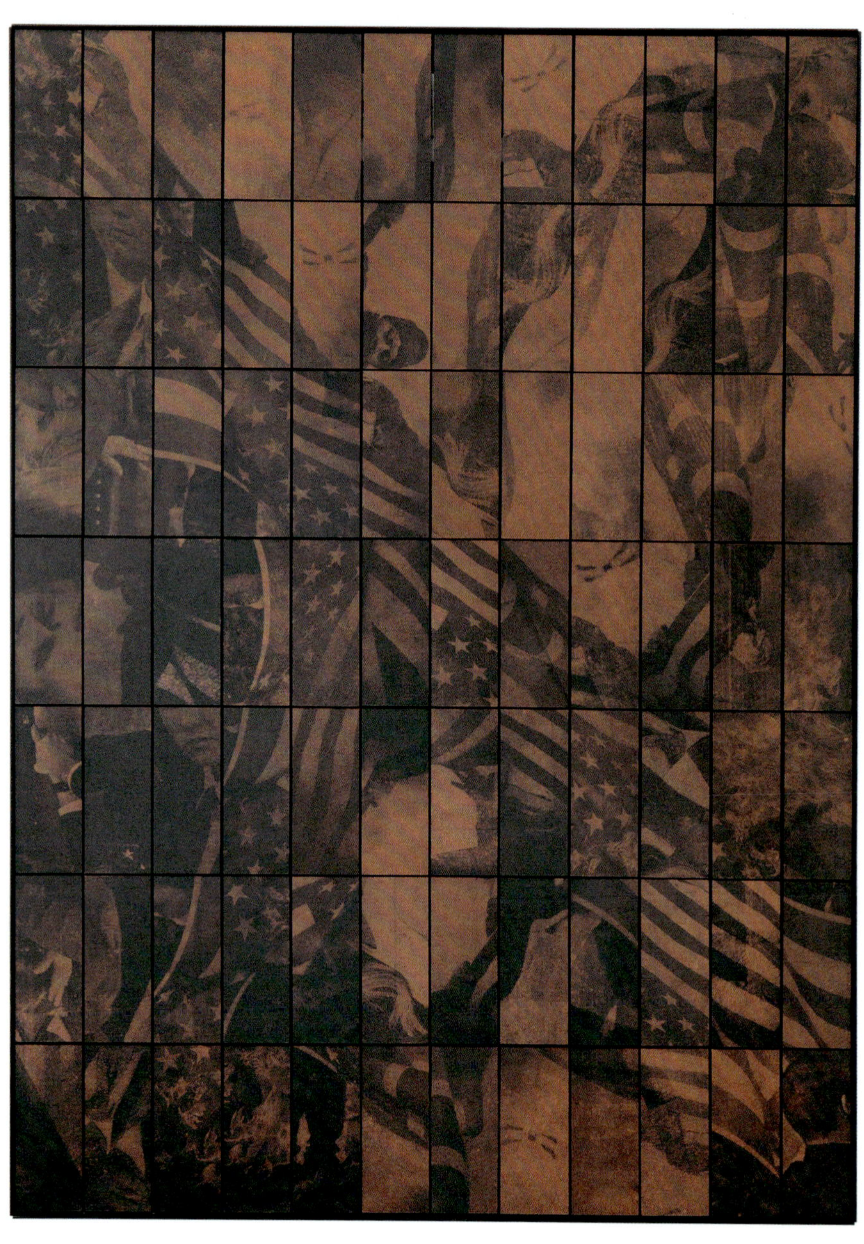

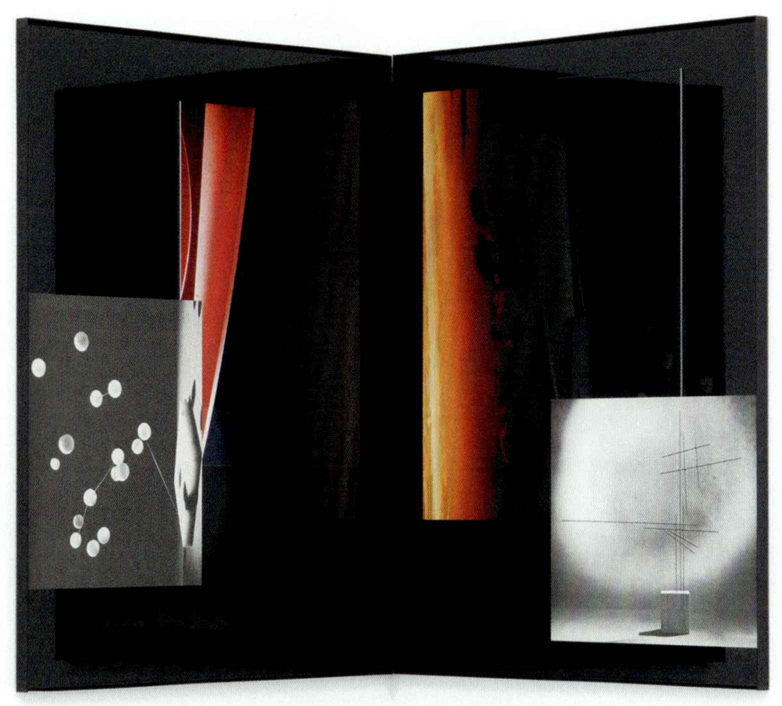

STYX 2021

In classical Greek mythology, Styx is a water goddess and a river, symbolising the boundary between the Earth and the Afterlife. In her work *Styx*, a co-commission by Photoworks and Ballarat International Foto Biennale, Australia, French artist Alix Marie explored the body and its representation, and alternative modes of image-making. Made during the Covid-19 pandemic, the work suggested the fragility of the body, via images exploring its cavities, and via an immersive labyrinthine installation which enveloped visitors in both inside and out. The installation also featured a text, voiced by Marie's long-term collaborator, performer and writer Nina Boukhrief, musing on death, light and life. *Styx* was shown at the National Centre for Photography, Ballarat, and at PHOXXI, Deichtorhallen in Hamburg.

Born in Paris in 1989, Marie studied fine art at Central St Martins, London, and an MA in photography at the Royal College of Art, graduating in 2014. Often focusing on the body and its representation, she pushes the surface of the photographic image, creating 3D sculptures and installations, and collaging and repeating her shots. In 2014, she was awarded residency at the Victoria & Albert Museum and in 2019 she won the Royal Photographic Society's Vic Odden Award.

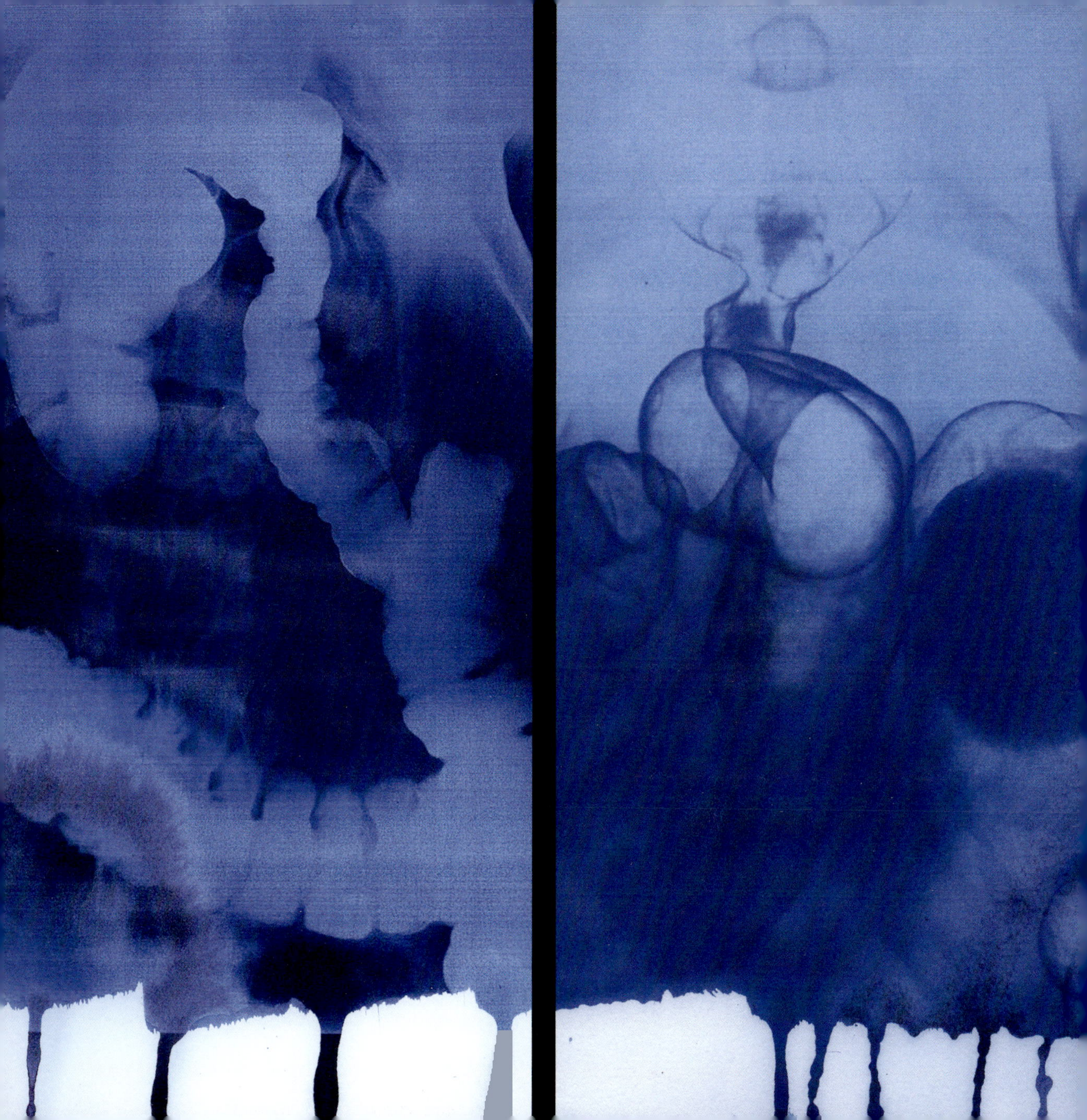

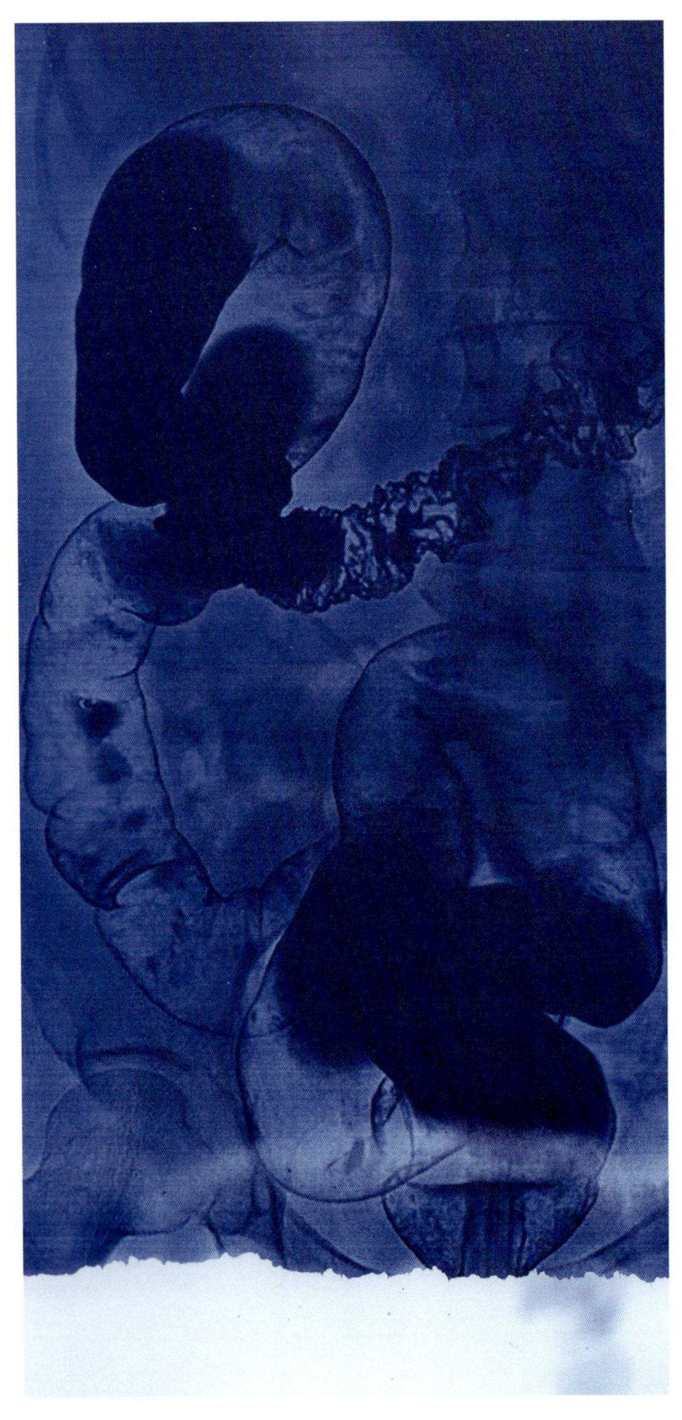

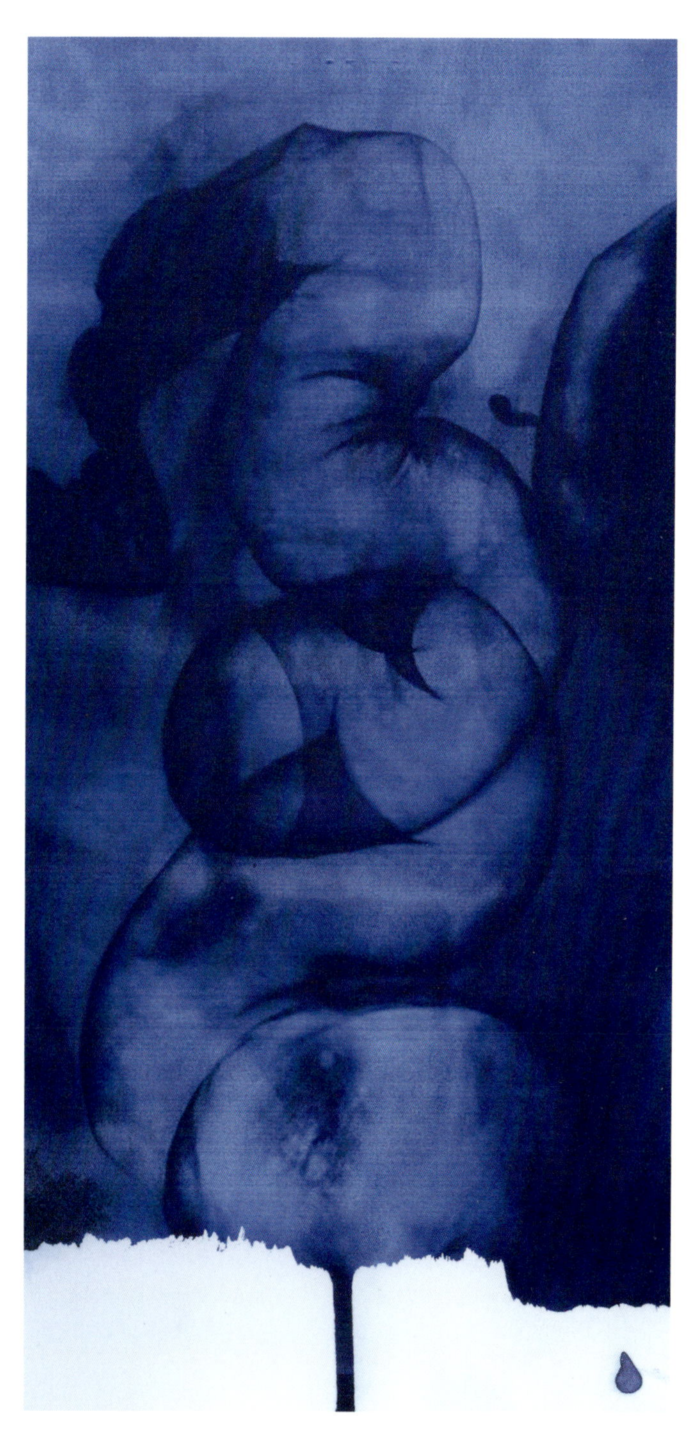

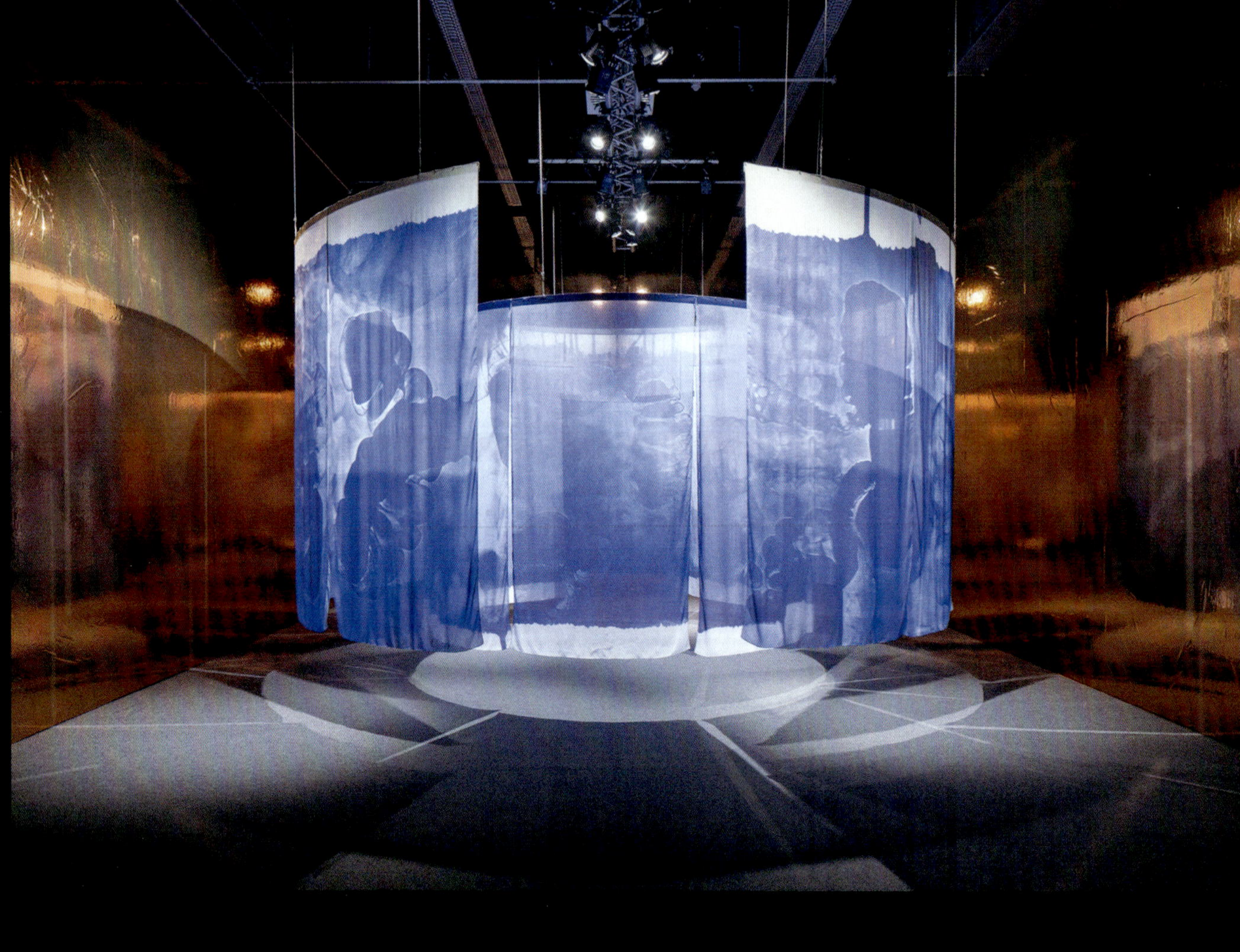

Styx (2021), PHOXXI, Deichtorhallen, Hamburg, 2022. Installation shot © Henning Rogge.

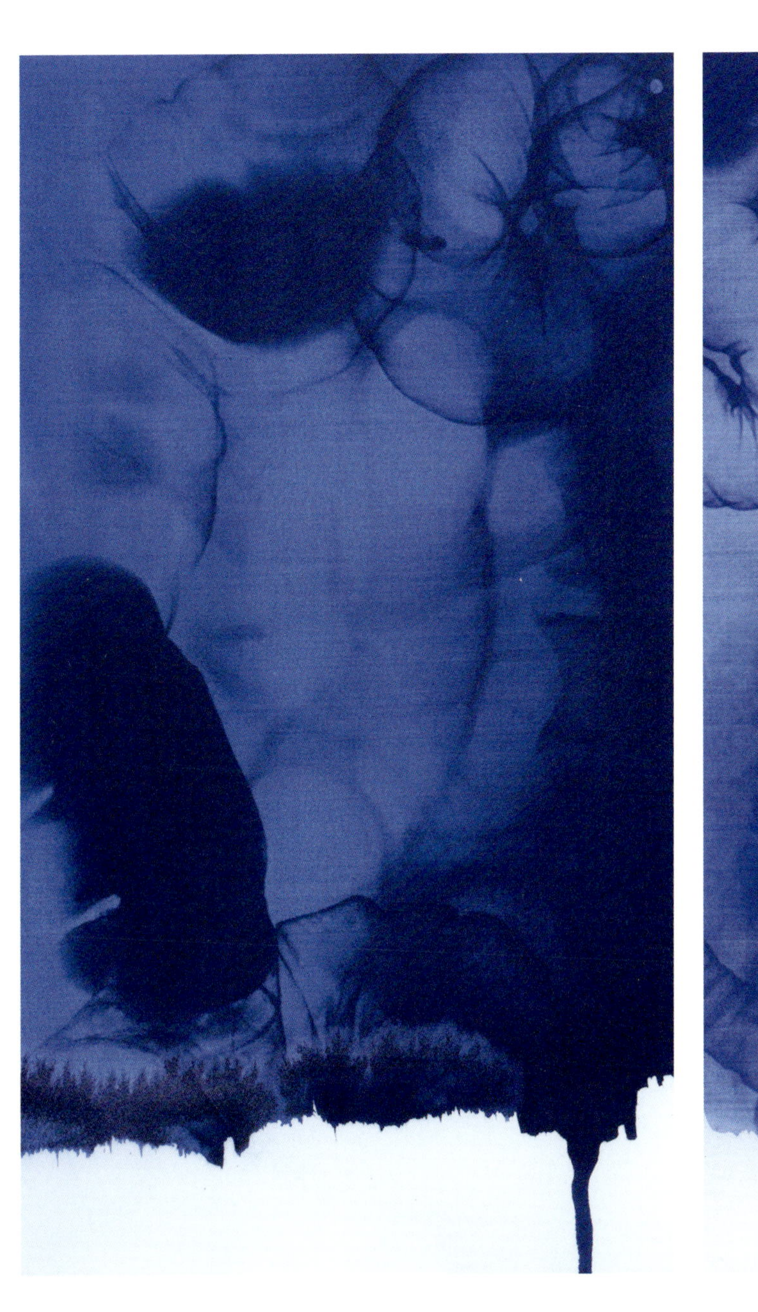

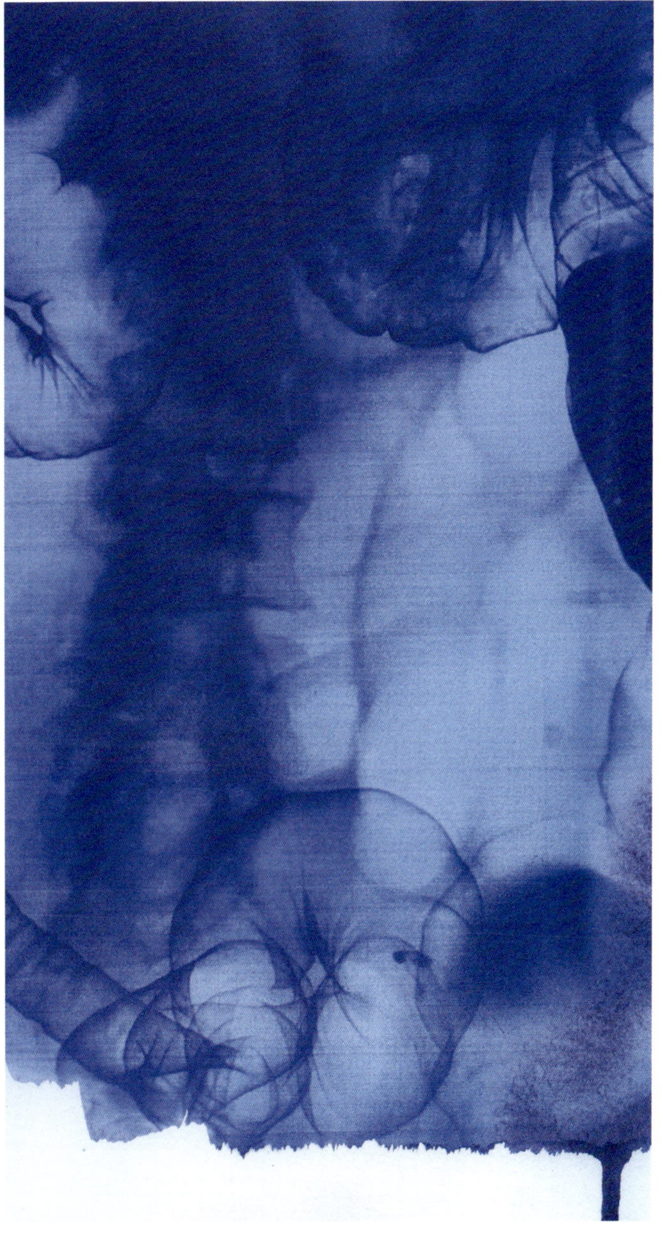

PRESENT CONTINUOUS

CLEOPATRAS SCORING CHANGE 2021

Drawing on her Egyptian upbringing and background in psychology and communications, photographer and visual artist Lina Geoushy tells stories that interrogate gender politics, patriarchal structures and perceptions of womanhood. In *Cleopatras Scoring Change*, commissioned in 2021 by the British Journal of Photography and the Against All Odds Malala Fund, Geoushy meditates on the power, quiet defiance and resilience of two Egyptian women in sport. Working collaboratively with her subjects, she shows Malak Hamza, the first Egyptian woman to become first reserve for the Olympic gymnastics finals, and Rooka Saeed, a footballer who overcame bullying and societal pressure to earn a place on Egypt's junior national team. Geoushy likens both to Cleopatra, for their power to overcome barriers and reclaim success on their own terms.

Born in 1990, Lina Geoushy lives and works between London and Cairo. She holds an MA in photojournalism and documentary photography from the University of the Arts London, graduating with distinction from London College of Communication in 2021. She featured in the 2021 Graduate Issue of Photoworks' *P+* online magazine, after being selected by a jury including artists Maryam Wahid and Photoworks curator Julia Bunnemann. Geoushy's series *Shame Less*, which focuses on women's experiences of sexual harassment, was also given a special award by global equipment platform MPB.

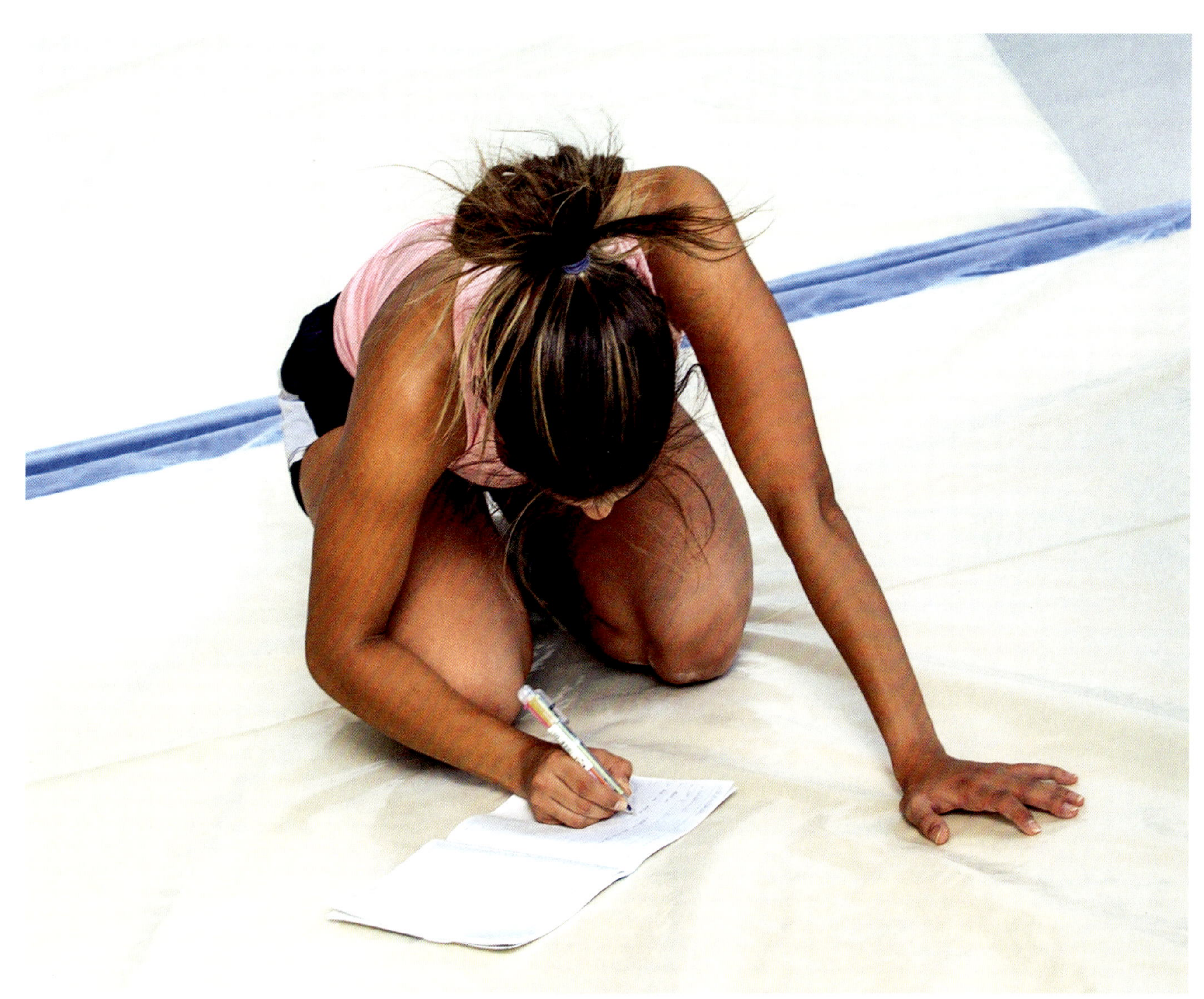

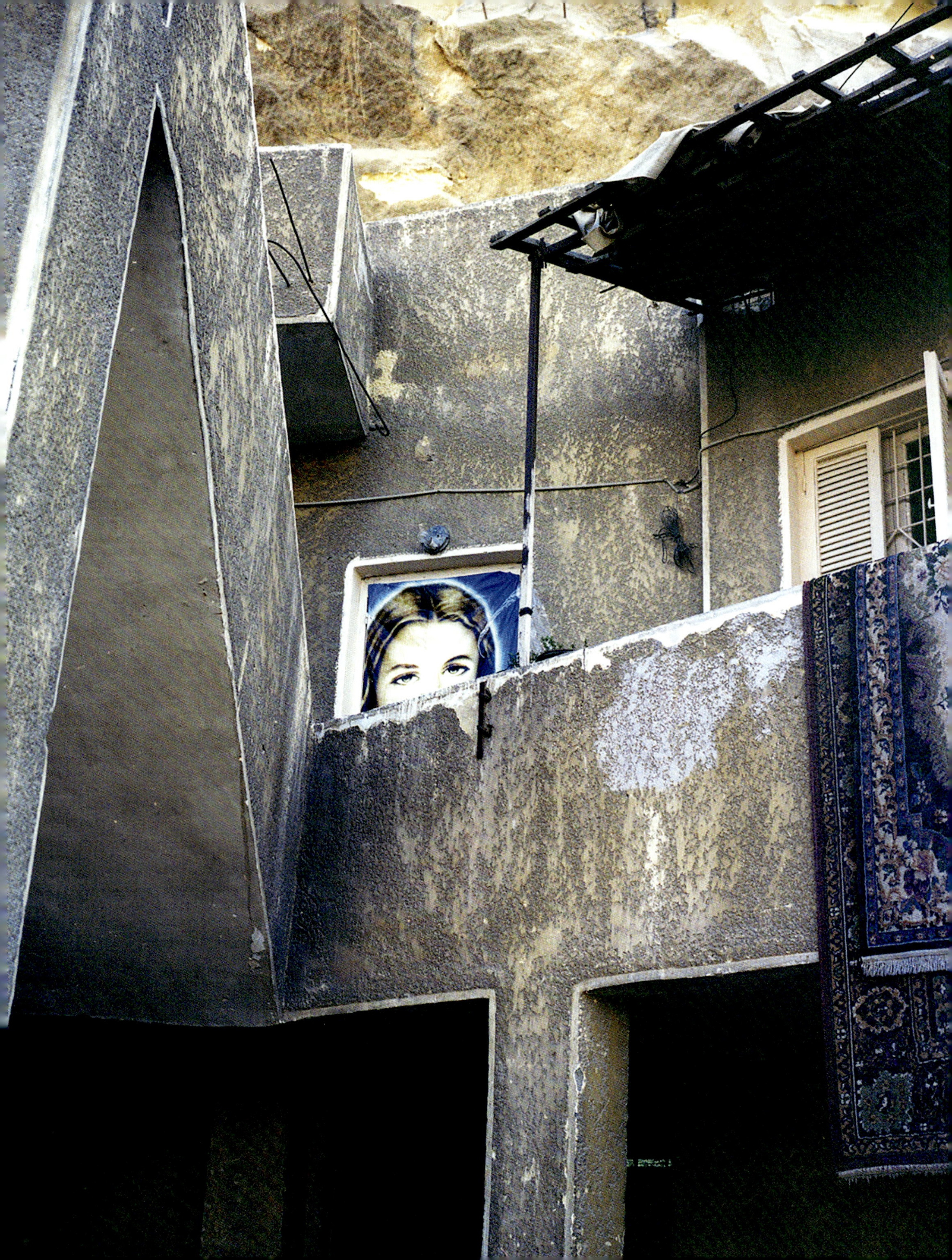

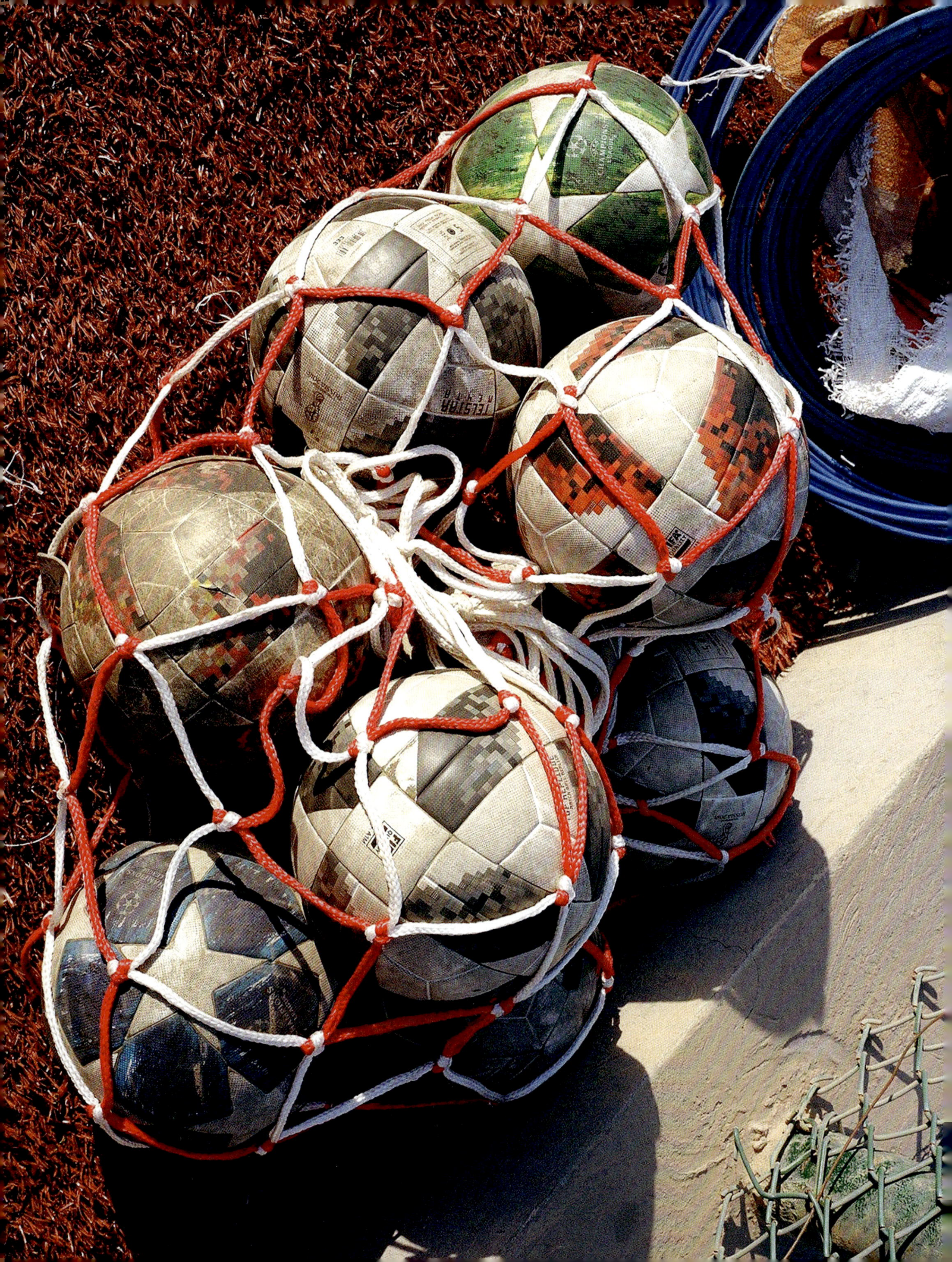

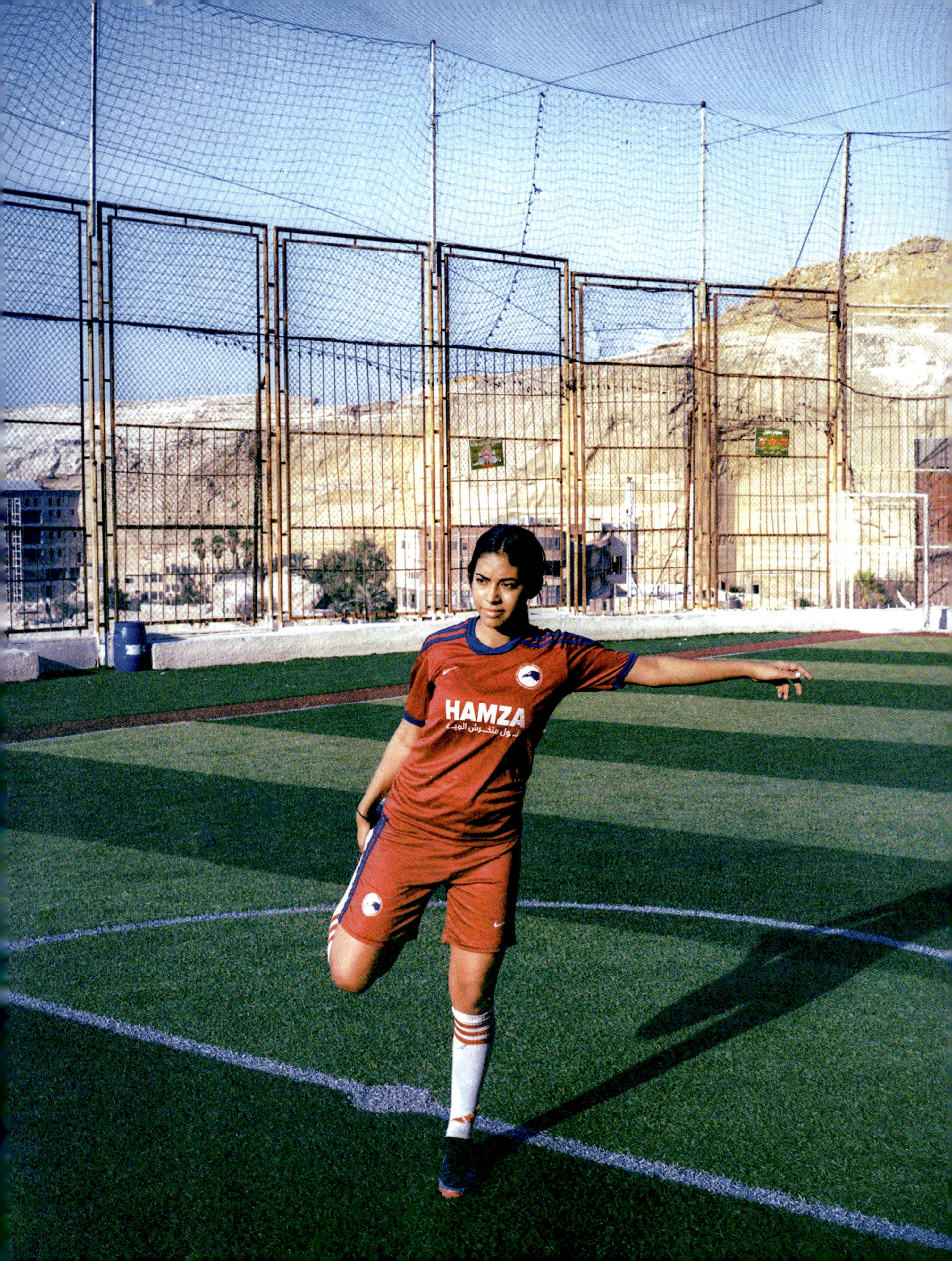
HAMZA

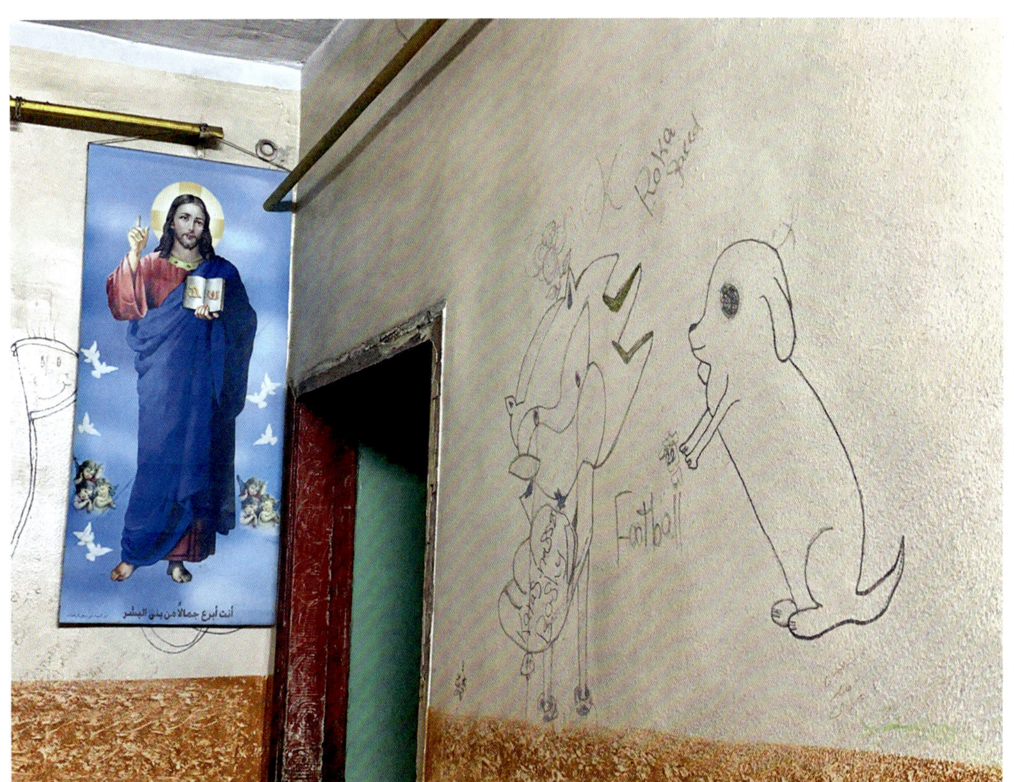
أنت أبرع جمالاً من بني البشر
Football

THINKING LIKE AN ISLAND 2024

Gabriele Chiapparini and Camilla Marrese are an artistic duo with a shared photographic practice. Combining their backgrounds as a film director (Chiapparini) and graphic designer (Marrese), their collaboration transforms individual thinking into matter for collective elaboration, to visually articulate complex questions.

In *Thinking Like an Island*, shot in an unnamed Mediterranean location, the duo avoided the temptation of representing an island as either a utopia or a dystopia, instead delving into the layered potential and confinement allowed by a place with no hospital, cars, religious leaders or police. When creating a book with the publisher Overlapse, they sought to formally reflect their ideas on geographical, social and temporal space, unconventionally binding four integrated books. The resulting publication highlights the relationship between the intangible and the tangible, the conceptual and the physical, which is so prominent in their practice.

Chiapparini and Marrese have exhibited their work at Fotografia Europea in Reggio Emilia, Espaço Alto in San Paulo and Kranj Foto Fest in Slovenia, among many more. Their work won the PhMuseum Criticae in 2022, and was shortlisted for the Luigi Ghirri Prize in 2024, and this year, Photoworks partnered with Luigi Ghirri, Forestry England and the Italian Cultural Institute of London to offer the duo a residency at Dalby Forest, North Yorkshire.

GABRIELE CHIAPPARINI and CAMILLA MARRESE

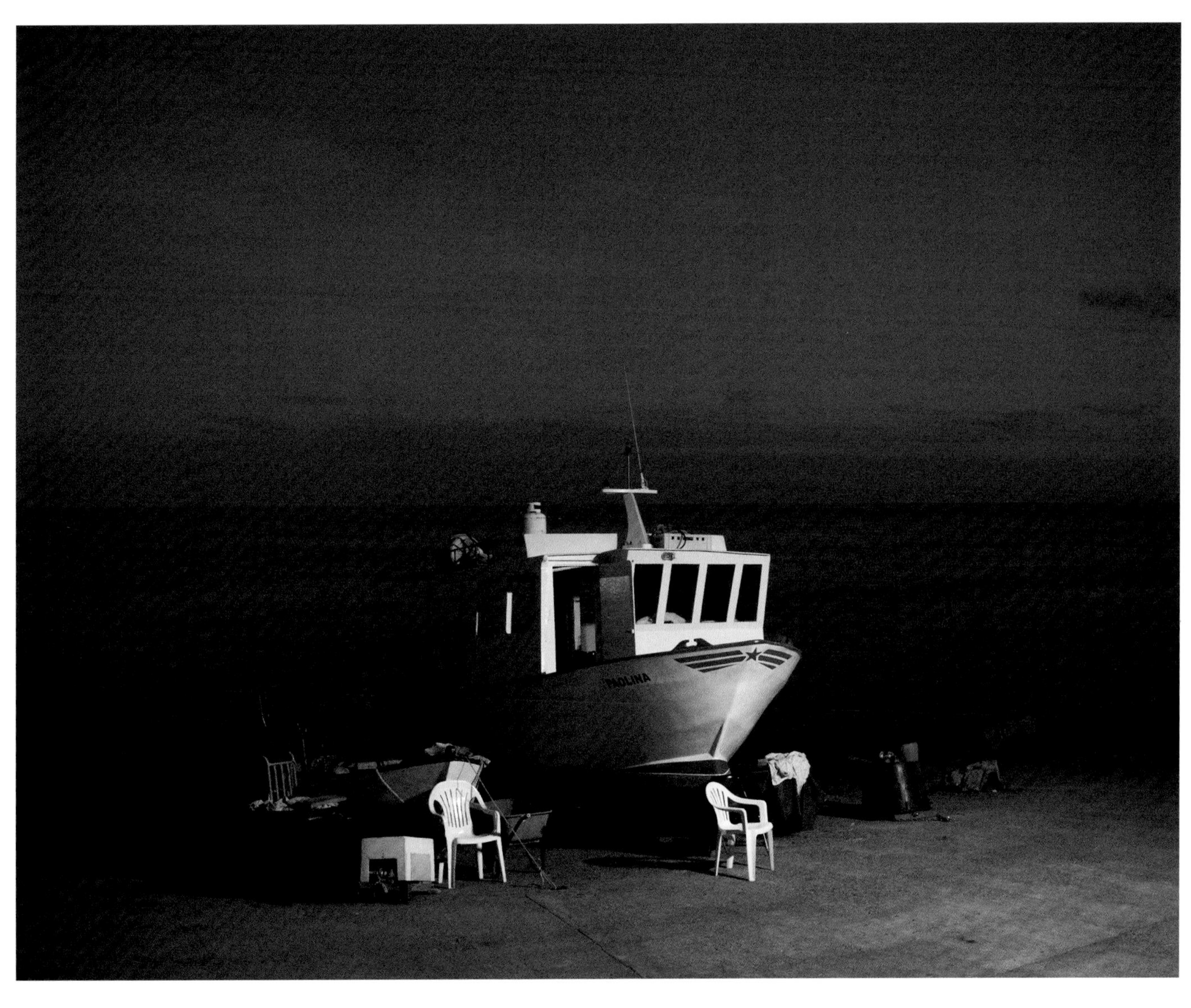

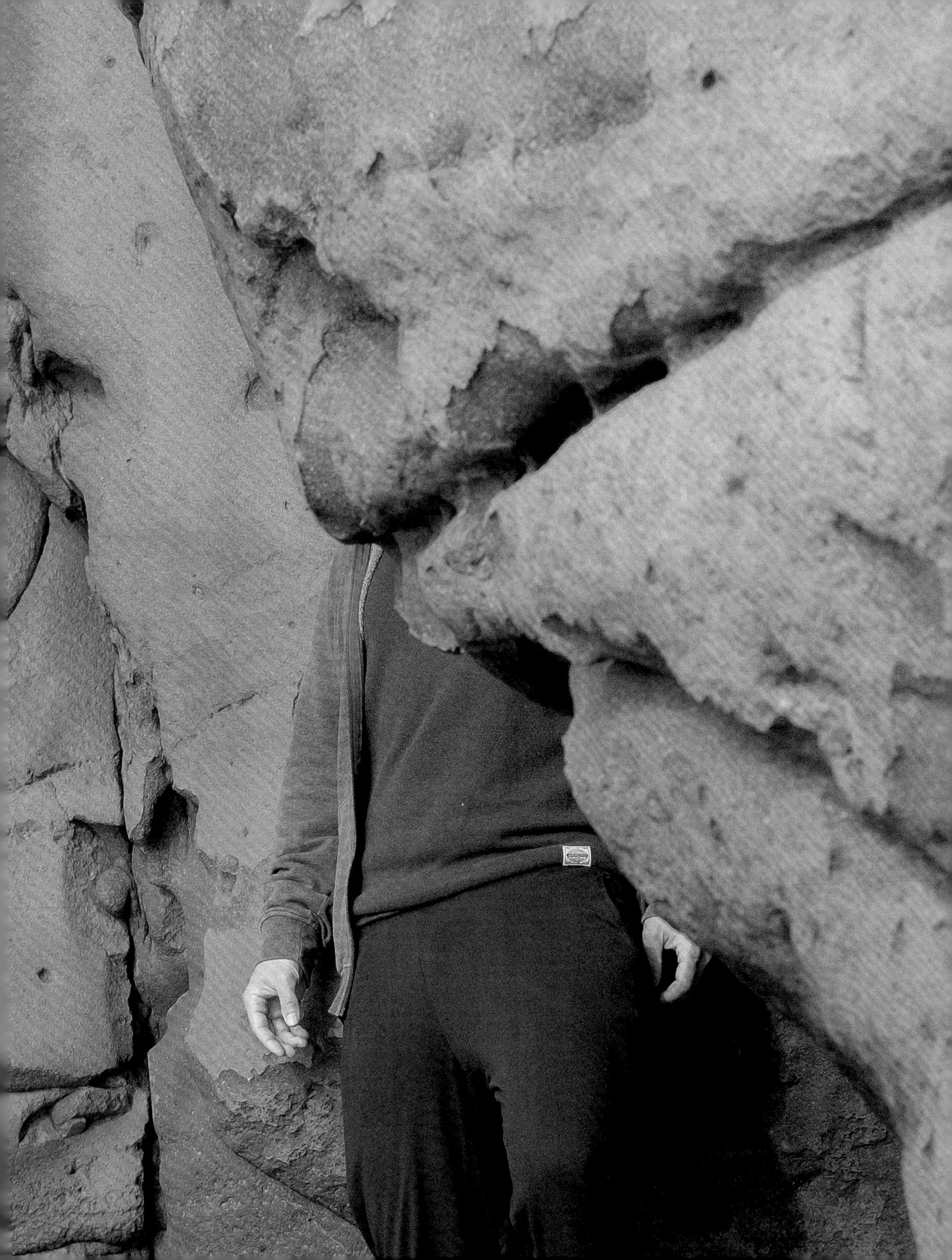

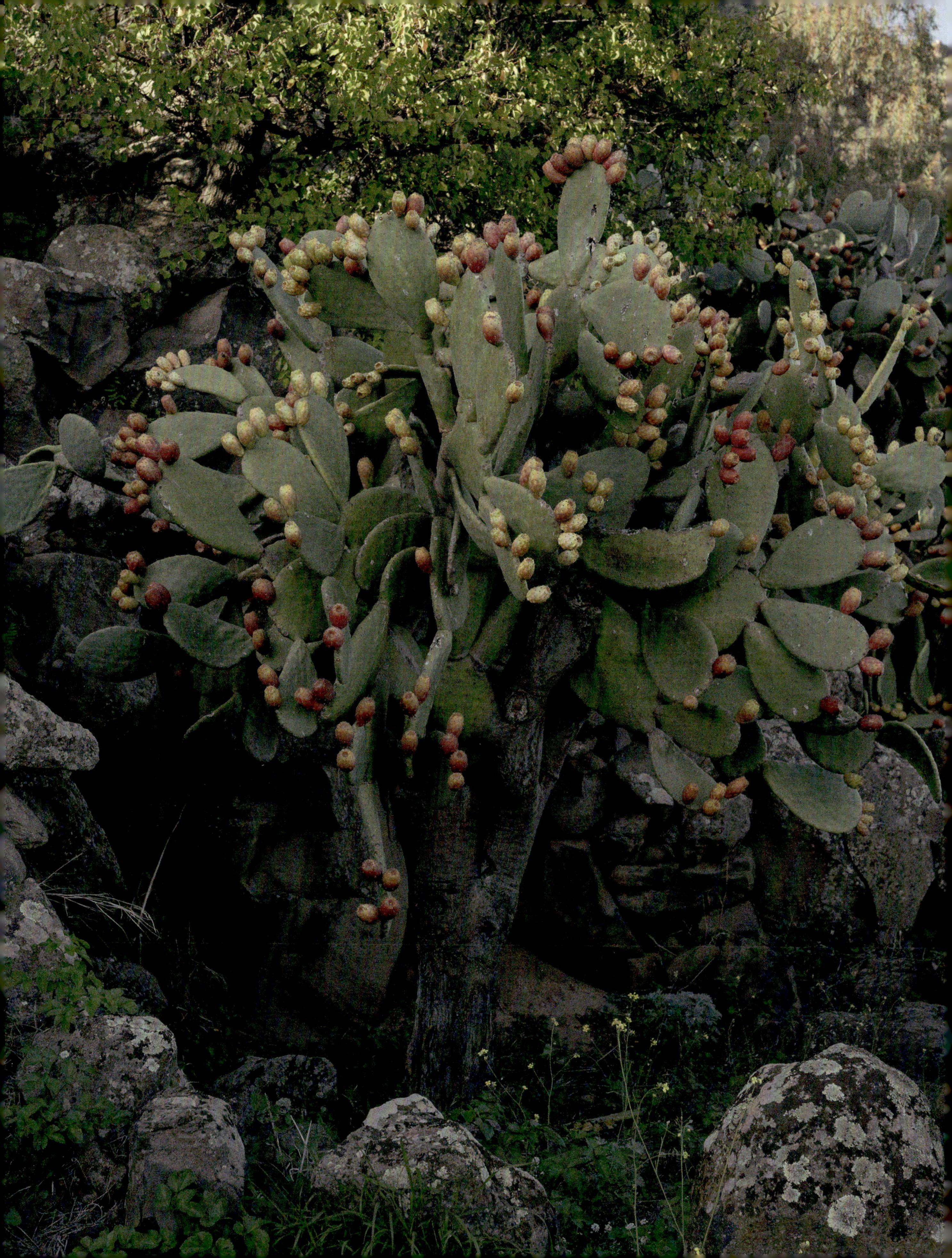

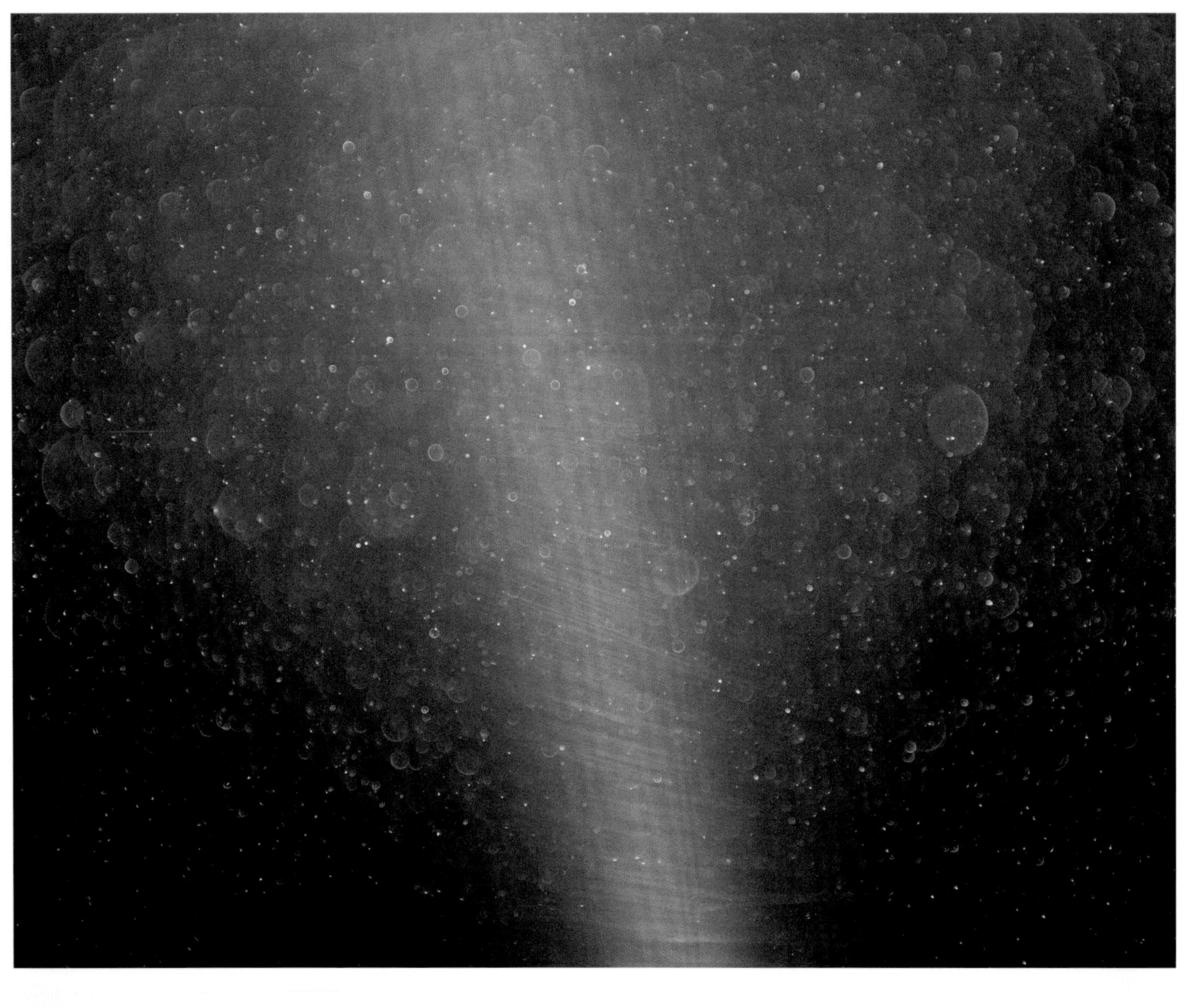

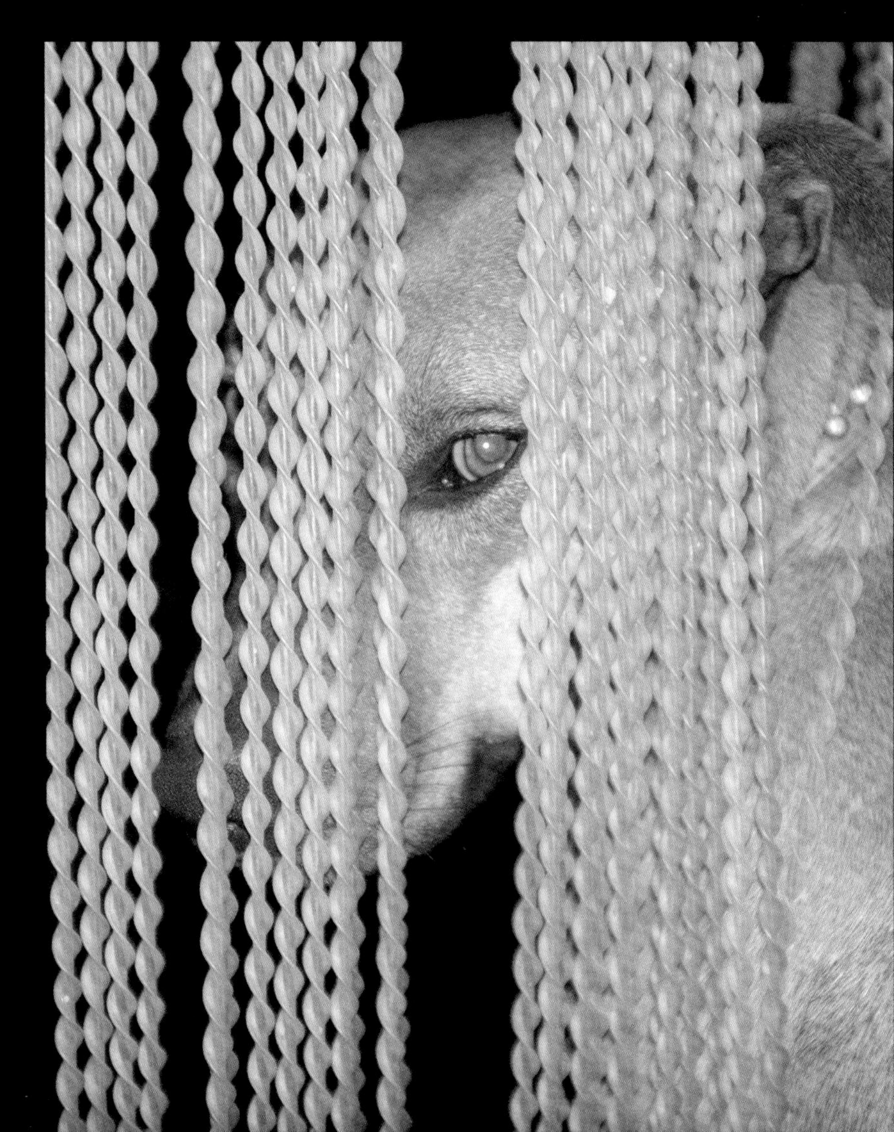

BLUEPRINTING OUR FUTURES 2024

London-born, Barbados-raised artist Myah Asha Jeffers was recommended to Photoworks by Heather Agyepong, who won the 2022 Jerwood/Photoworks Awards alongside Joanne Coates. Born in 1994, Jeffers makes work spanning photography, theatre and film, focusing on documenting daily life in diasporic communities. She has chosen to show the mixed-media project *Blueprinting Our Futures*, which she made in 2024 on residency at Knowle West Media Centre, Bristol. Jeffers set up a series of workshops, inviting locals to reflect on their sense of self both in their current neighbourhood and the homes they have left behind. The cyanotypes here are all self-portraits, showing local women who have migrated to the UK from elsewhere. The project also includes sound and textiles, to explore "the sonic and visual frequencies of hope", says Jeffers, as well as the complexity of the diasporic experience.

Jeffers mostly works in analogue and often develops and prints her own monochrome images. Her images have featured in publications such as *Vogue*, *The Guardian* and the *British Journal of Photography*. Jeffers currently works at The Uncertain Kingdom, a film short funding project, and her debut narrative short, *Bathsheba*, was shown at Toronto's Inside Out film festival and the S.O.U.L film festival at the British Film Institute. In 2024, Jeffers won the Joan Wakelin Bursary.

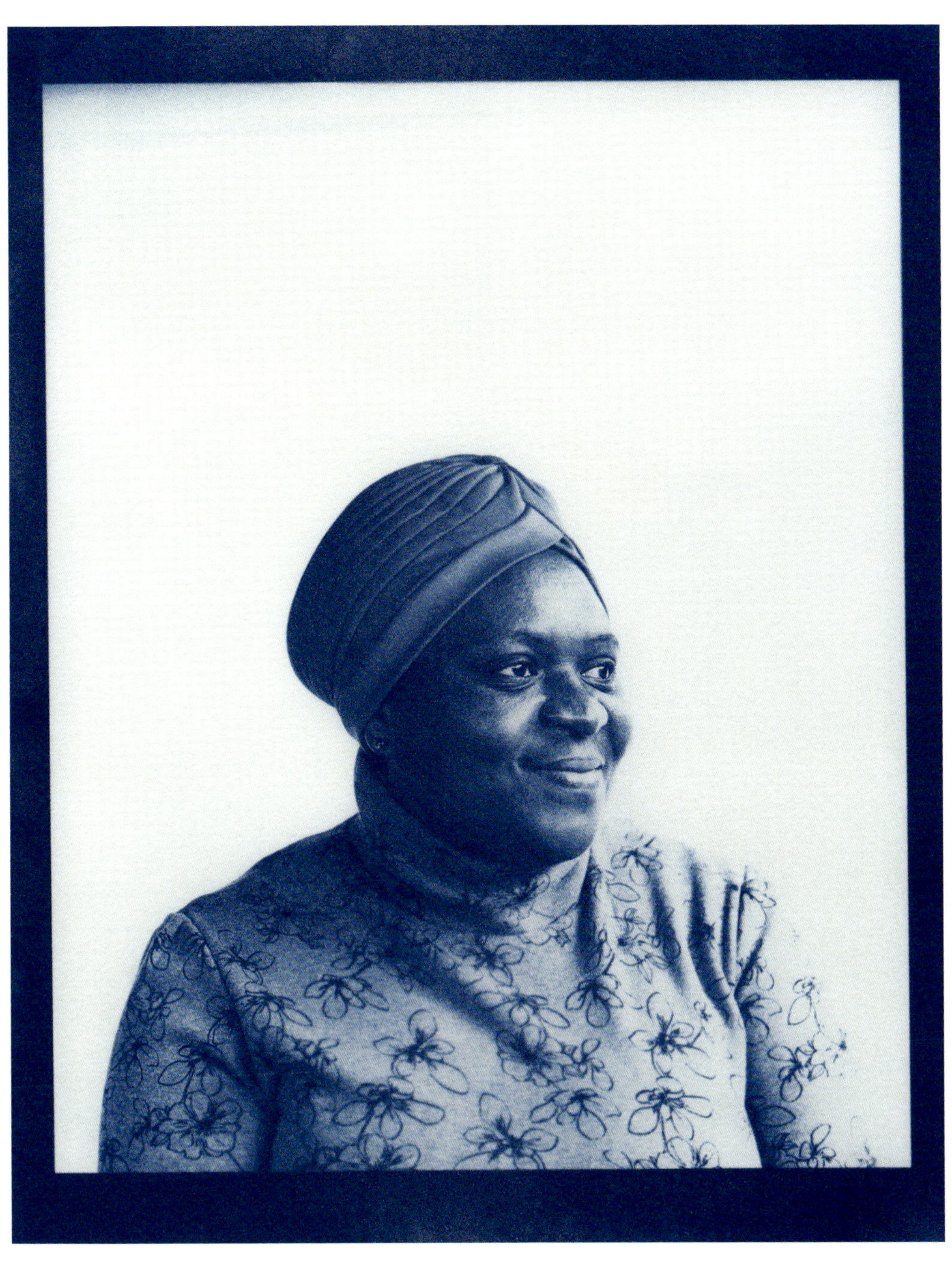

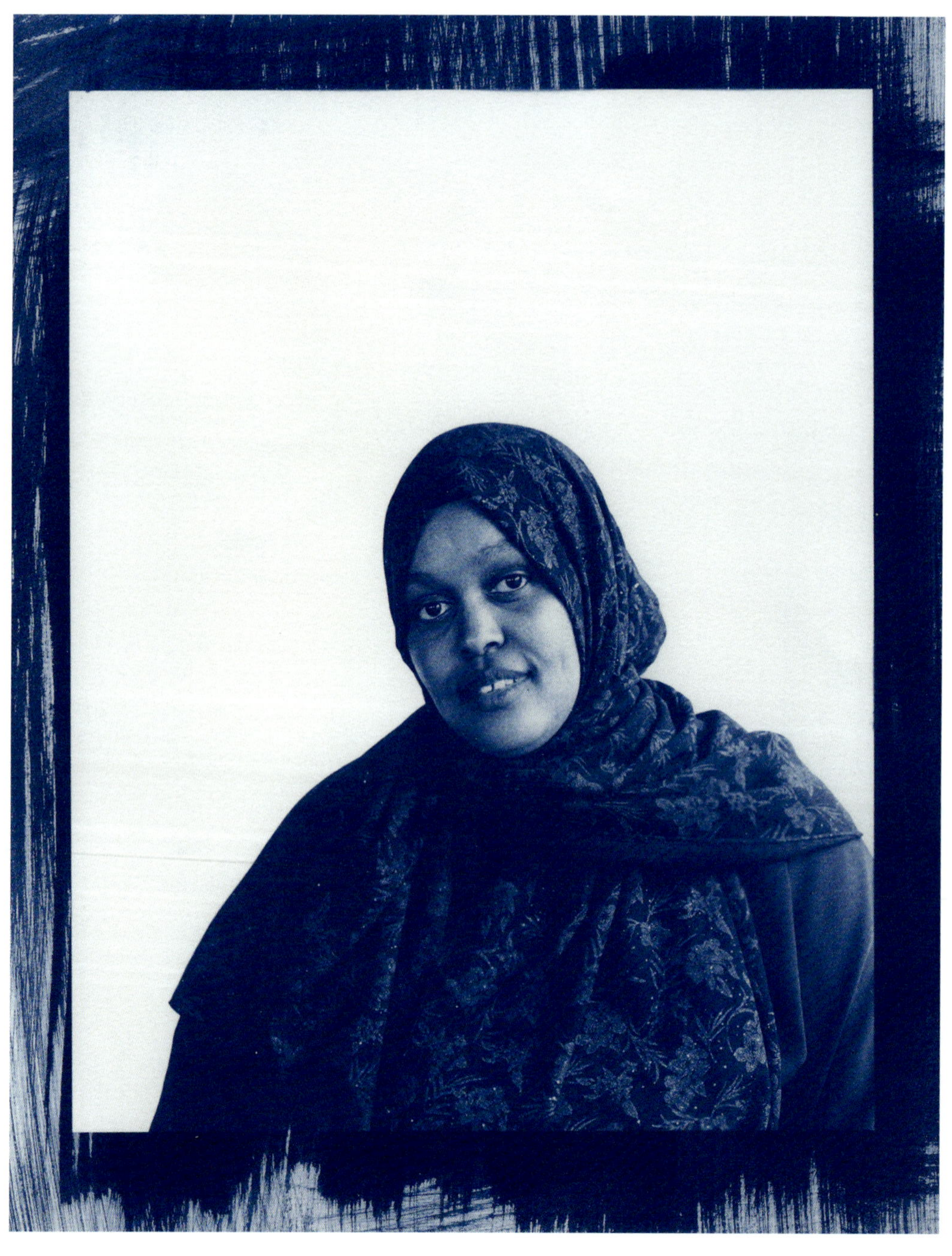

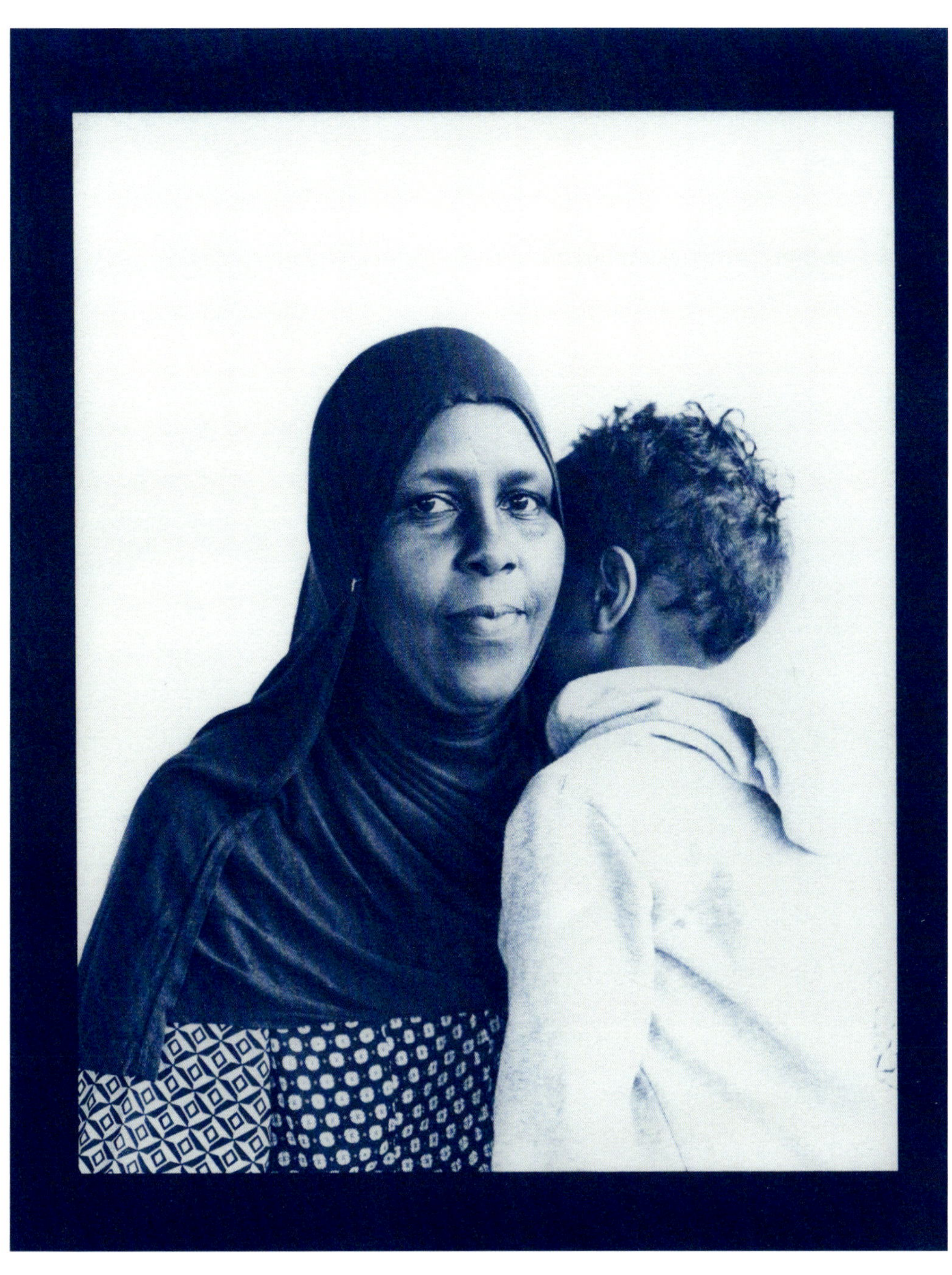

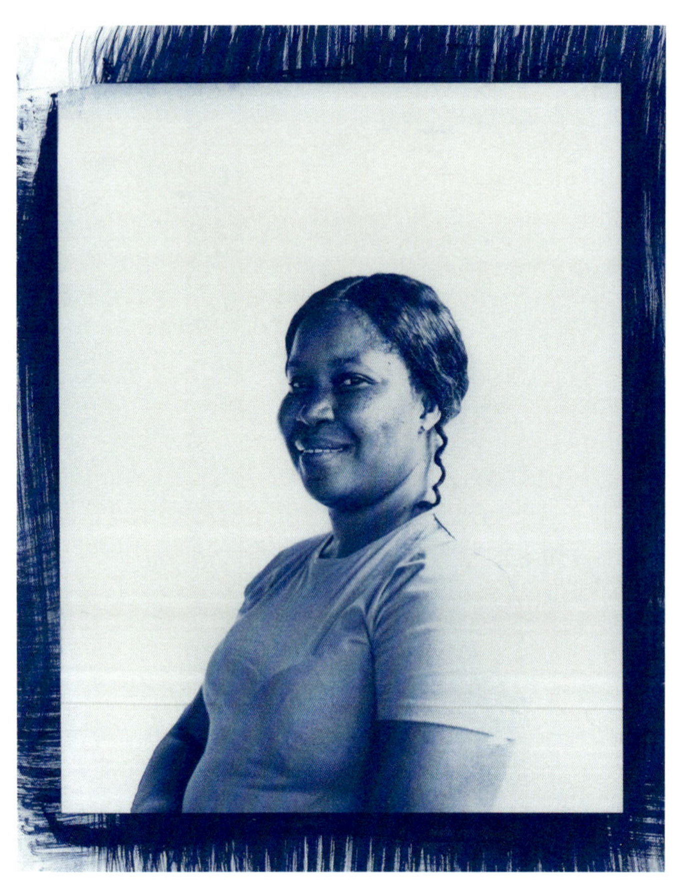

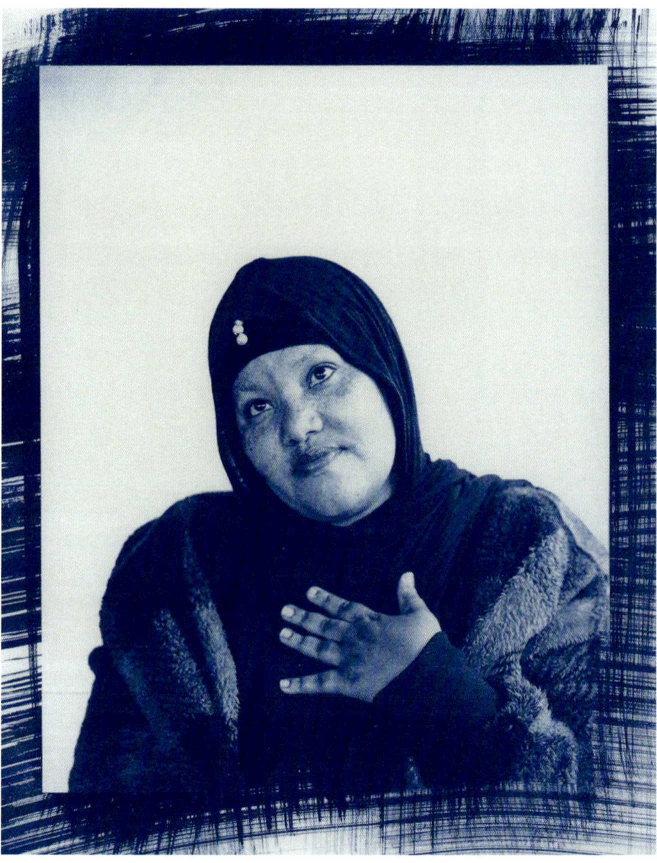

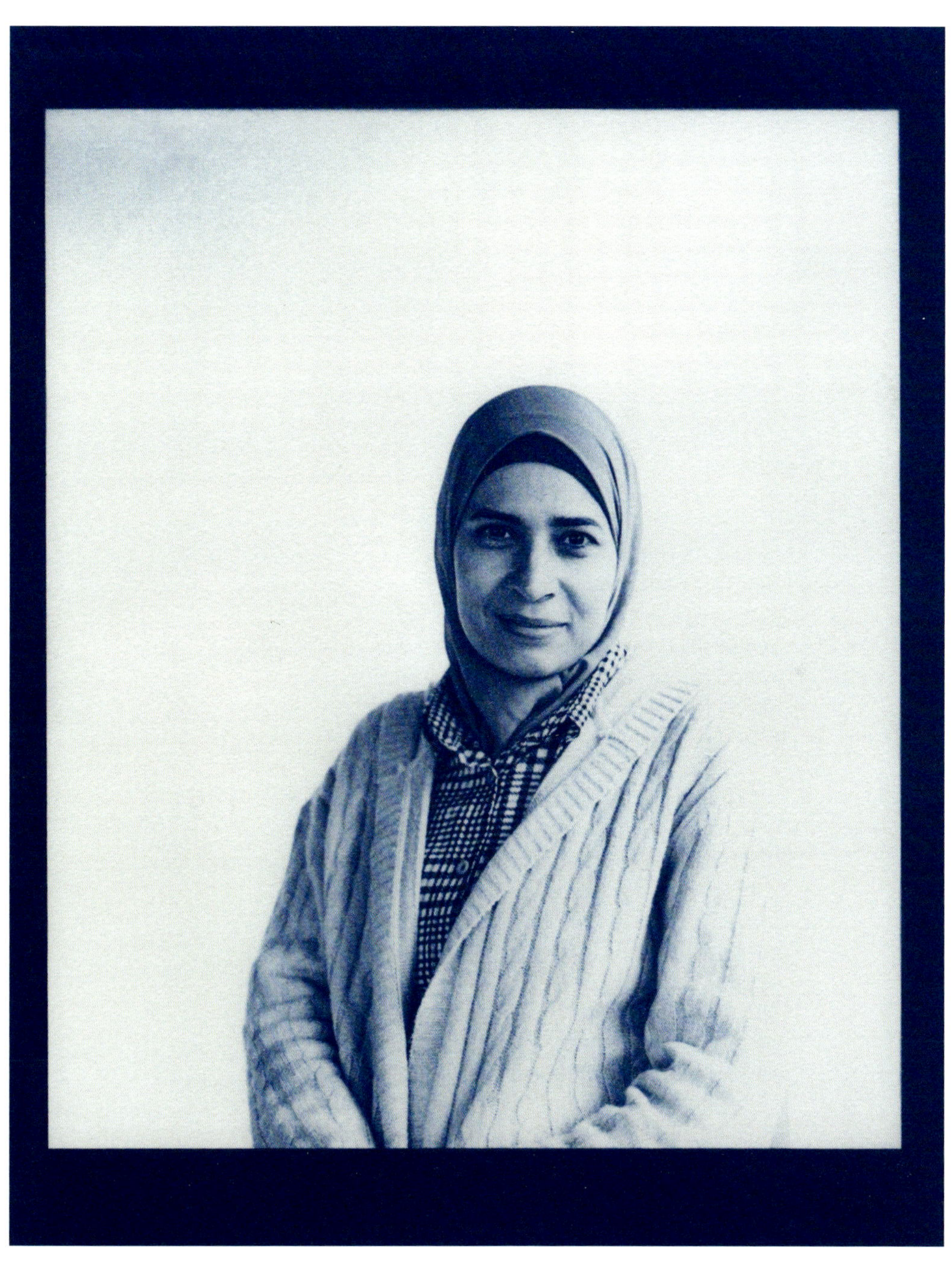

FOR SO MANY YEARS WHEN I CLOSE MY EYES Since 2024

Billy HC Kwok's series *For So Many Years When I Close My Eyes* represents various aspects of Yu Lai Wai-ling's struggle for answers about her son, Yu Man-hon, a teenager who disappeared in 2000 at the China-Hong Kong border. Kwok's intimate portrayal of the Yu household combines with images of Chinese landscapes to deepen the narrative; Yu Lai Wai-ling's Polaroids of unhoused children wandering the streets are shown pinned to a map in her home, for example, exploring photography as a means of evidence in her quest for truth. *For So Many Years When I Close My Eyes* was published by Aperture in 2024, but it is an ongoing project to which Kwok plans to add elements such as satellite images.

Based in Hong Kong and Taiwan, Kwok works between art and documentary, to reveal rapid shifts in geopolitical relationships and structures of power in his region. Kwok was a Magnum Foundation Fellow in 2018 and a VII Academy Fellow in 2023, selected for his project investigating national archives in Taiwan and family archives in Hong Kong. His work has been exhibited at The Royal Photographic Society, UK, Foam, Amsterdam, and Landskrona Foto Festival, Sweden. Photoworks director Louise Fedotov-Clements has selected him to be included in this publication.

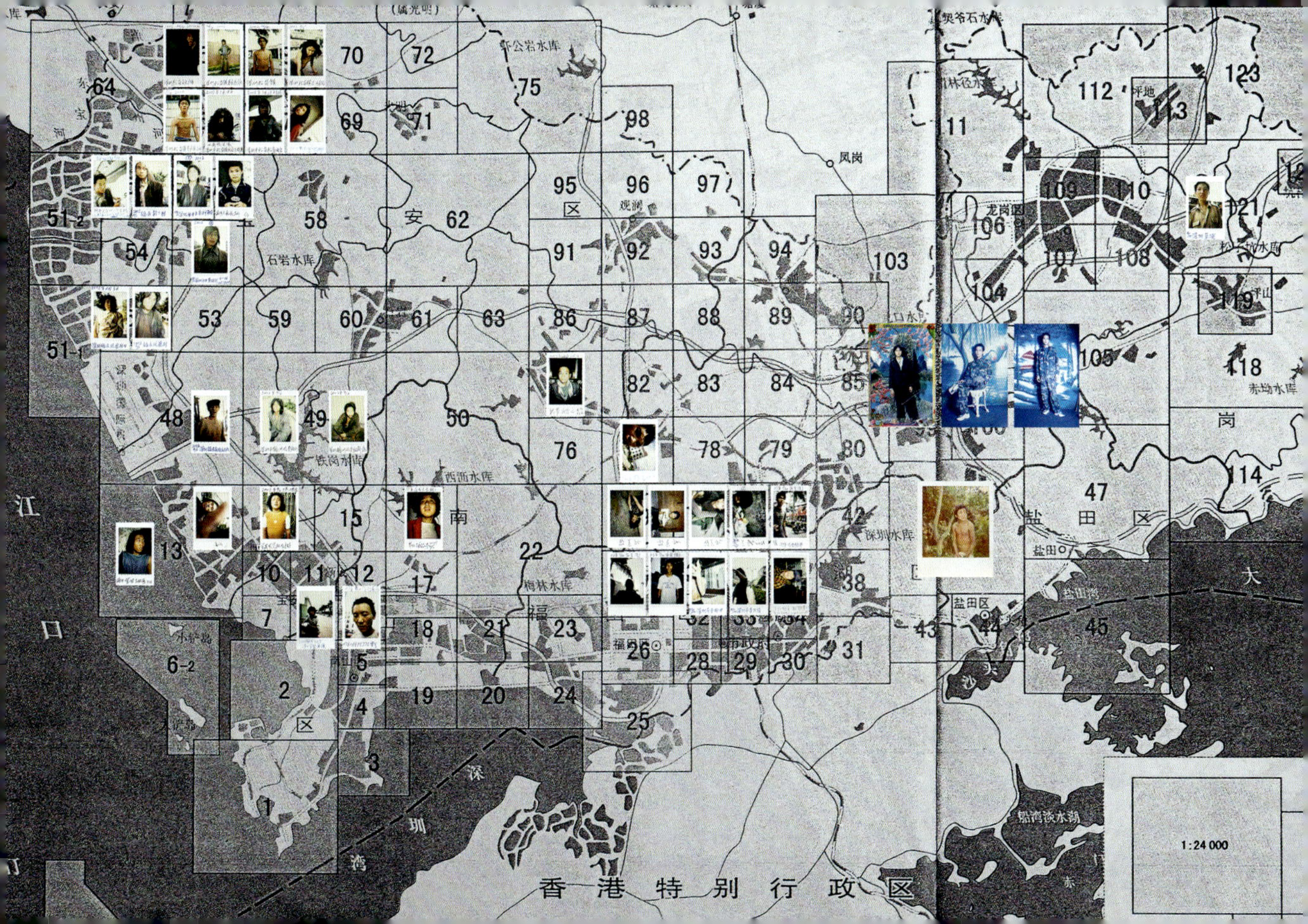

石岩水库
铁岗水库
西沥水库
梅林水库
深圳水库
凤岗
观澜
龙岗区
赤坳水库
盐田区
盐田
盐田区
市政府
香港特别行政区
1:24 000

致翰兒

我朝夕念掛的翰兒，你還安在嗎？是母親的生命之舟把你帶來這世界，原本以為在我們這個平凡平靜的家中一家人可以平安愉快地生活，過安穩溫馨的日子。

自從2000年8月24日中午11:20我們母子在地鐵站失散後，你被香港入境處人員錯誤地強行遣送到深圳以至在內地失蹤。從此改變了翰兒你的命運，也改變了我們家的一切。沒有你的日子，原本暖暖的充滿笑聲的家變得冷冷的甚是凄清，母親我從此被困在無底的痛苦之窟。翰兒啊，你這無辜被強迫離群的孤雁到底在哪裡？父母和親友們踏破鐵鞋走遍南北東西就是不見你的蹤影。翰兒啊，餓了你吃甚麼？冷了有衣嗎？病了怎麼辦？你可否聽到母親悲切的呼喚？快回來吧我的翰兒，千萬記住請求有心人幫助你回到母親身邊來，母親將會繼續努力尋找你。

懸念翰兒愁緒如麻無處問生死，引頸以待五中儘裂，疲憊不堪的殘軀百病纏生遠征艱難，母親拜托清風捎去我的祝福，祝翰兒平安無恙早日歸家。倘若你已離開這世界，記住要托夢告訴母親你在天國是否安好，母親會祈求神佑你安康快樂，來生我們再續母子緣，到那時我們會共同享有平安 健康幸福快樂！

母親泣字

二零二二年十月八日

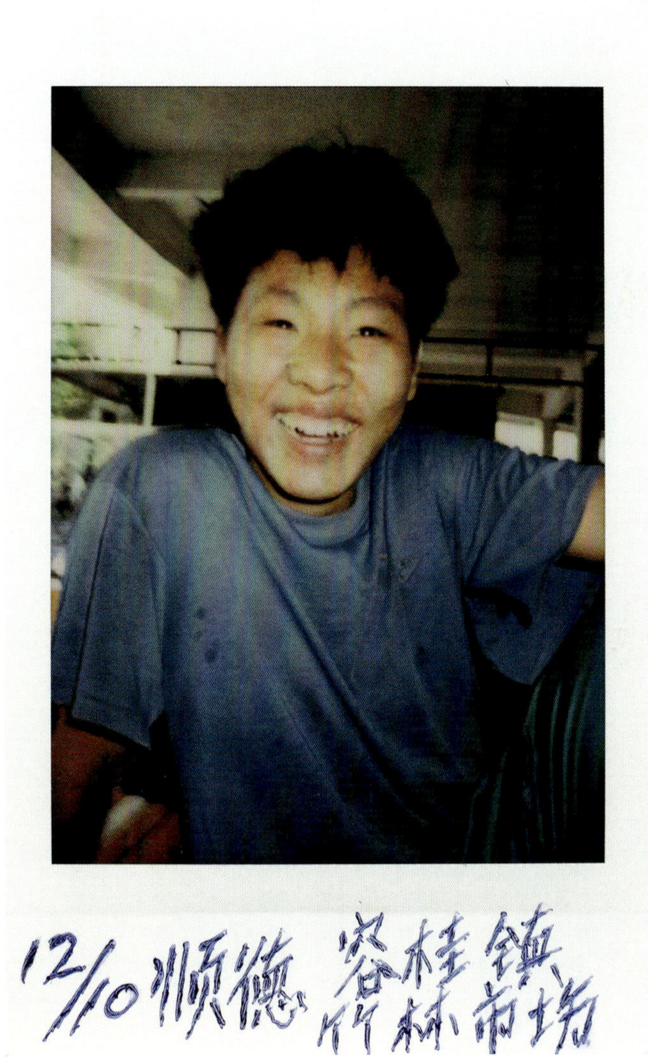
12/10 顺德 容桂鎮
竹林市场

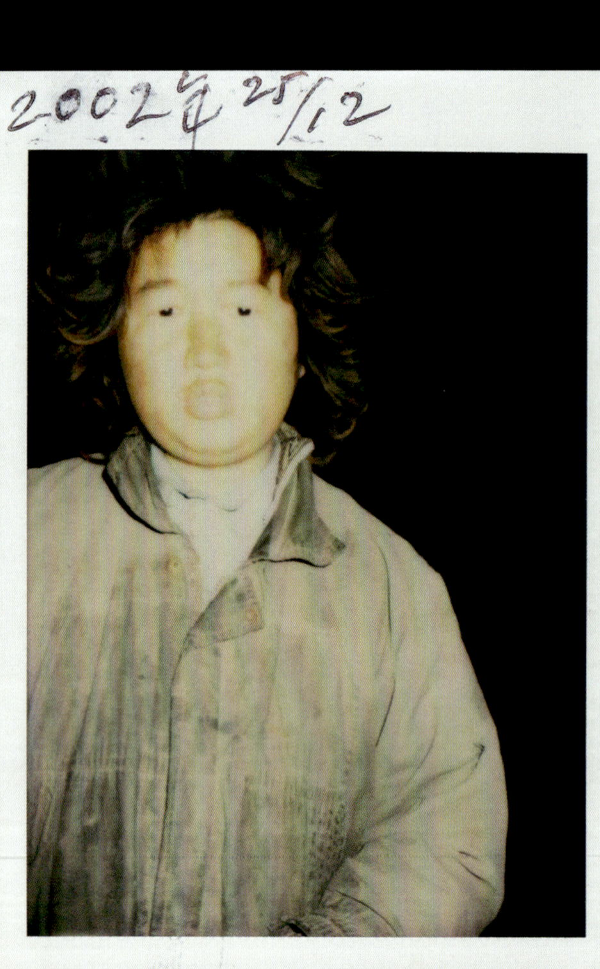
2002年25/12

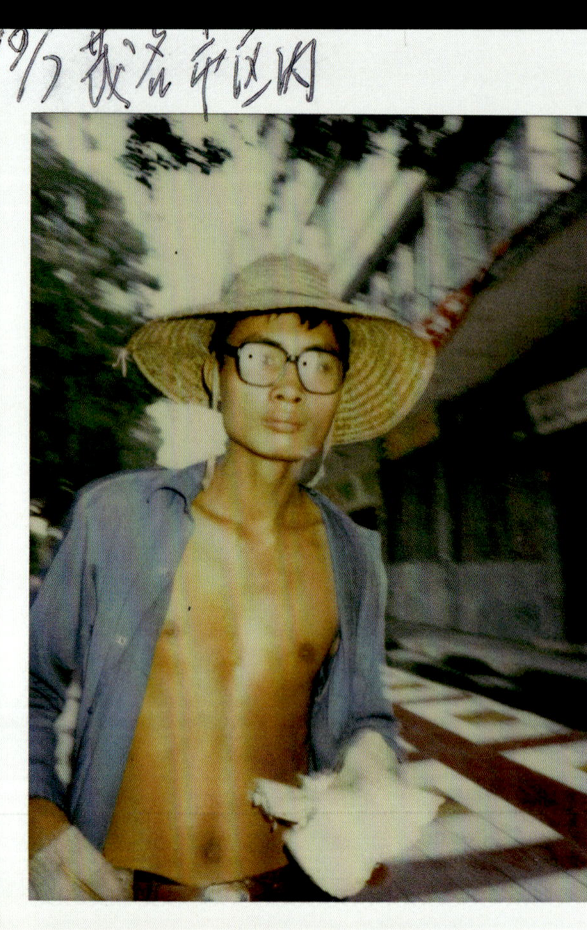

2002年 1/12

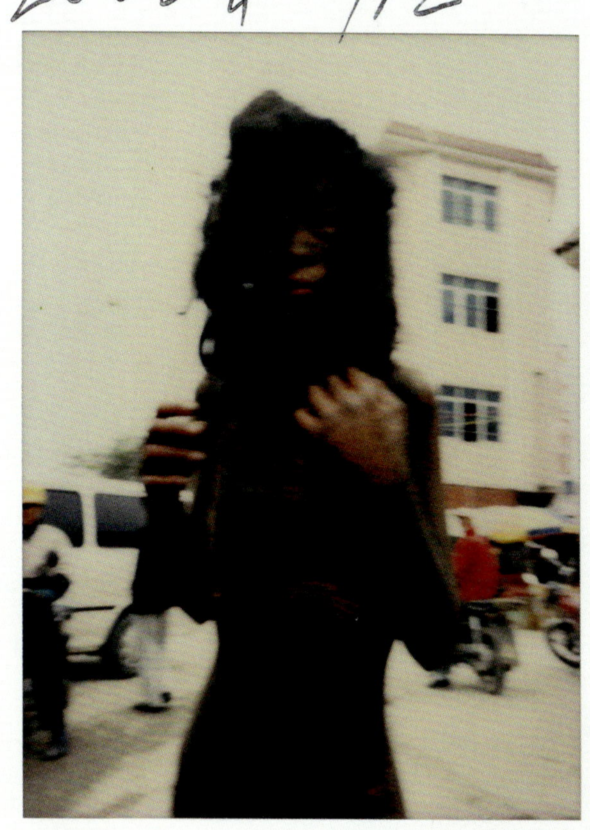

惠东吉隆派出所

STOPPING BY THE WOODS
Since 2024

Named after Robert Frost's poem *Stopping by Woods on a Snowy Evening*, Ārun's *Stopping by the Woods* is an ongoing meditation on solitude, memory and the natural world, shaped by personal experience and literary influence. In late 2024, Ārun was invited to join a darkroom residency organised by Photoworks and Chennai Photo Biennial, and opted to work on this project by making gum oil prints. An early photographic process that combines gum bichromate process with oil printing techniques, gum oil is a technically demanding approach. Learning through trial and error, Ārun created 17 prints, each of which he says tells its own story of struggle, discovery and the acceptance of imperfection.

Ārun presented his prints in an exhibition in Chennai in January 2025 titled *Alt:Analog*, which also featured the two other invited darkroom residents – Holly Birtles and Soham Joshi. A self-taught freelance photographer, Ārun specialises in black-and-white medium format image-making, with a particular interest in archival photographic processes. Based in Chennai and represented by the Kalinka Art Gallery, he has had solo shows at Kalinka and at the Centre d'Art Gallery in Auroville, an experimental township founded in Viluppuram district, India, in 1968. He has also taken part in group shows in Angkor Photo Festival and D Emptyspace, South Korea, among others.

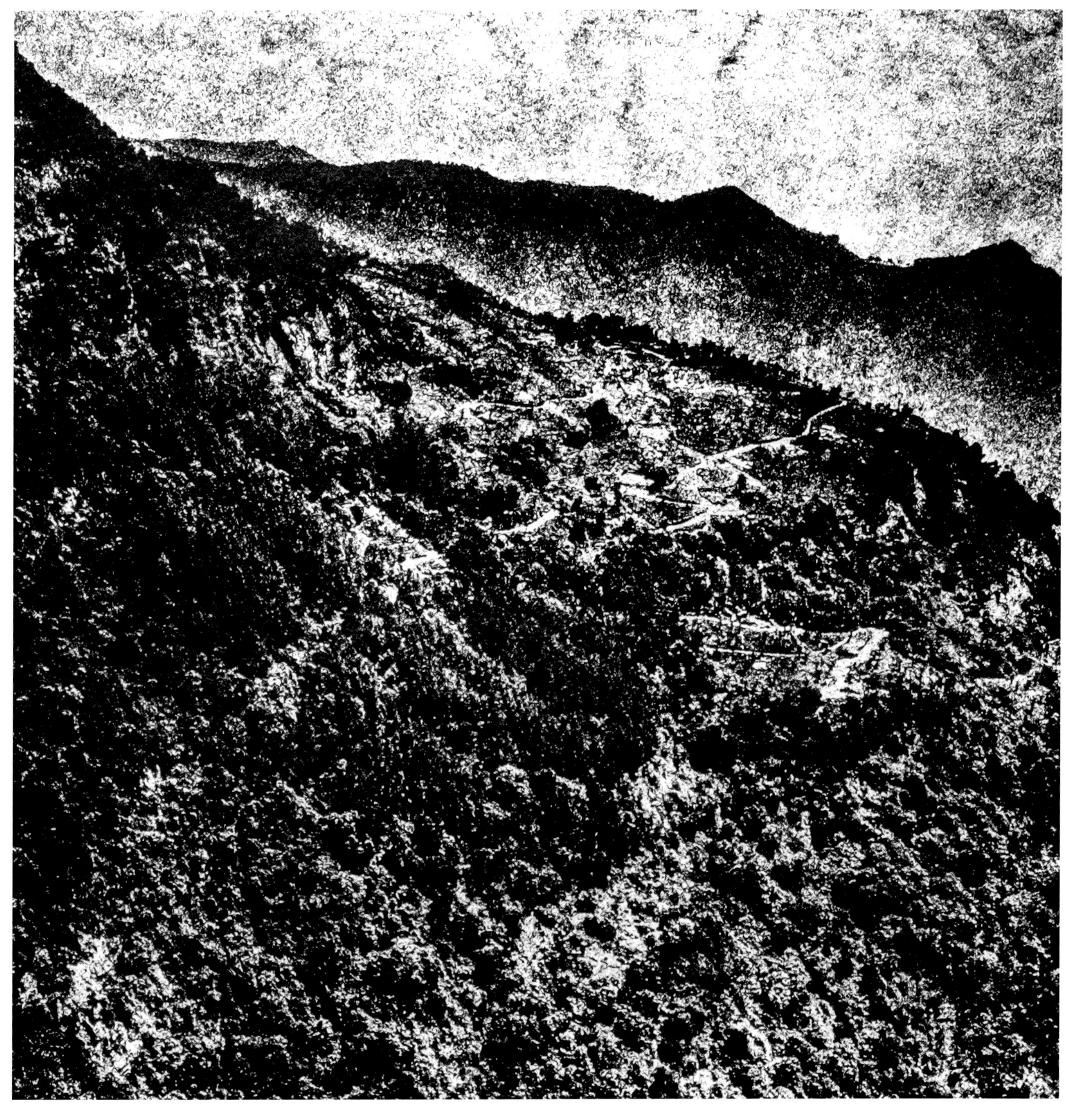

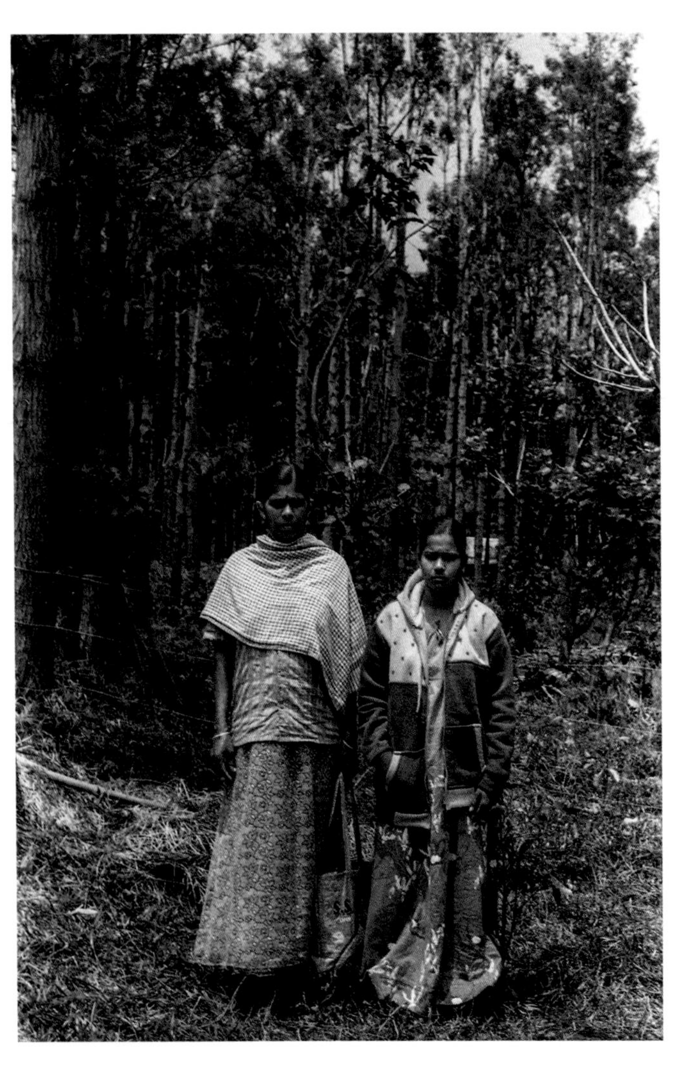

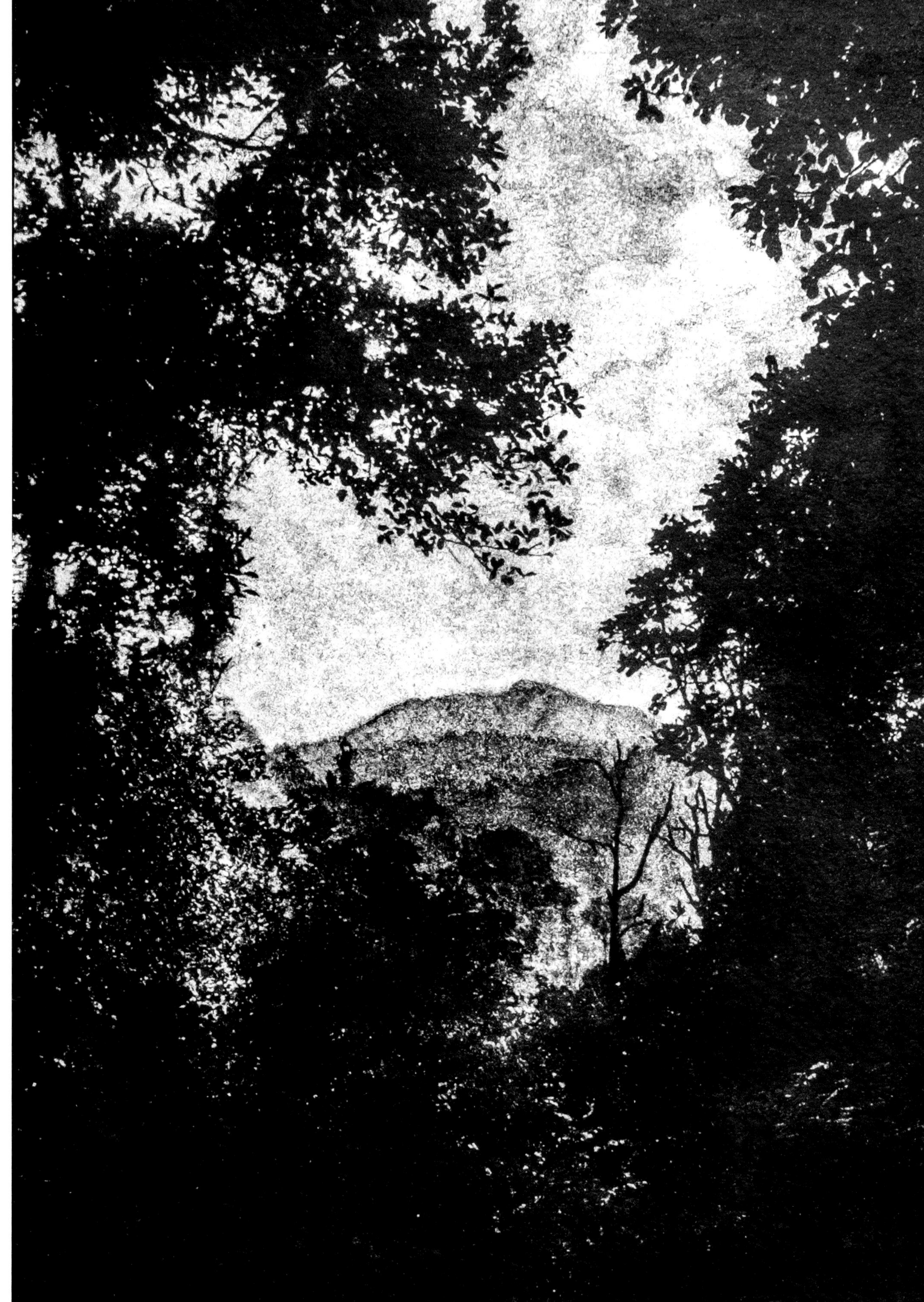

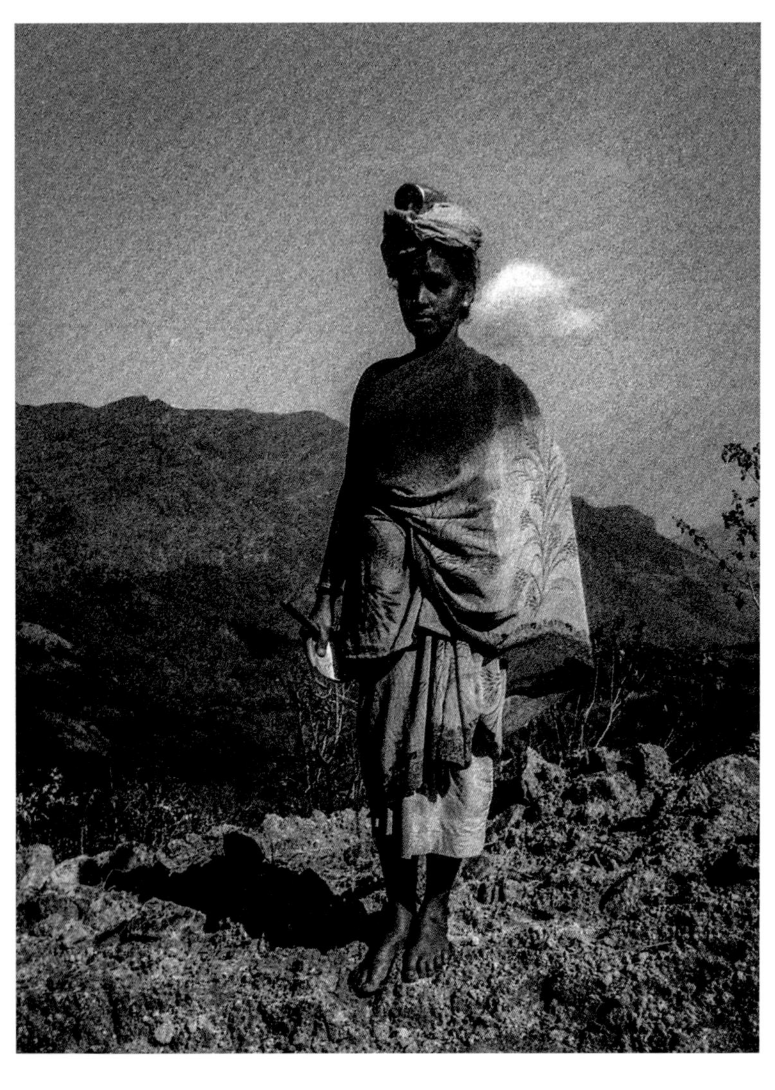

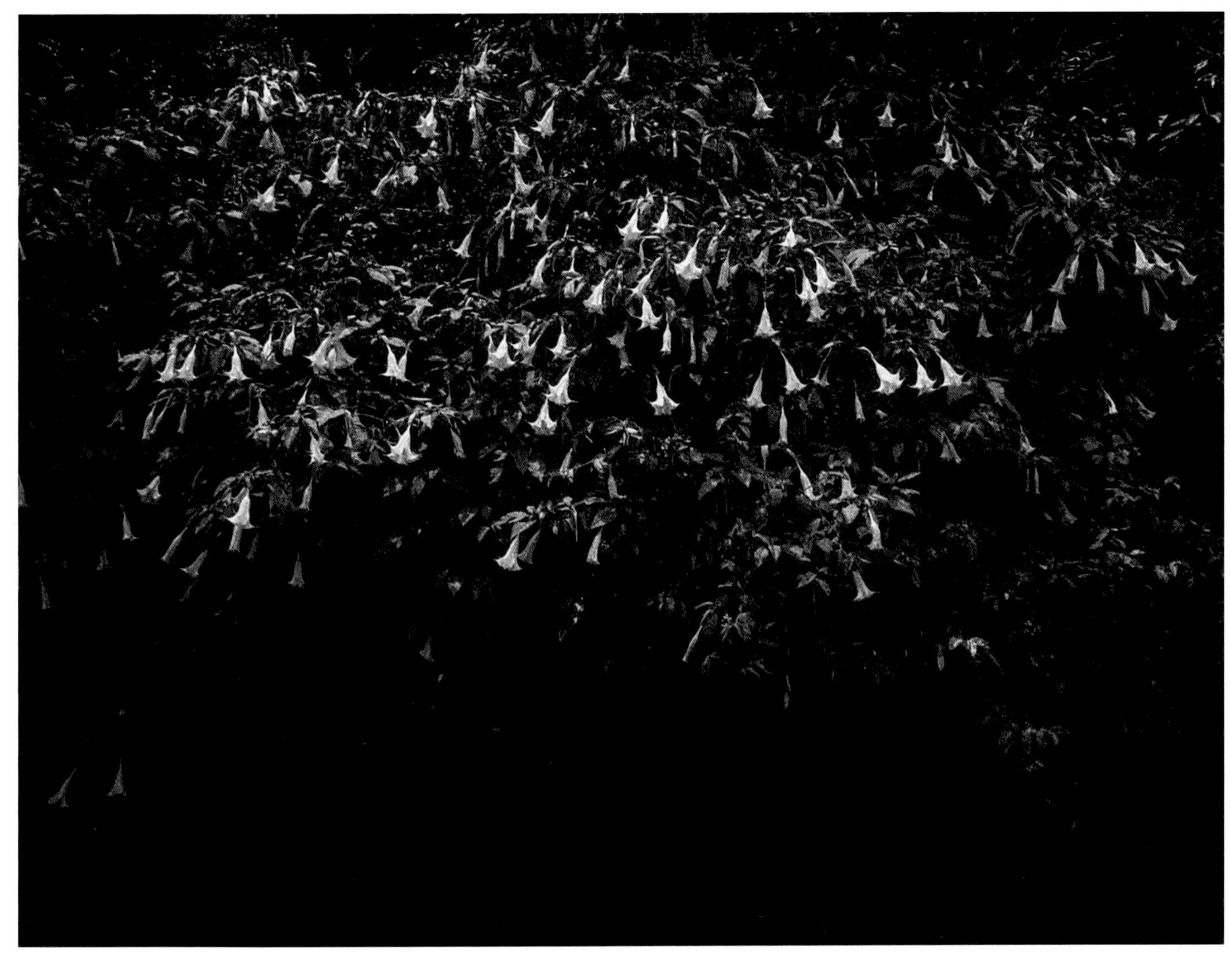

118

UNFIXED 2025

Anna Sellen was born by the sea and, though she has migrated halfway around the world, still lives by the sea today. The ocean is in her blood, she says, but it is also facing an urgent crisis as manmade chemicals and agricultural runoff are dumped into the water. Some 80% of global marine pollution comes from these sources, and scientists warn it has already reached a tipping point. In *Unfixed*, Sellen aims to show this apparently invisible problem, gathering seaweed, plants and objects near her home in Wales and making contact prints with common household pollutants, agricultural runoff water and seawater. Recording the chemical reactions of the pollutants, she uses pages of the Stockholm Convention on Persistent Organic Pollutants (2004), chemical safety data sheets and expired photography paper as substrates for her prints.

Based on the west coast of Wales, Sellen makes multidisciplinary work that includes conceptual and documentary photography. Focusing on the environment, climate change, and personal histories within wider socio-political stories, she is interested in the power of human agency in changing our landscapes and reimagining our relationship with nature. Sellen's work has been exhibited internationally and was awarded a portfolio award at FORMAT in 2021, and the Sidney Nolan Trust Prize at Earth Photo 2023. In 2022 she was one of 10 artists featured in Photoworks' *P+* Graduate Issue.

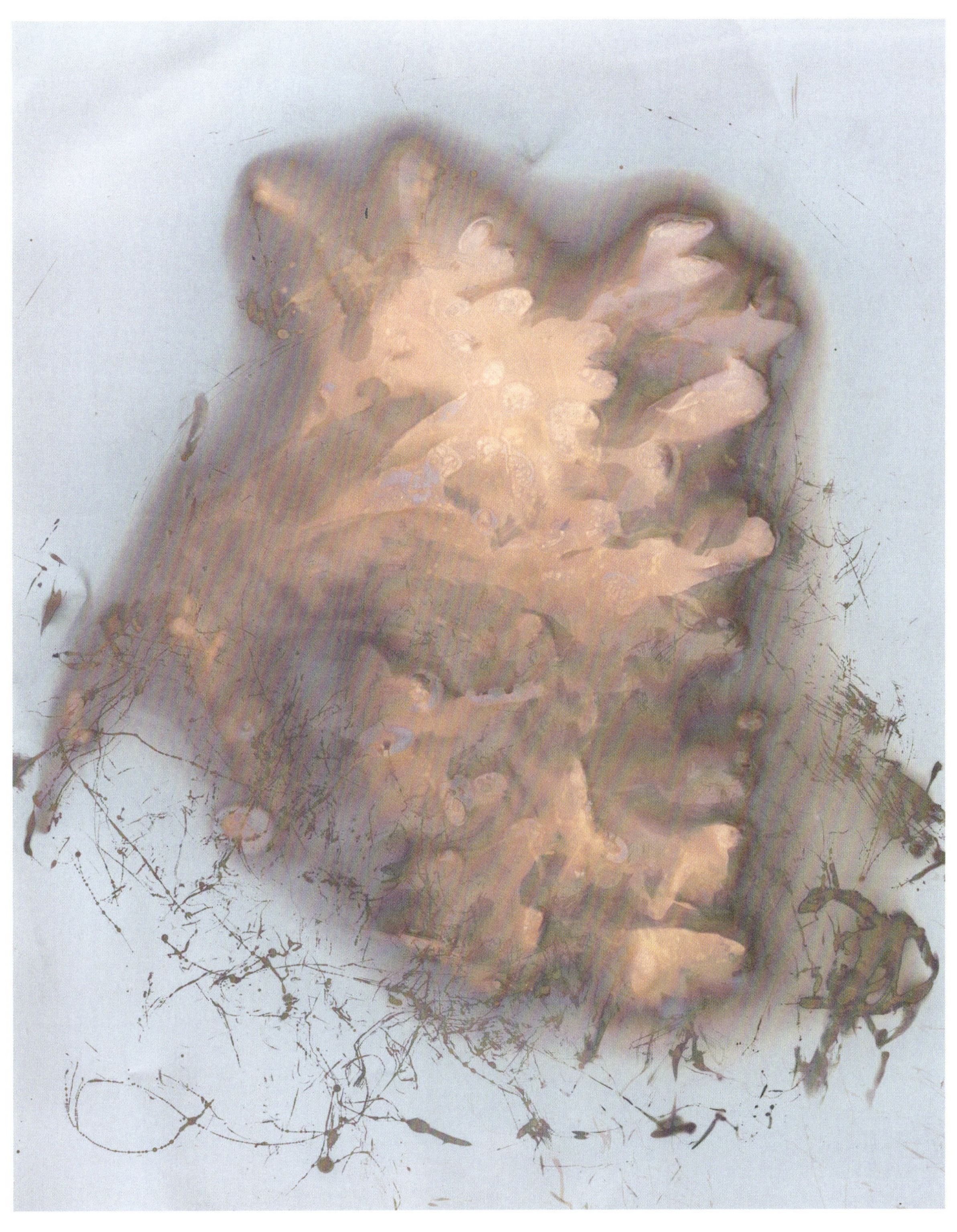

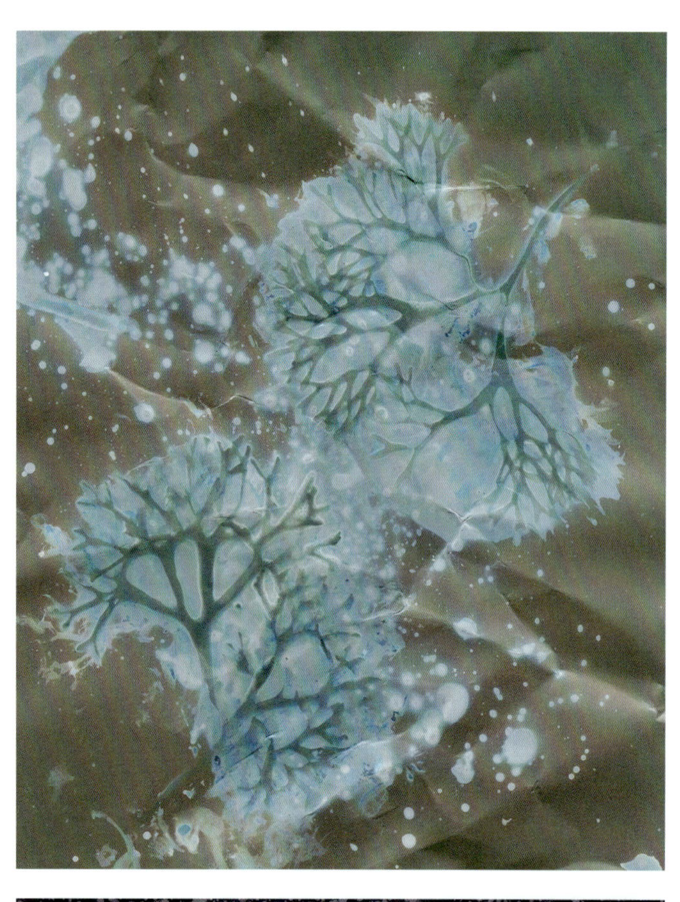

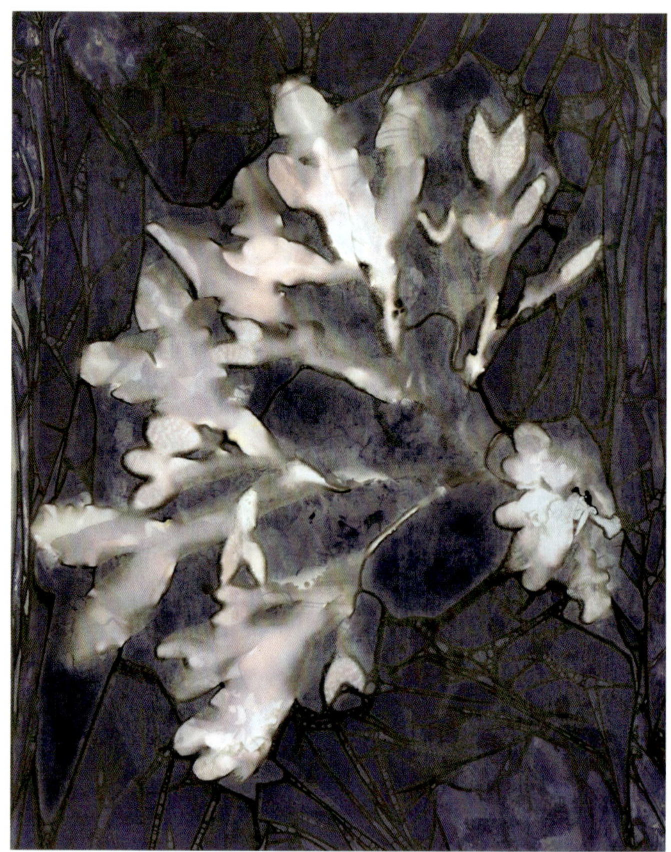

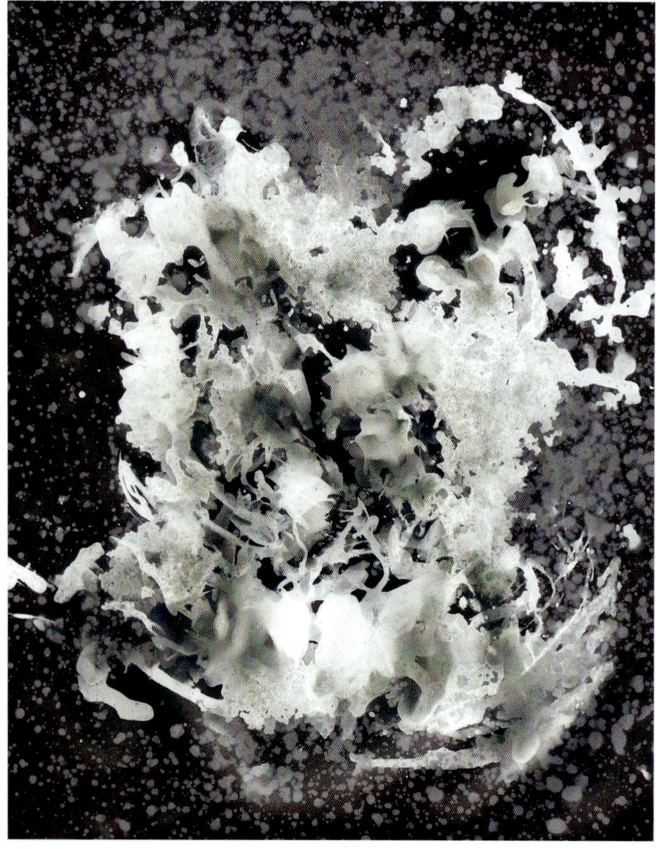

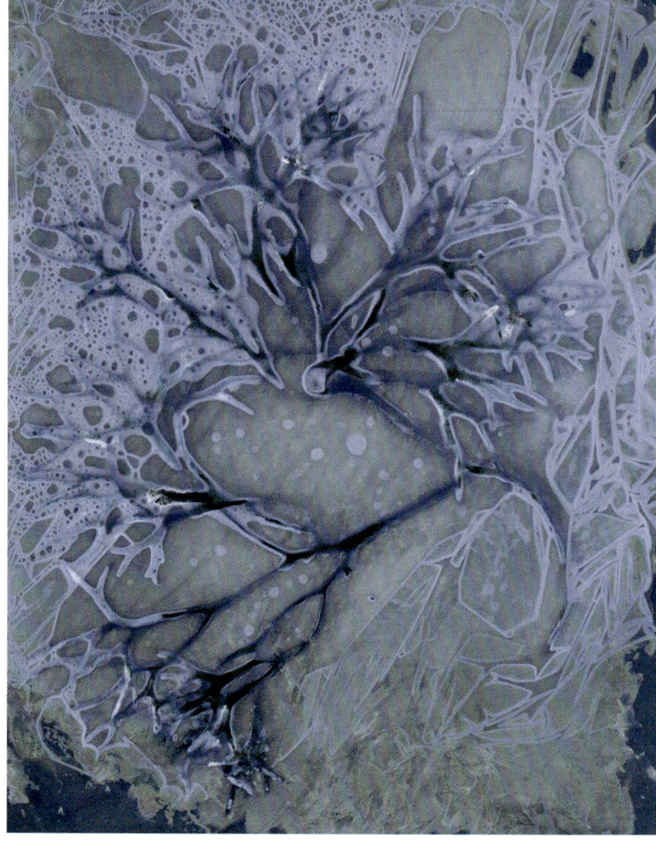

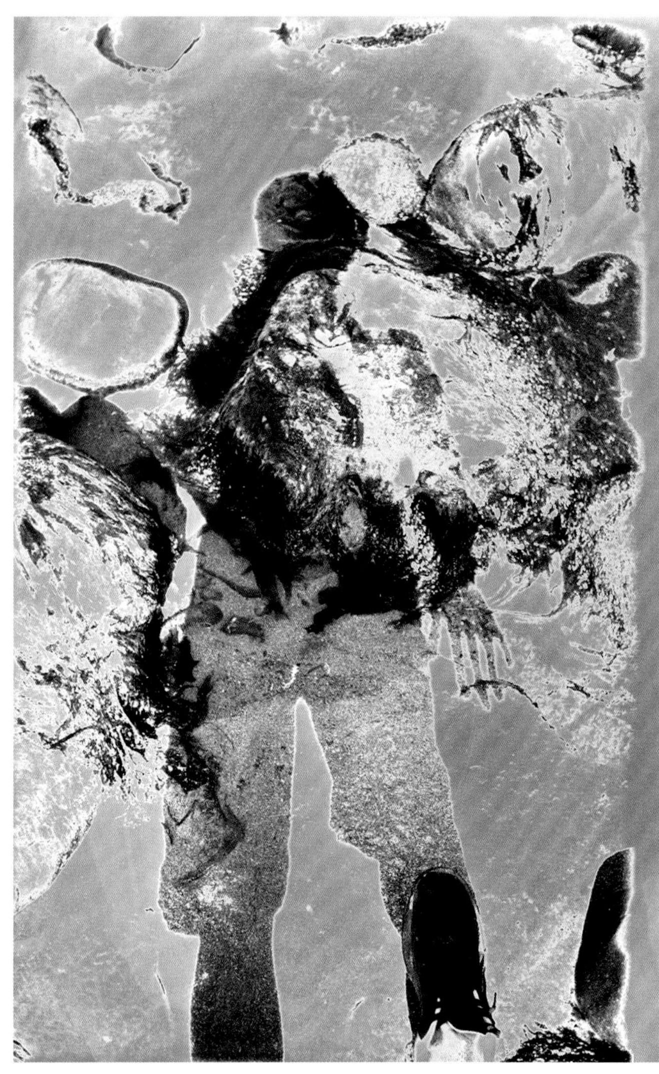

120 Clockwise, from top left
Cleaning Spray With Bleach
Metal Polish
Washing Up Liquid
Carpet Freshener
121 *Untitled*

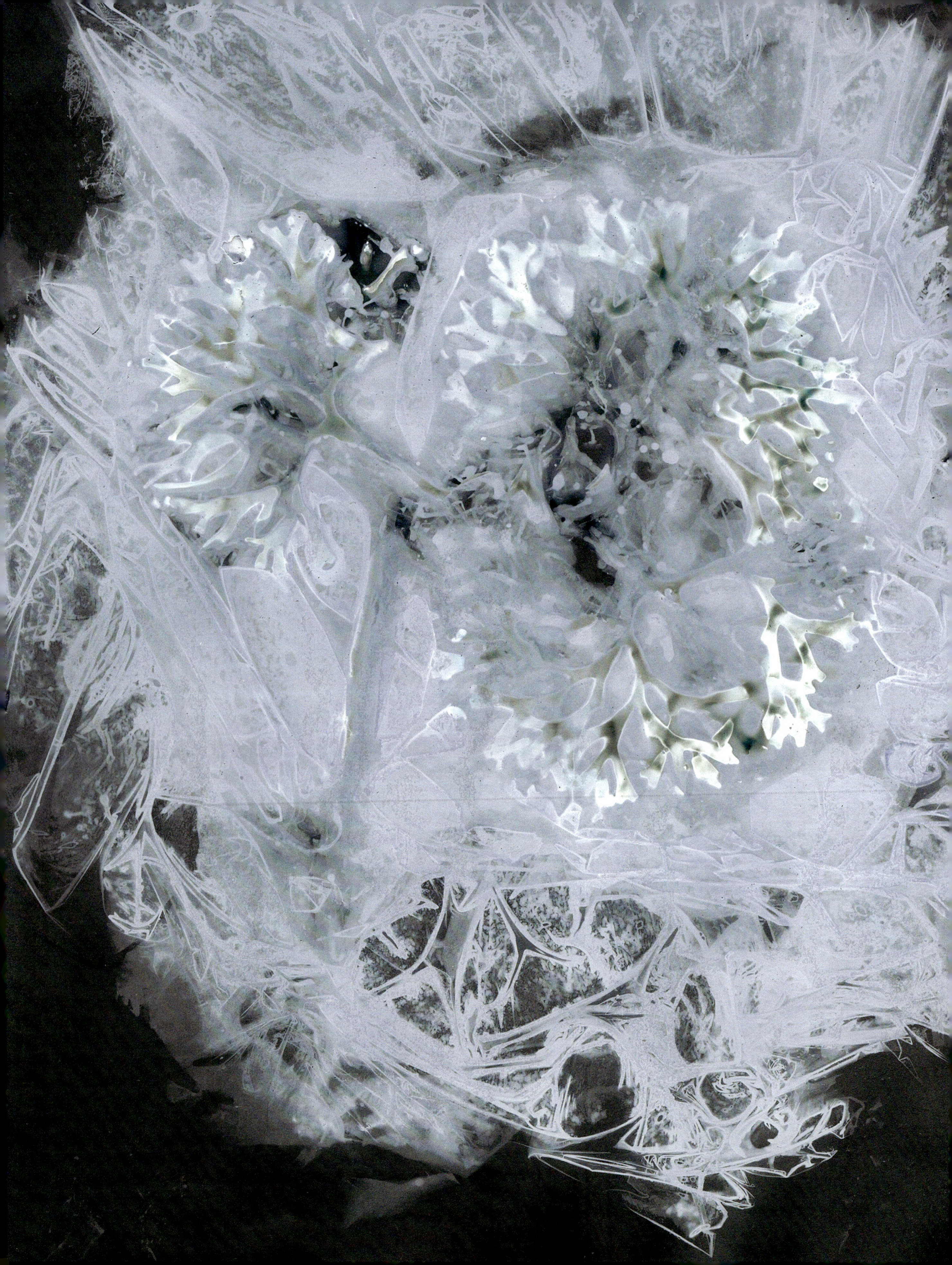

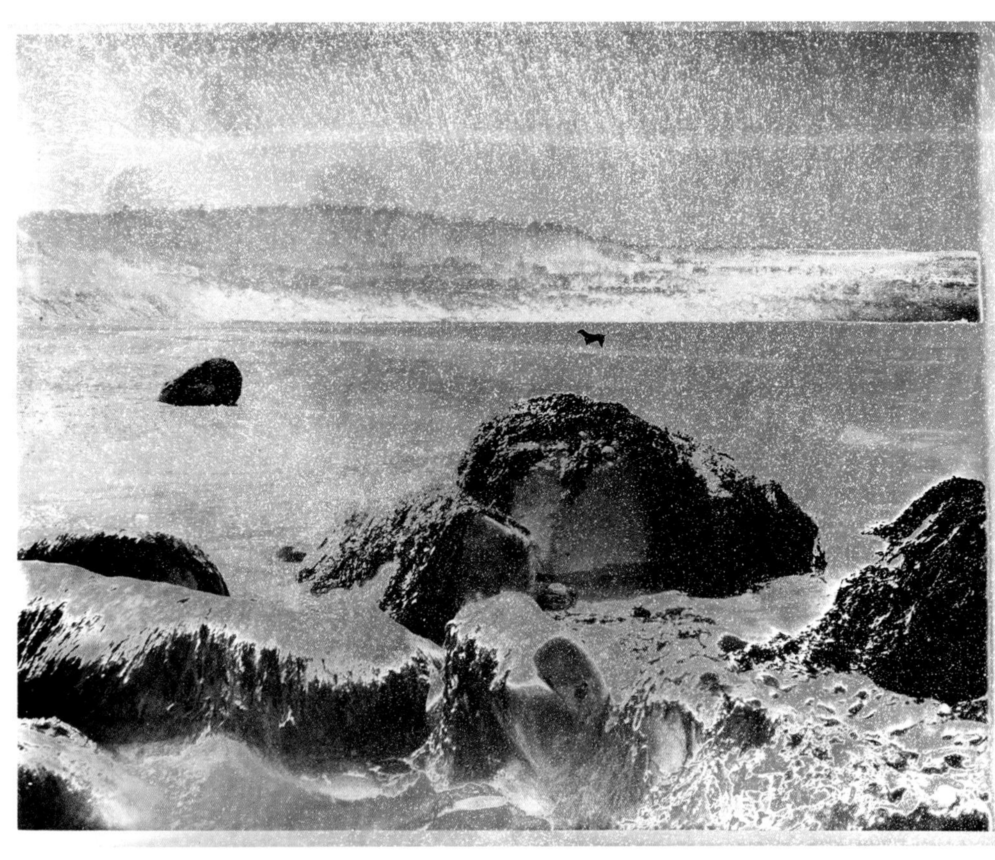

122 *Stain Remover*
123 *Untitled*

空席 KUSEKI, 'EMPTY SEATS' 2025

Japan is facing a rapid population decline and, with birthrates falling and towns shrinking, schools are quietly closing down. Nearly 9,000 schools disappeared between 2002 and 2020, and 450 continue to shut every year. Sayuri Ichida grew up in a small town in Niigata, one of the worst-affected areas, where two of three elementary schools have already closed, and the junior high is scheduled to follow suit. Winning the Jerwood/Photoworks Award in 2024, alongside Roman Manfredi, she embarked on a project documenting the now-empty school buildings in Niigata. Reimagining the structures as fragmented visual forms, composed from cut, rearranged and reassembled photographs, she echoes the instability and fragmentation the closures are bringing to the local community. Ichida plans to screenprint these images onto freestanding chalkboards, combining memory and presence with disappearance and decline.

Born in 1985 in Fukuoka, Japan, Ichida graduated from the University of Westminster with an MA in photography arts in 2022. In 2023, she won the Benrido Award as part of the Hariban Award and took part in the Light Work artist-in-residence programme in New York. Her work has been shown at venues such as the Daiwa Foundation in London, Ibasho in Antwerp, and the Princeton University Art Museum in New Jersey, and is held in the Verbund Collection and Museum Voorlinden. Ichida is now based in Margate, UK.

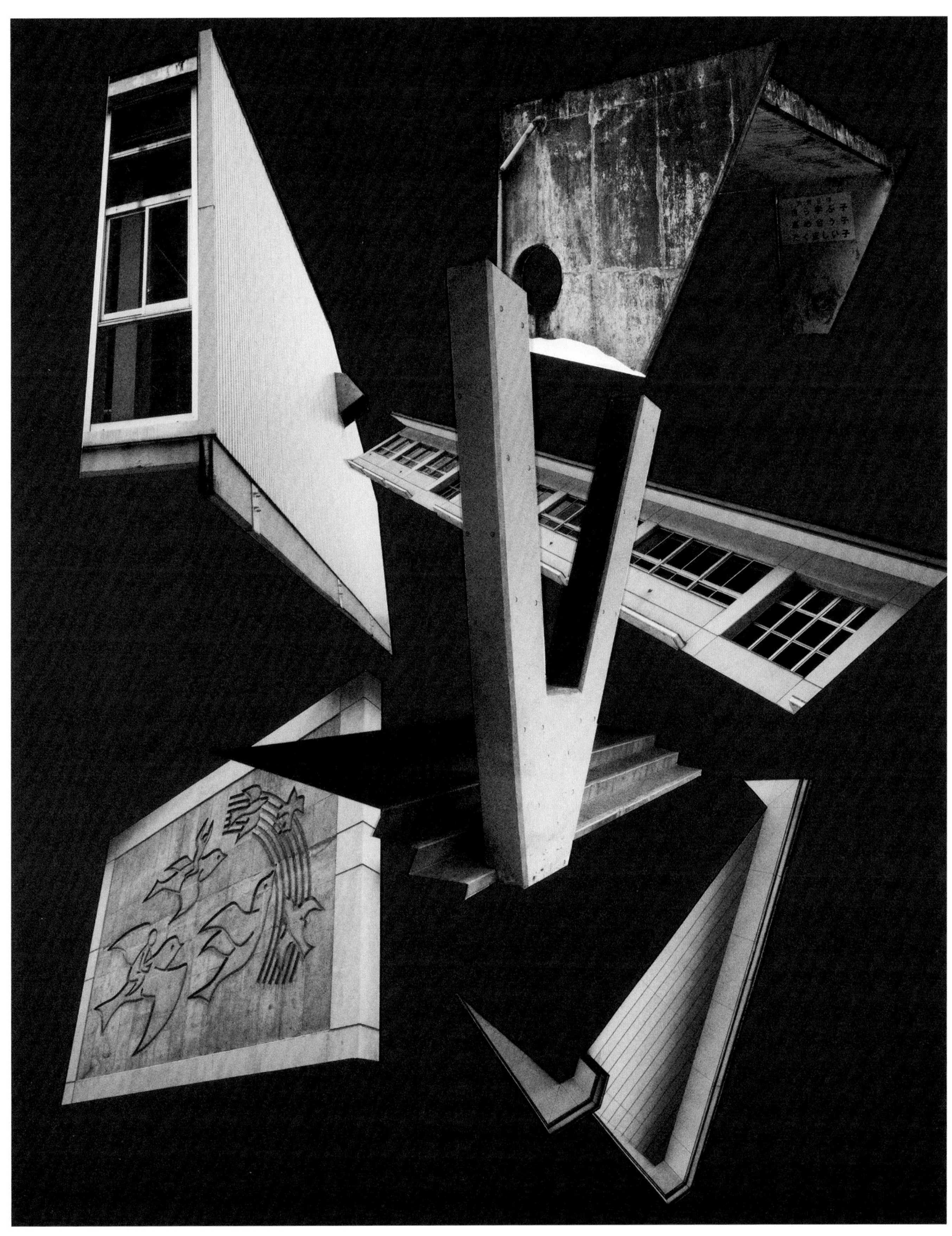
たくましい子

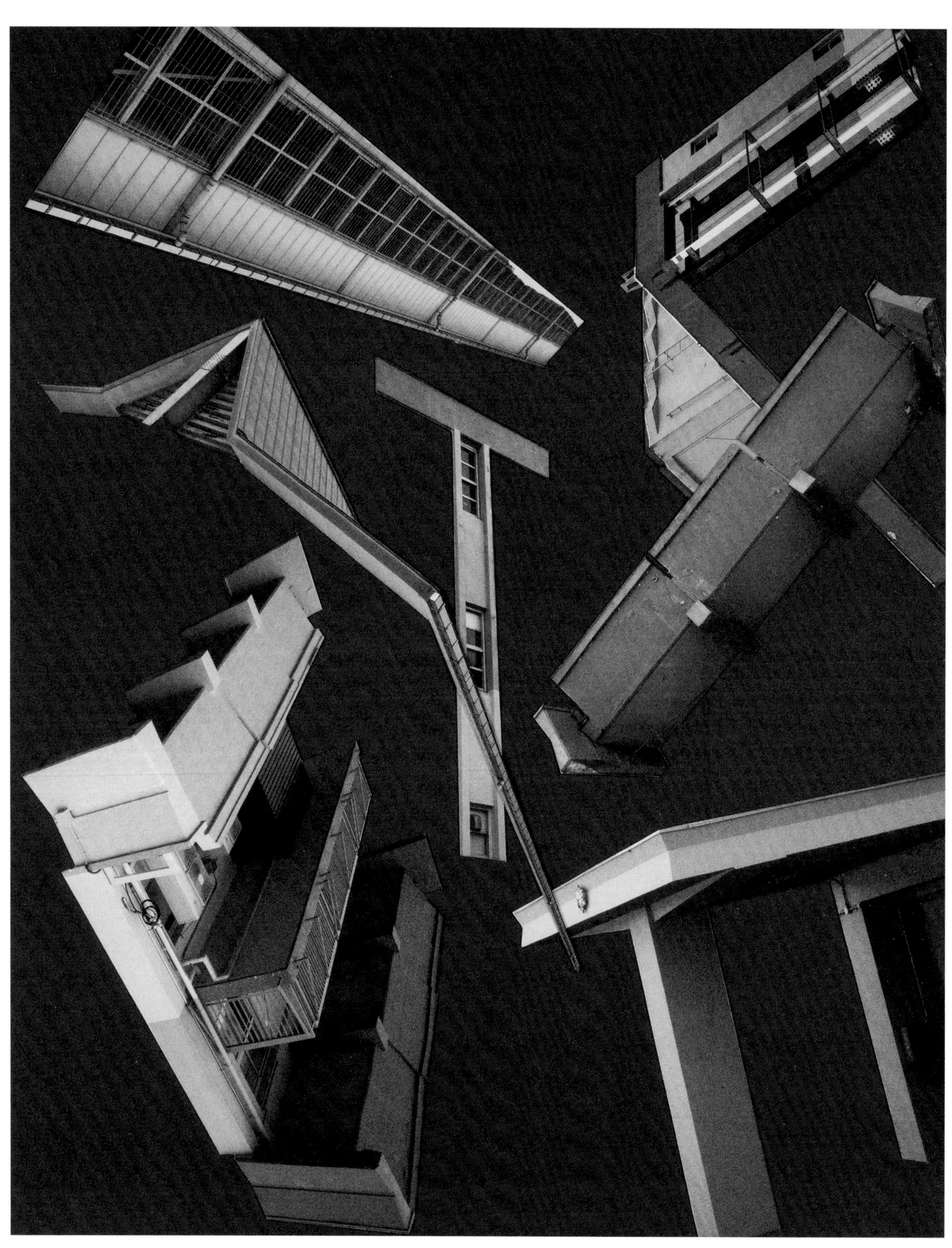

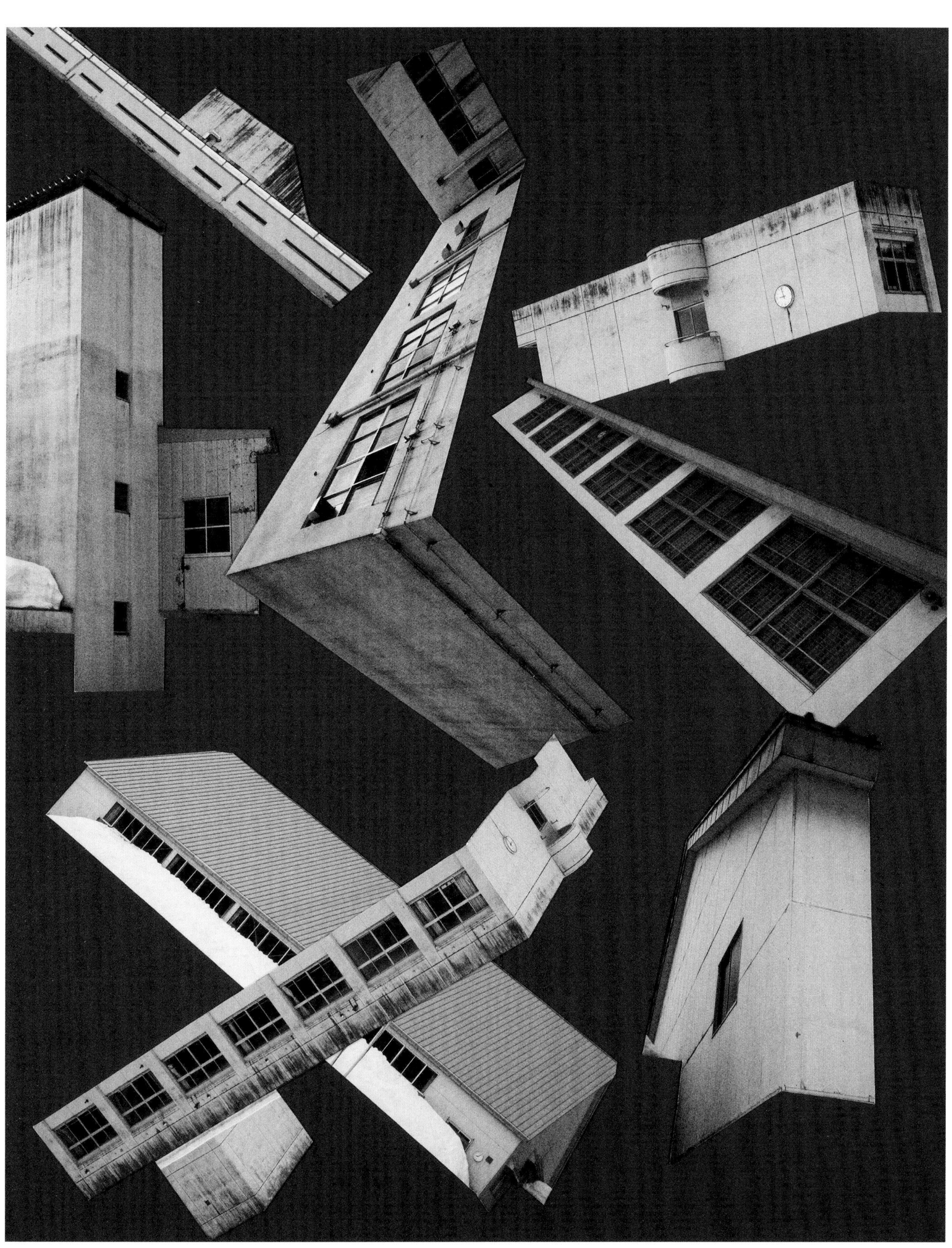

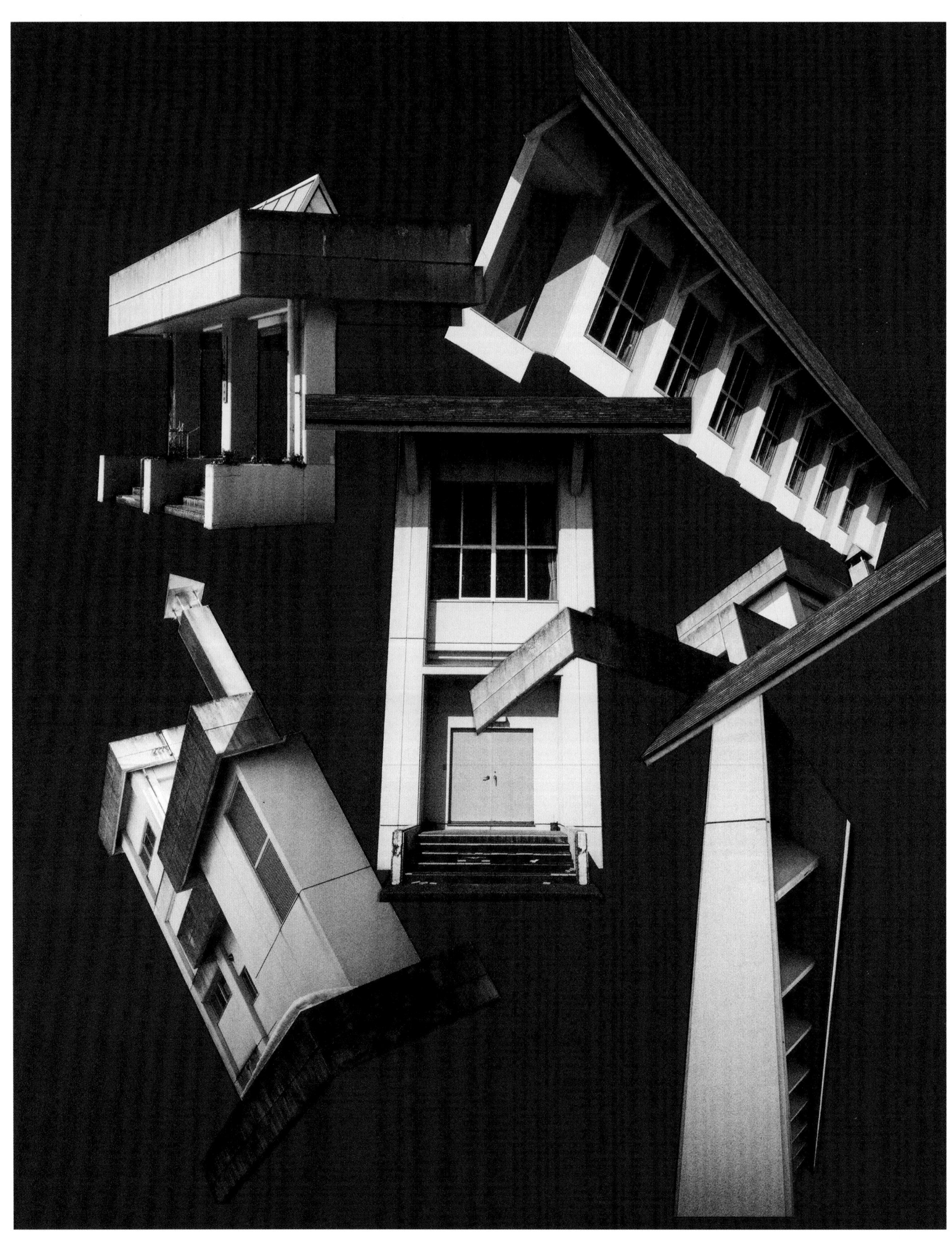

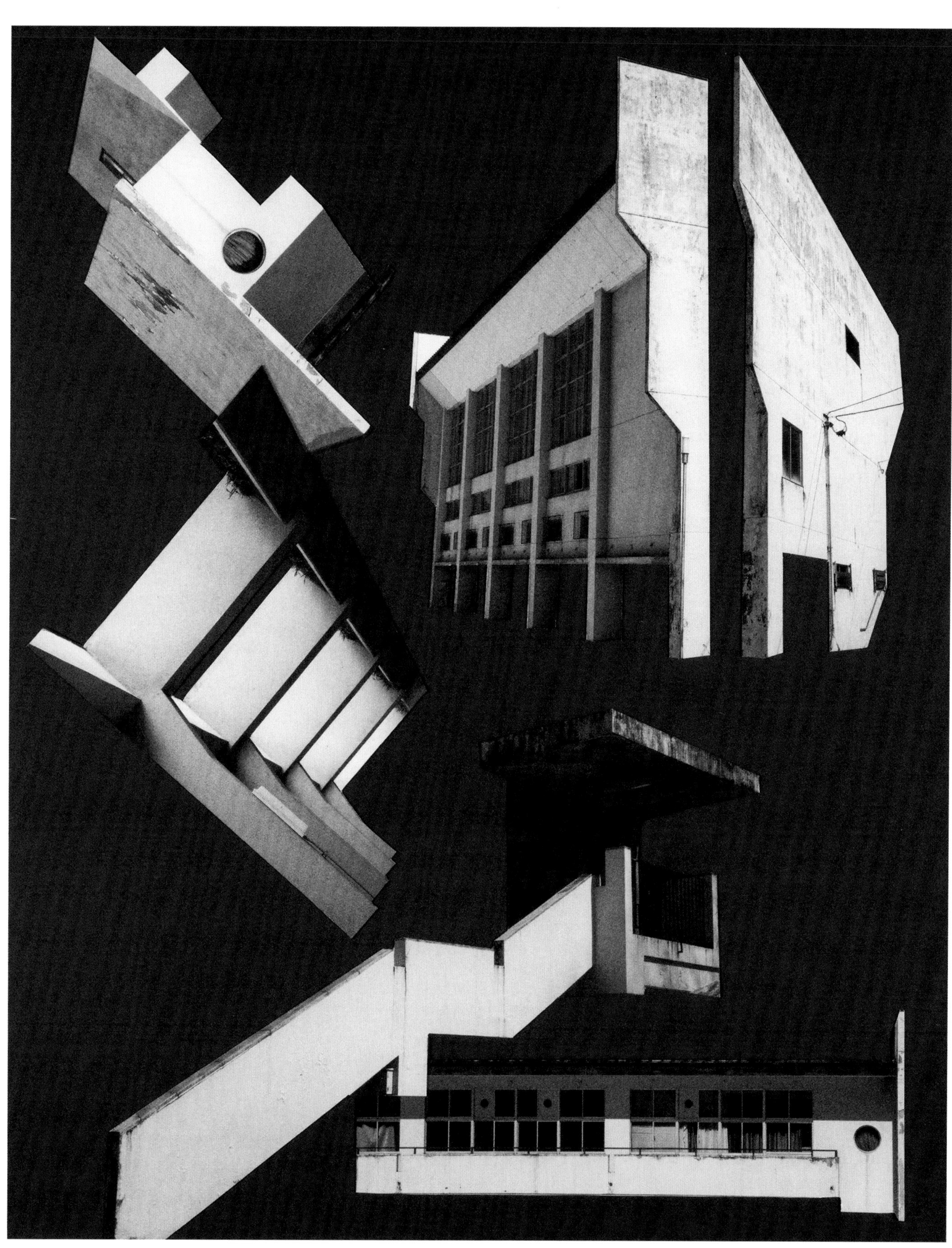

IL SOLE MUTO, 'THE SILENT SUN', BRIGHTON 2025

Born in Bari, Piero Percoco couldn't afford to study photography. But he did buy the occasional photobook and, inspired by image-makers such as Stephen Shore and William Eggleston, started to shoot on the street. In 2025, he won a residency in Brighton organised by Photoworks and PhEst International Festival of Photography and Art, supported by the Italian Cultural Institute. Percoco responded to the energy he found in the city, observing the light, people's gestures, abandoned objects and quiet moments. He was particularly drawn to the beach, which he found similar to Bari, although with its own English flavour. Suffering from an ear infection, he experienced Brighton "as if moving through a soft, surreal layer of perception".

Percoco first found fame via Instagram, where he posts as @therainbow_is_underestimated and now has more than 100k followers. He has published three books. His work has been shown across Europe, and the images he made in Brighton are now part of Photoworks' and PhEst's public programming. Percoco believes photography can reveal a world that combines dreams and reality, which is often missed by the distracted eye. He now lives near Bari in a small country village, where there is nothing but olive and almond trees.

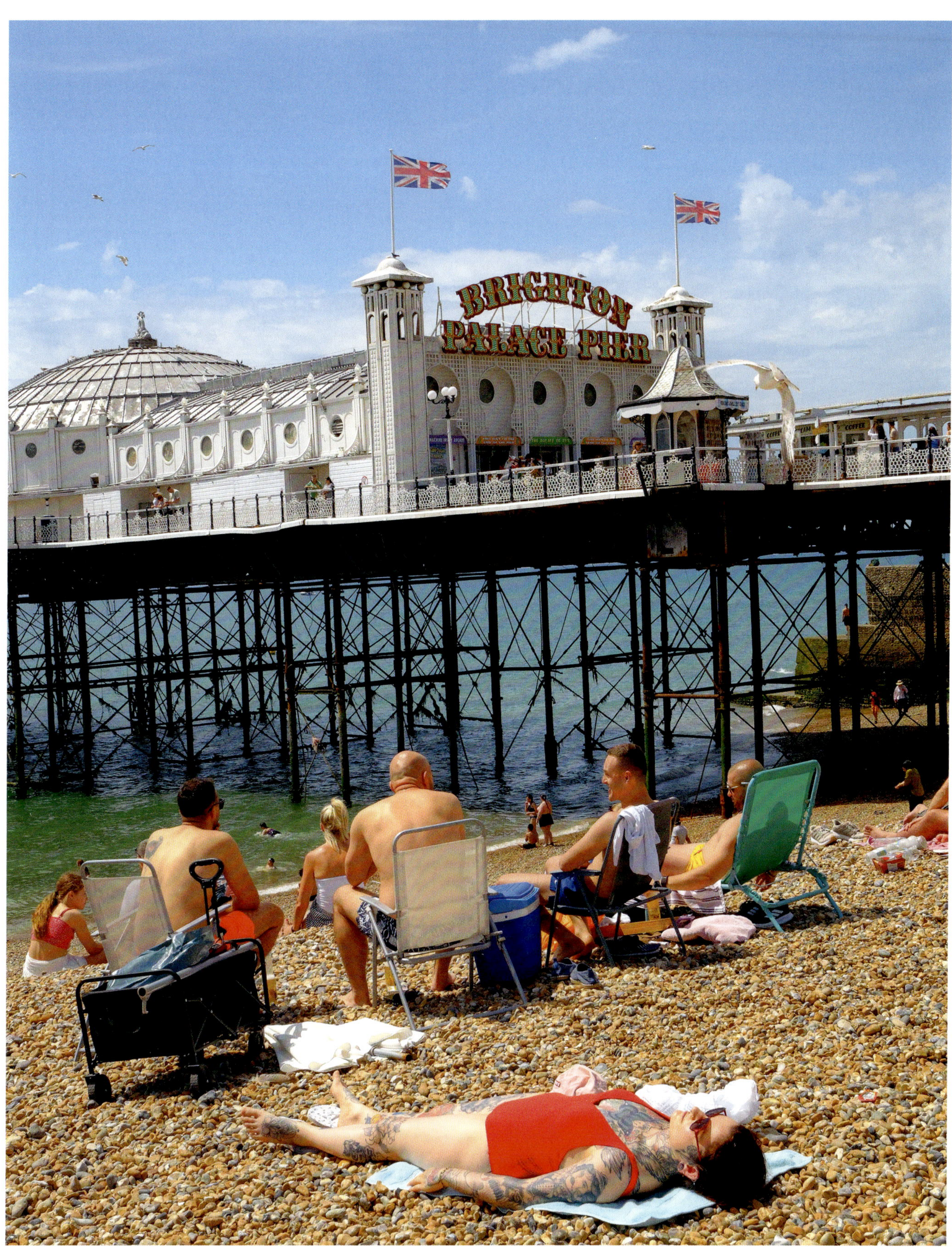
BRIGHTON
PALACE PIER

IL SOLE MUTO, 'THE SILENT SUN', BRIGHTON

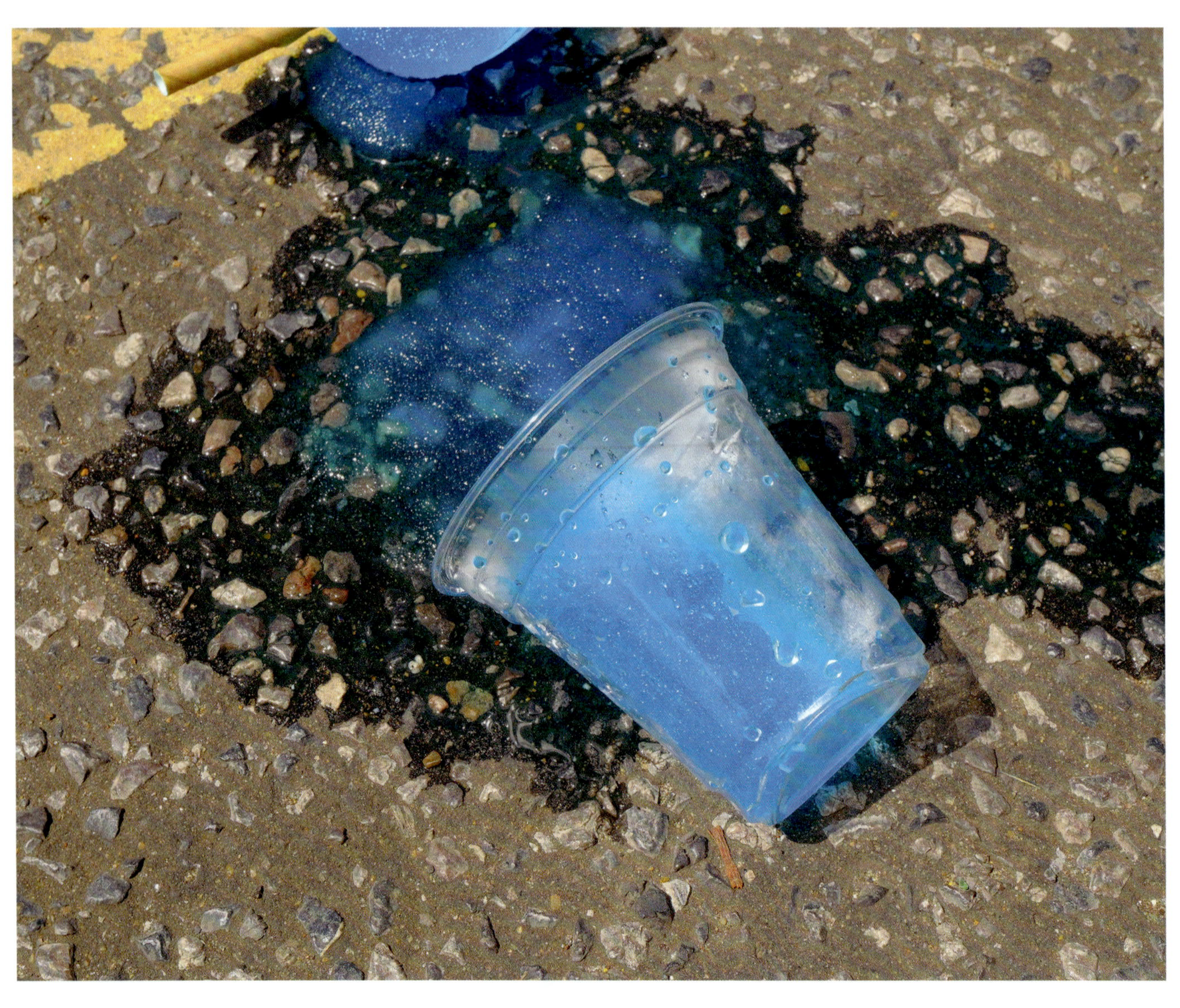

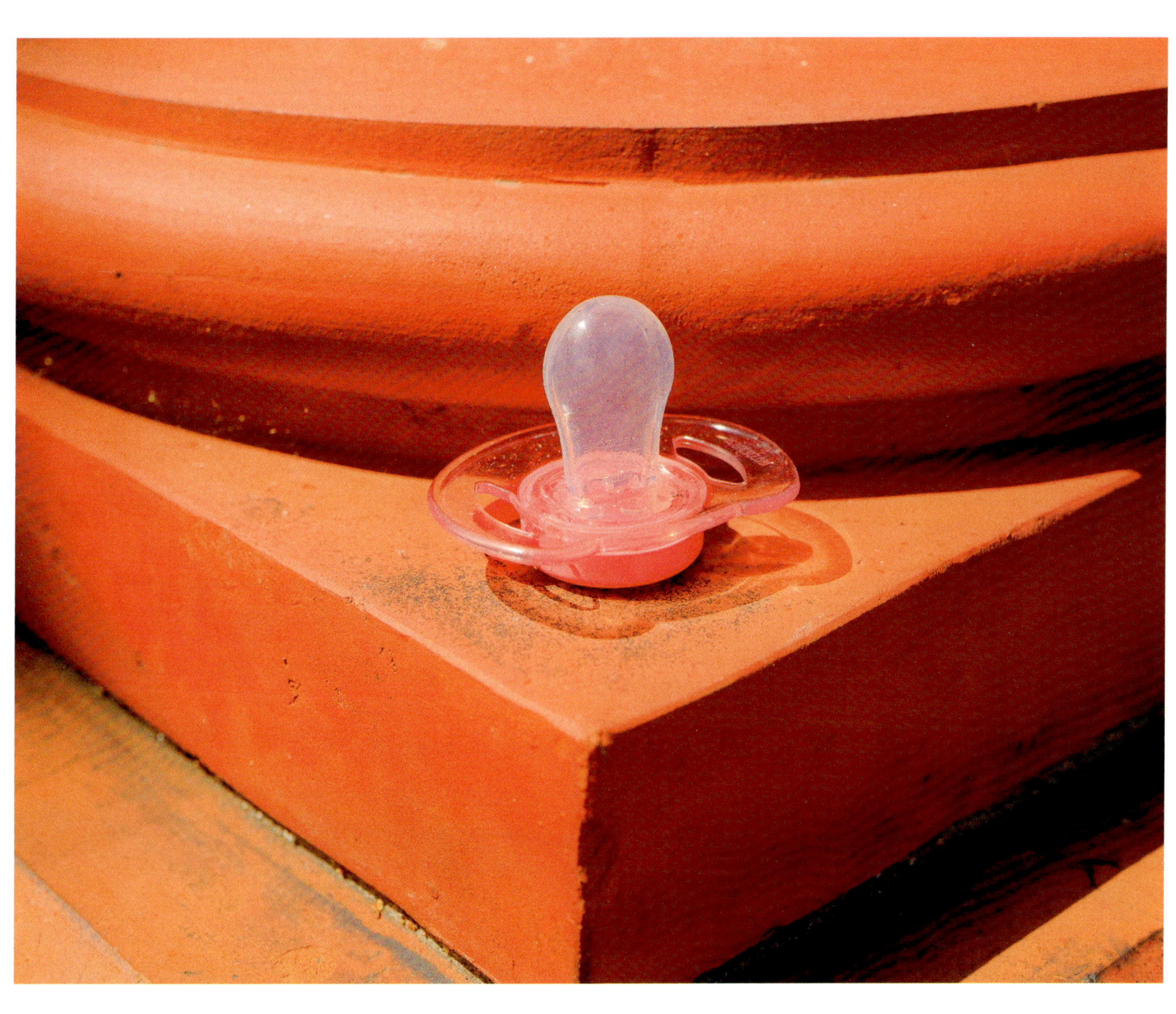

IL SOLE MUTO, 'THE SILENT SUN', BRIGHTON

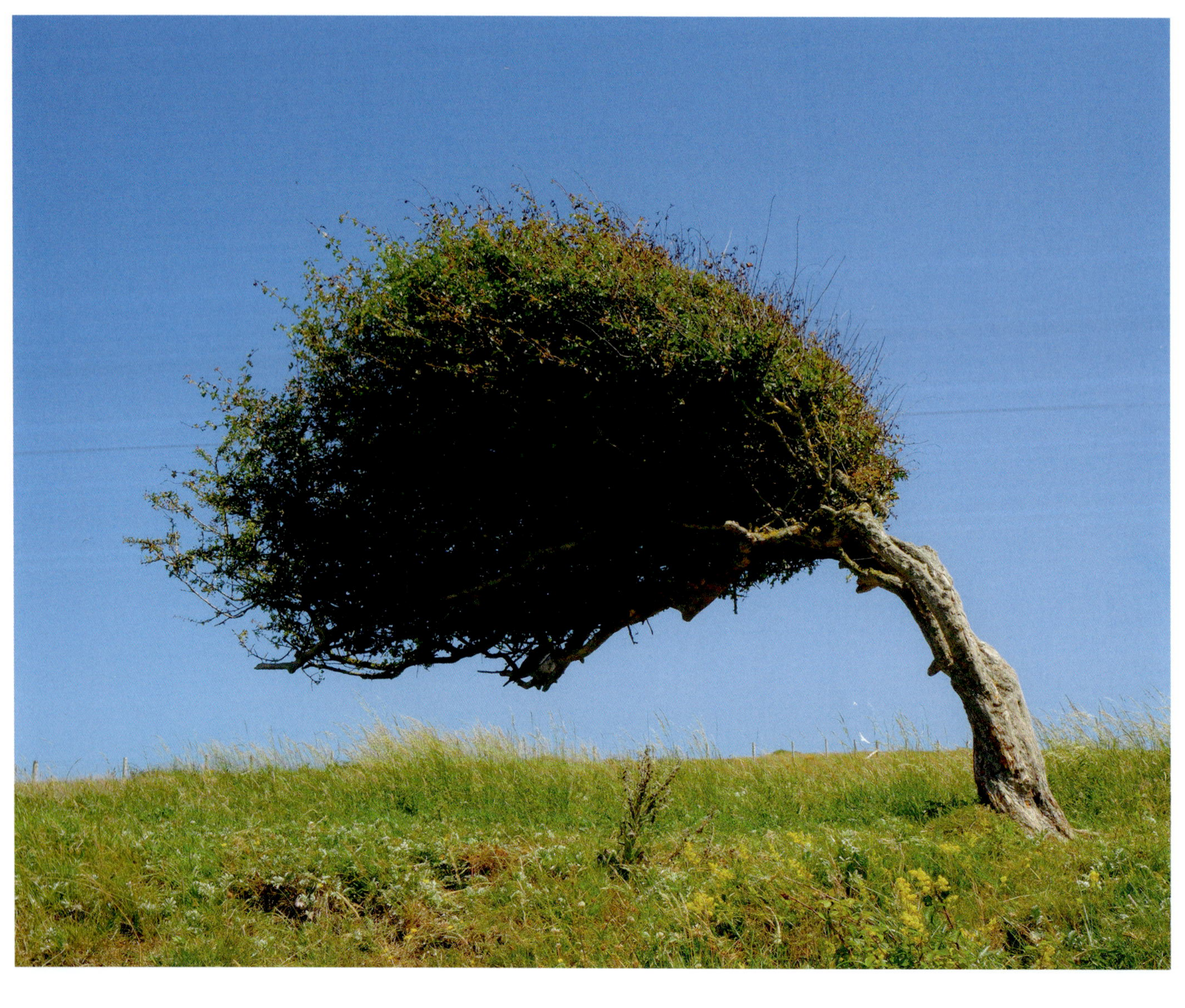

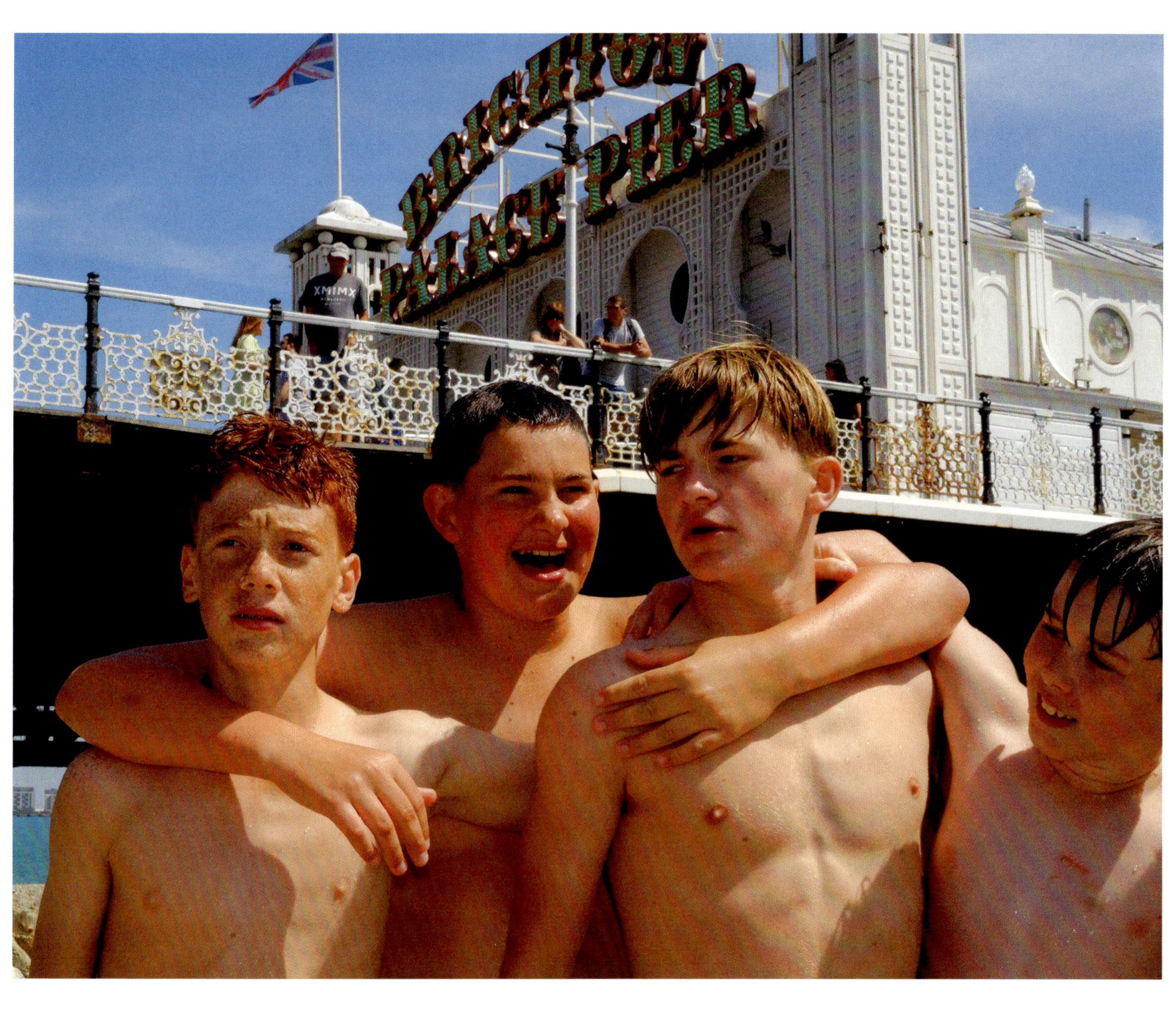
BRIGHTON
PALACE PIER

THREADS OF BELONGING
Since 2025

Within a multidisciplinary series that explores migration, identity and belonging, Mohamed Hassan navigates his experience as an Egyptian artist now based in Wales. Rooted in collaborative portraiture, landscape and archival research, Threads of Belonging sheds light on narratives of continuity, movement and adaptation across generations and geographies. Within co-created portraits, participants from long-established Welsh communities and those newer to the country share their stories, while in shots of the environment, the Welsh landscape is shown to be diverse and ever-changing, suggesting metaphors of emotional transition and the search for place.

Originally from Alexandria, Hassan has lived and worked in Pembrokeshire since 2007. After graduating with a first-class degree in photography from Carmarthen School of Art in 2016, he completed a master's in documentary photography with distinction at University of South Wales in 2023. His work has been exhibited at the National Museum of Wales, National Library of Wales, National Portrait Gallery and Oriel Davies, among others, and was included in the Photoworks *P+* Graduate Issue in 2024. Hassan also won the STAR Award for a photobook dummy in 2024, after being nominated by Photoworks director Louise Fedotov-Clements. His first photobook was published in spring 2025.

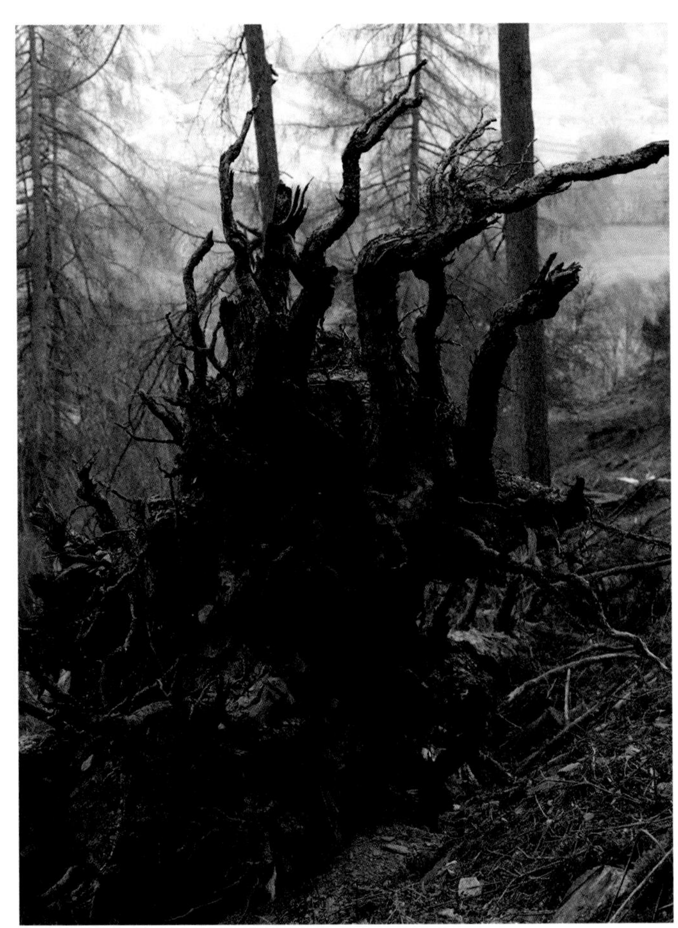

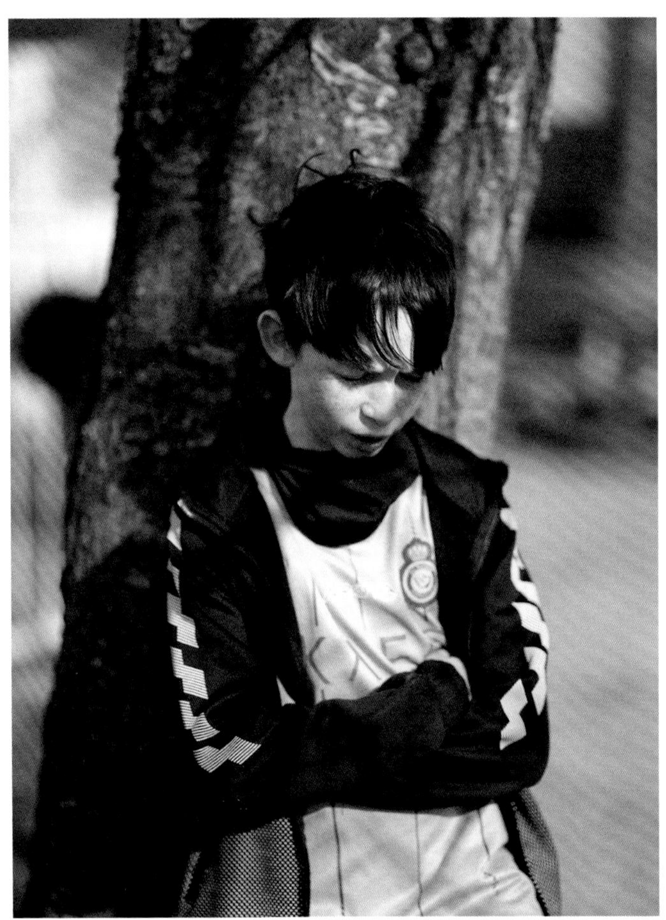

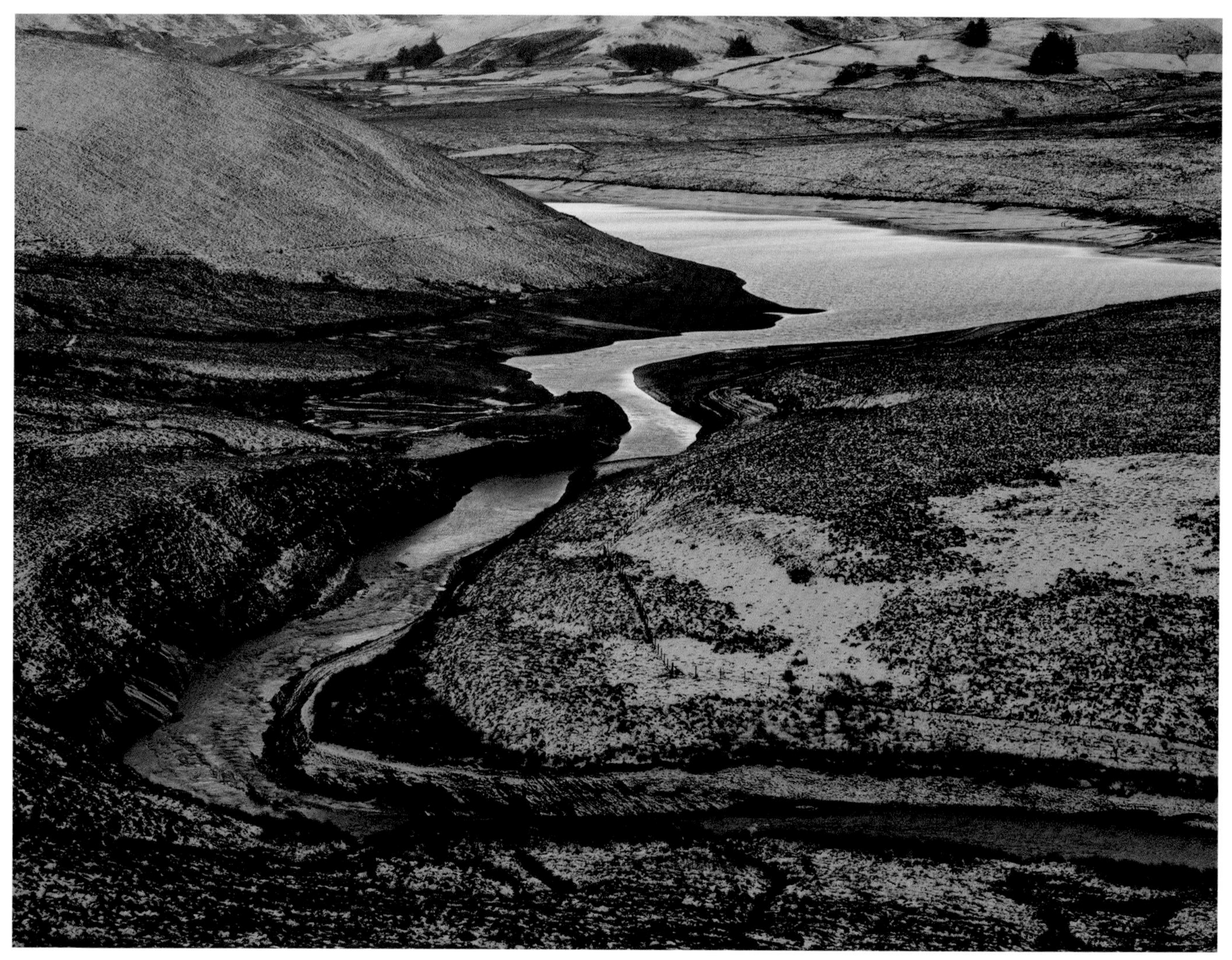

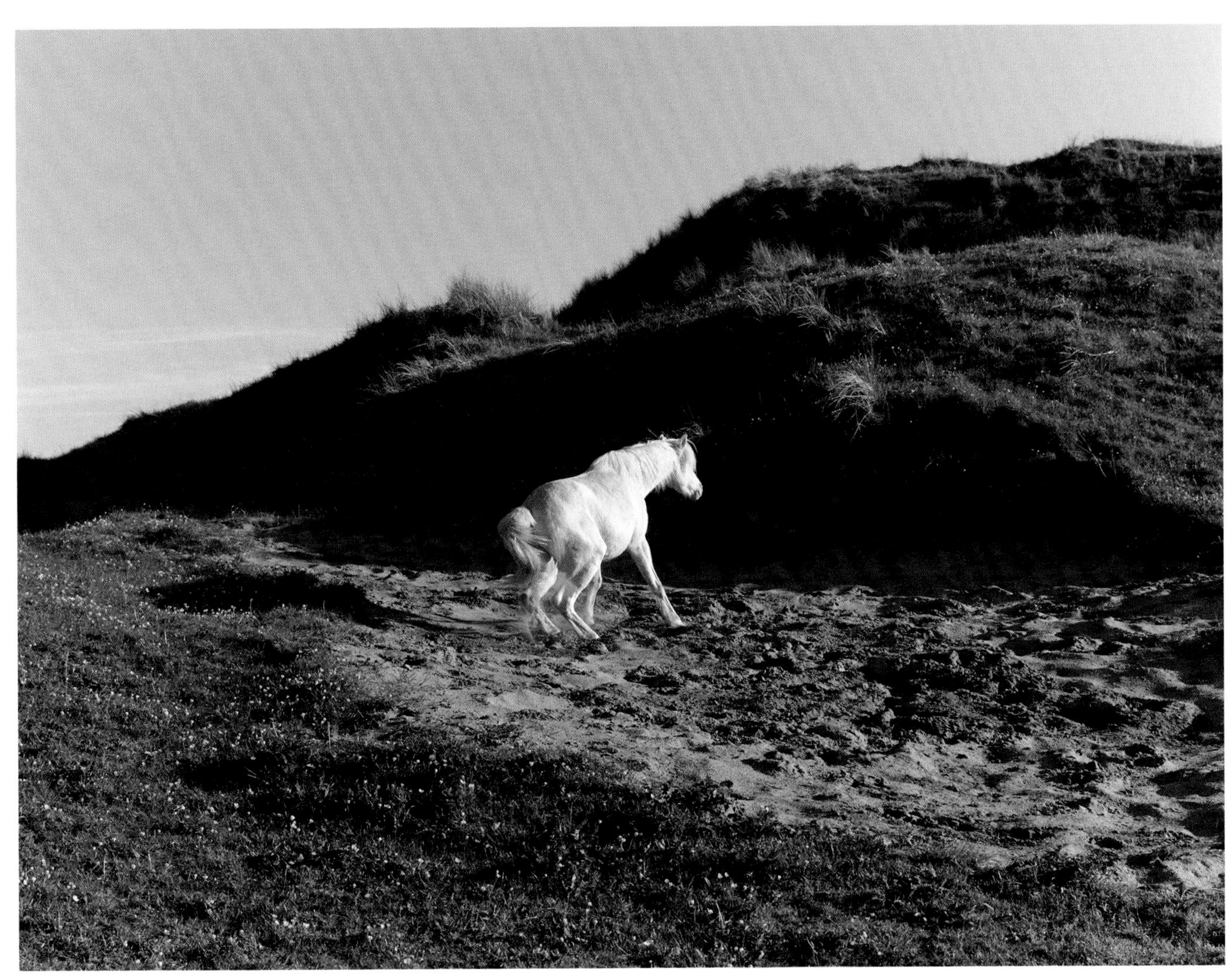

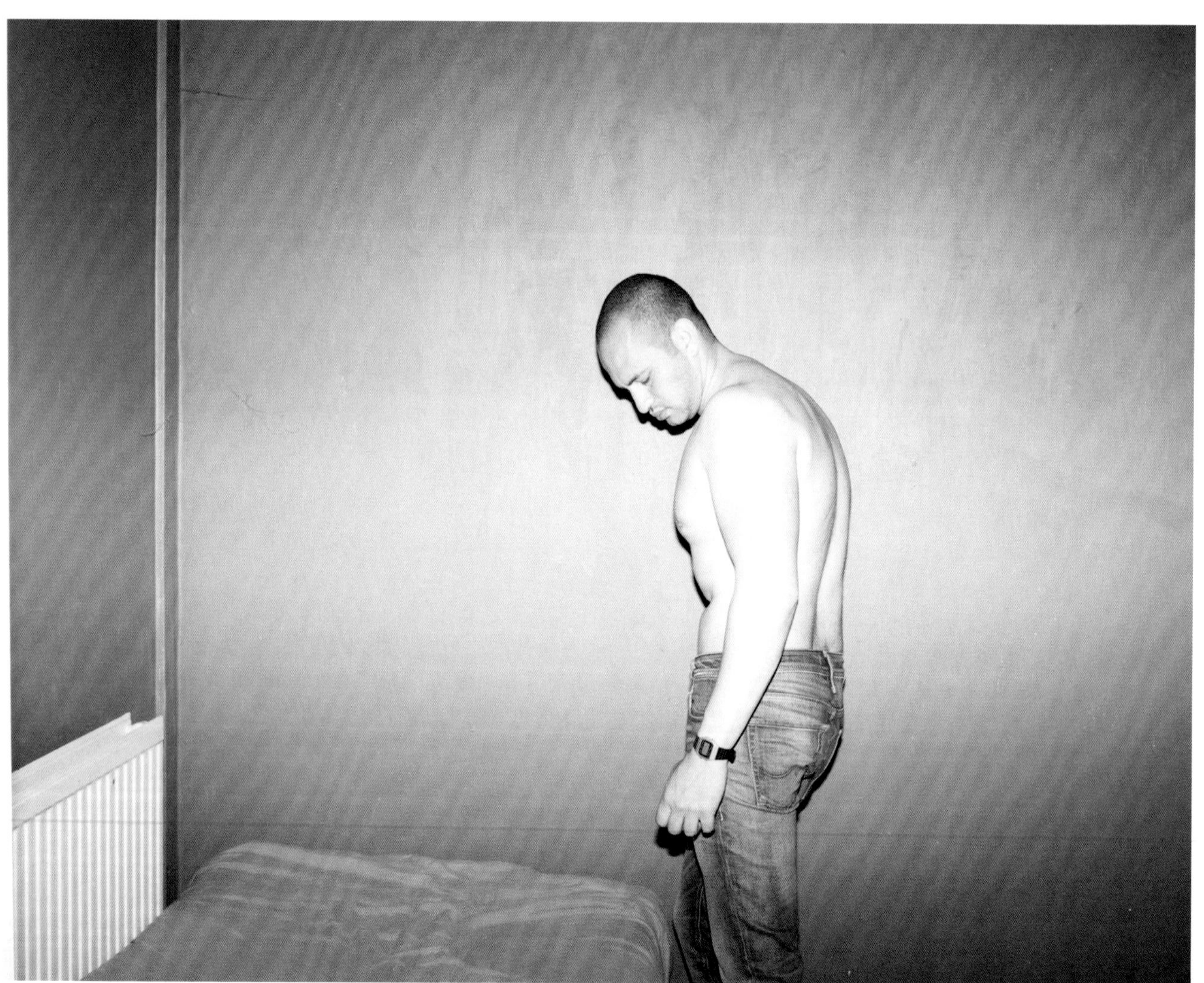

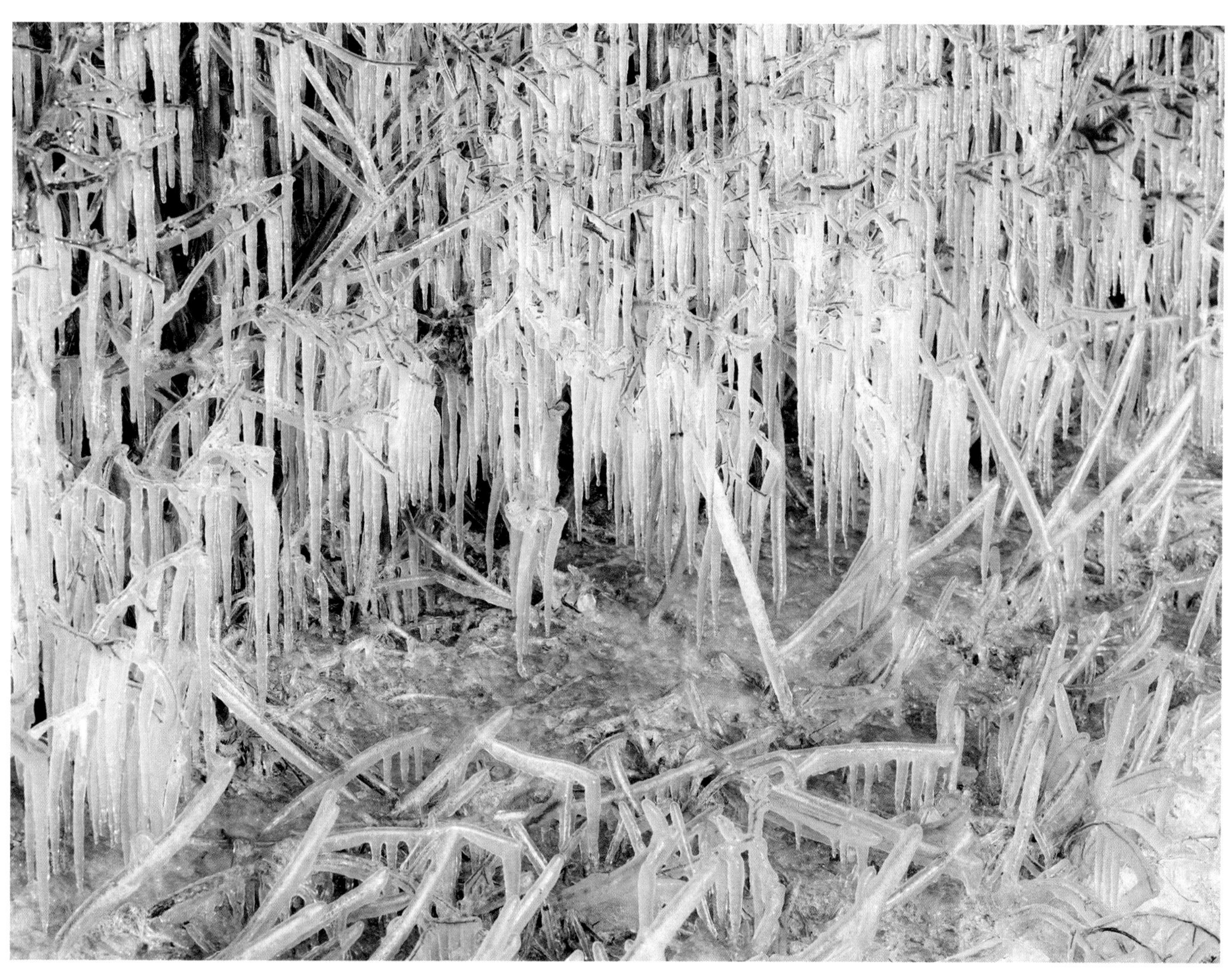

A SORRY STATE
Since 2025

Does your condition affect your washing and bathing? Does your condition affect you using the toilet or managing incontinence? These are just two of the questions UK citizens are asked when applying for aid from the welfare state, queries typically posed by strangers. Jack Moyse finds the process intrusive and demeaning and has fought back with his work, mapping the relevant scenarios with his own body then shooting at a distance. Peeping through doorways or watching long-distance through trees, his imagery suggests the surveillance to which he and others are subjected; using images to raise awareness, he also suggests the camera as a liberatory tool. Moyse's staged still lifes materialise the rhetoric that surrounds disability, meanwhile, and his layered artworks the trappings of bureaucracy. Here he is presenting new images of his installations, especially made for Photoworks.

Born in 1996, Moyse is based in Swansea, Wales, and holds an MA in photography from Plymouth College of Art. His practice focuses on the lived disabled experience, providing insight into and exposure for those marginalised in the UK, and the oppressive systems they encounter. Moyse has exhibited at Ffotogallery in Cardiff, Mission Gallery in Swansea, and Belfast Exposed; he was recommended to Photoworks by Joanne Coates, who won the 2022 Jerwood/Photoworks Award alongside Heather Agyepong.

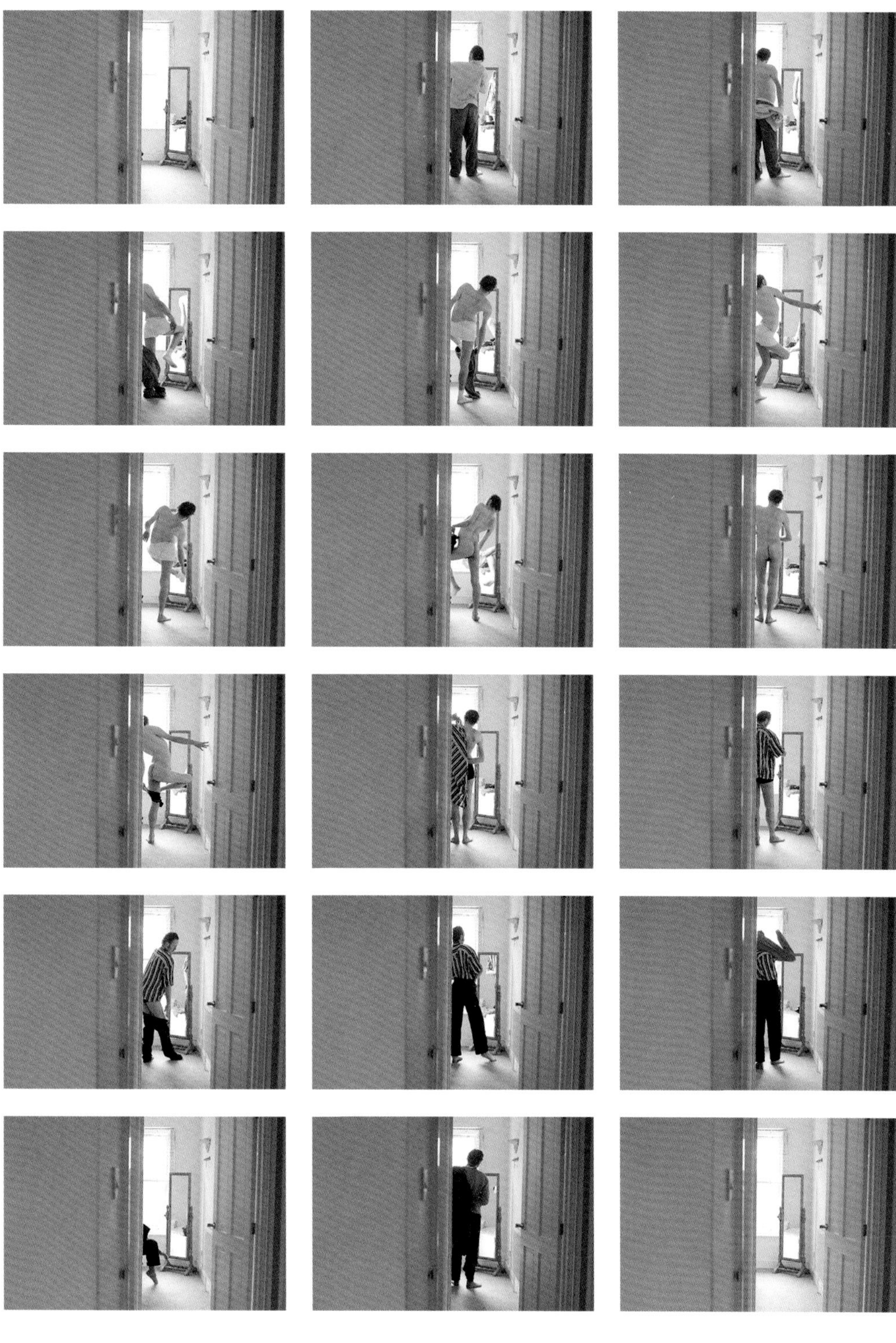

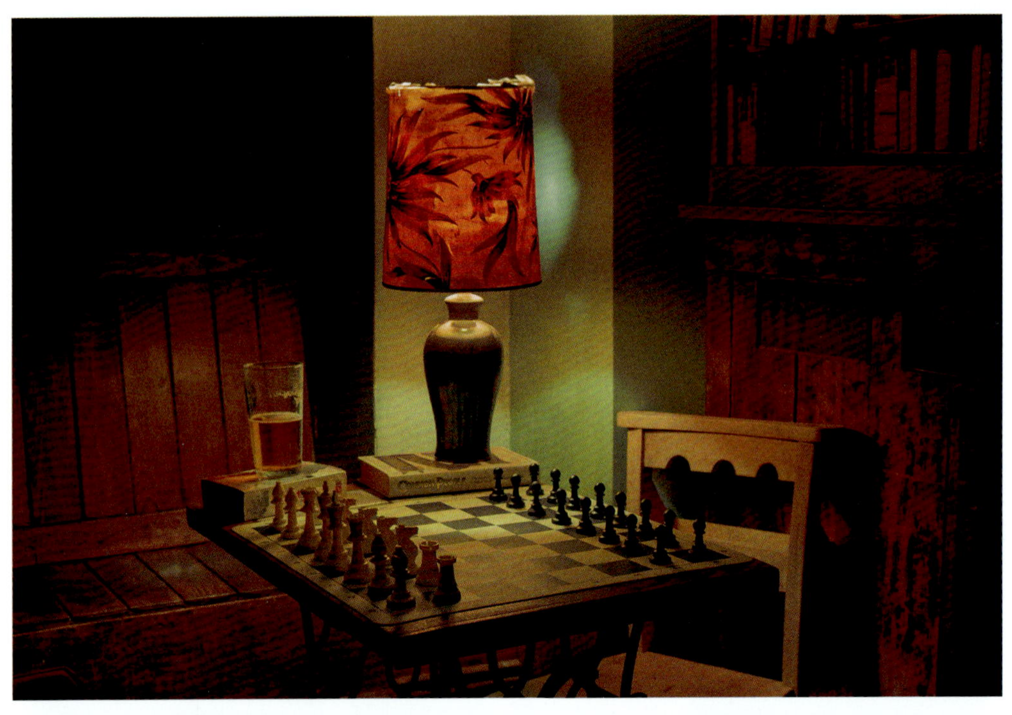

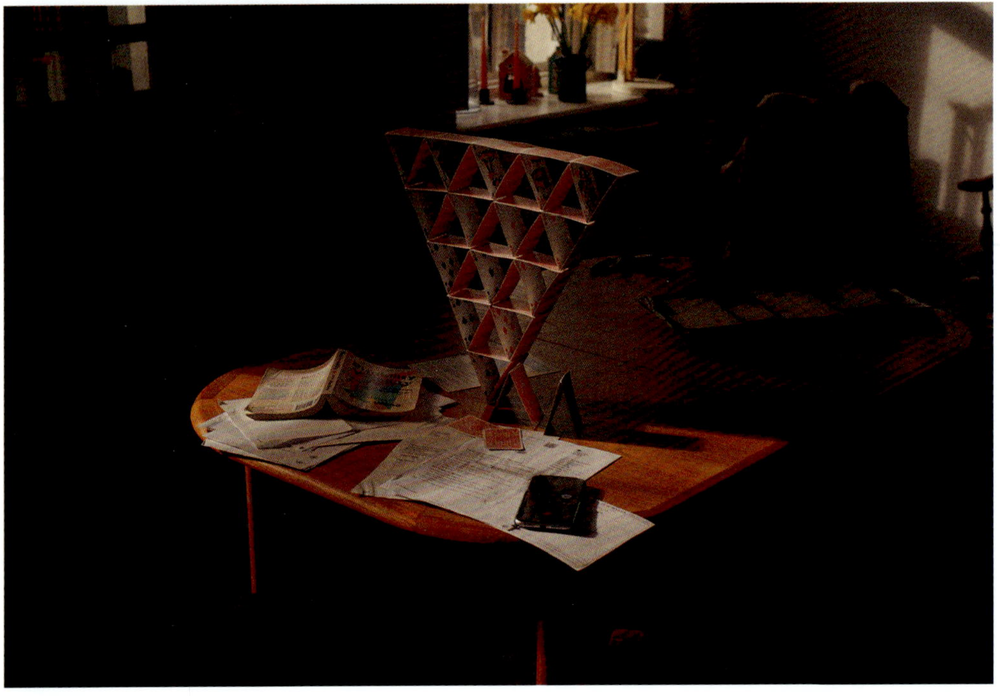

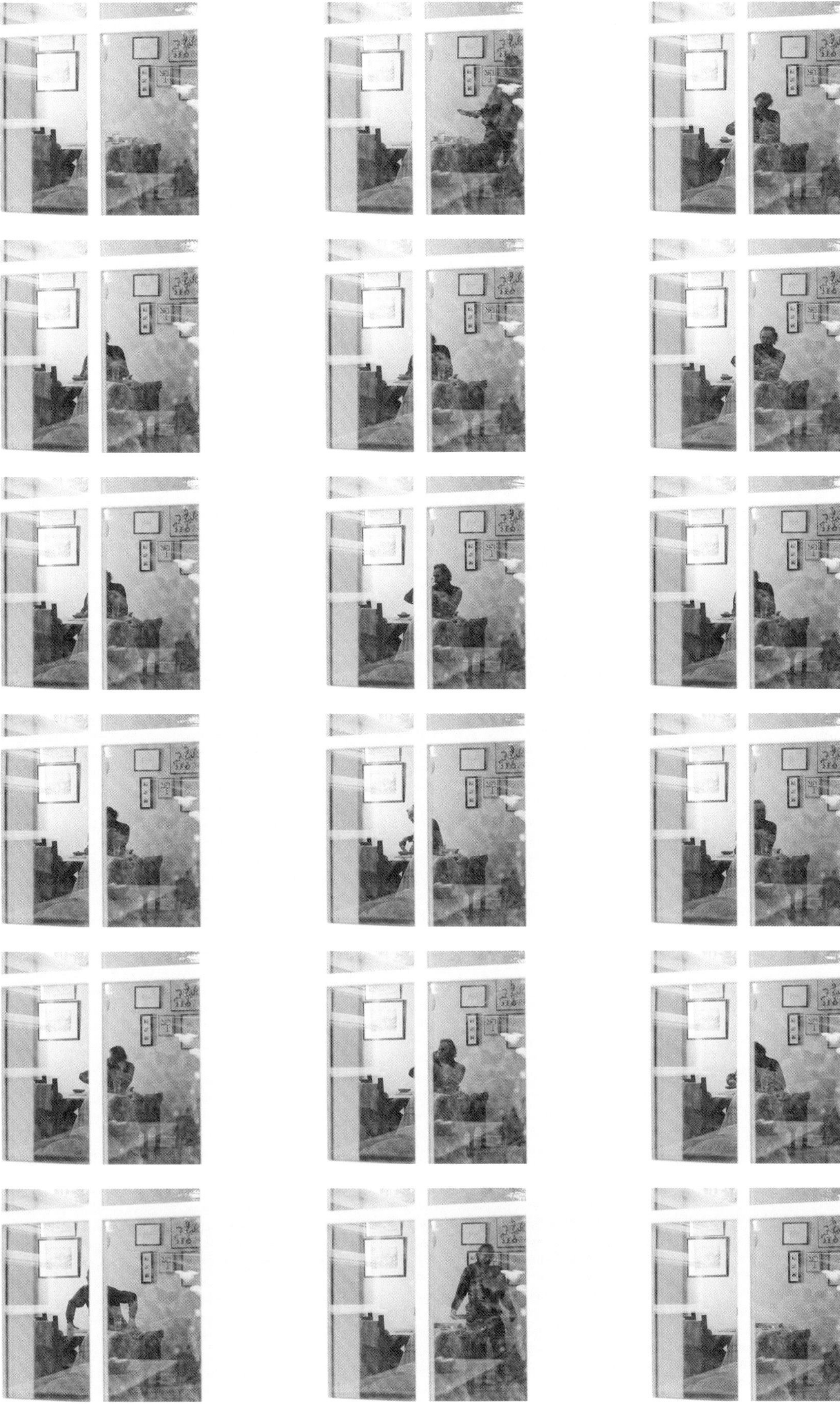

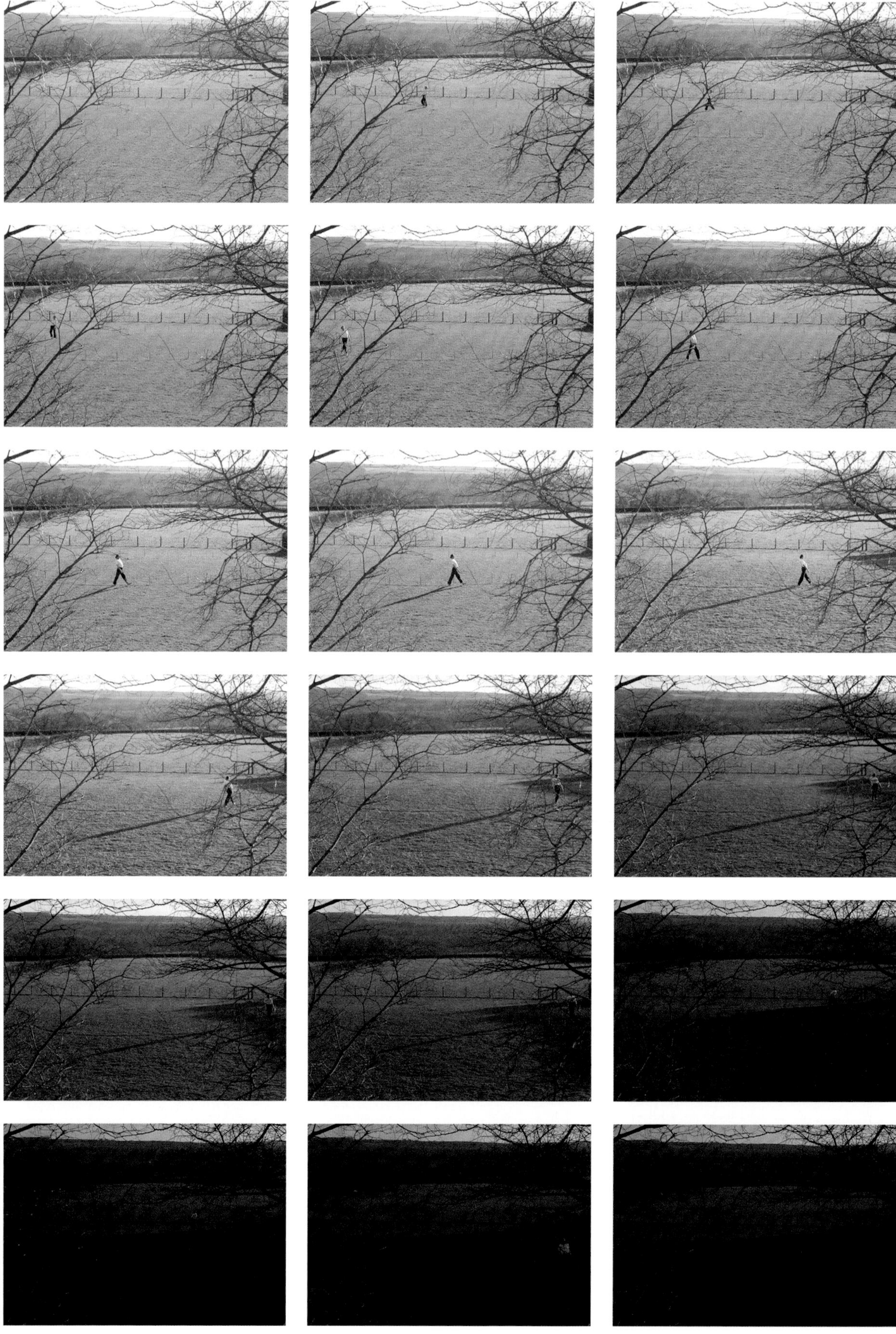

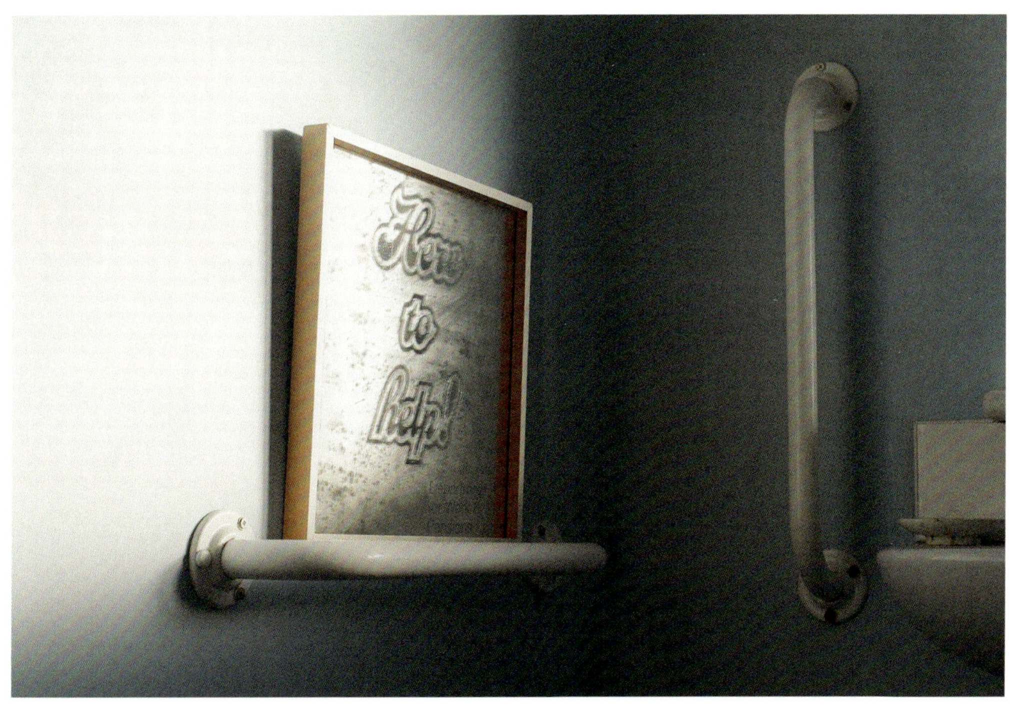
to
help!

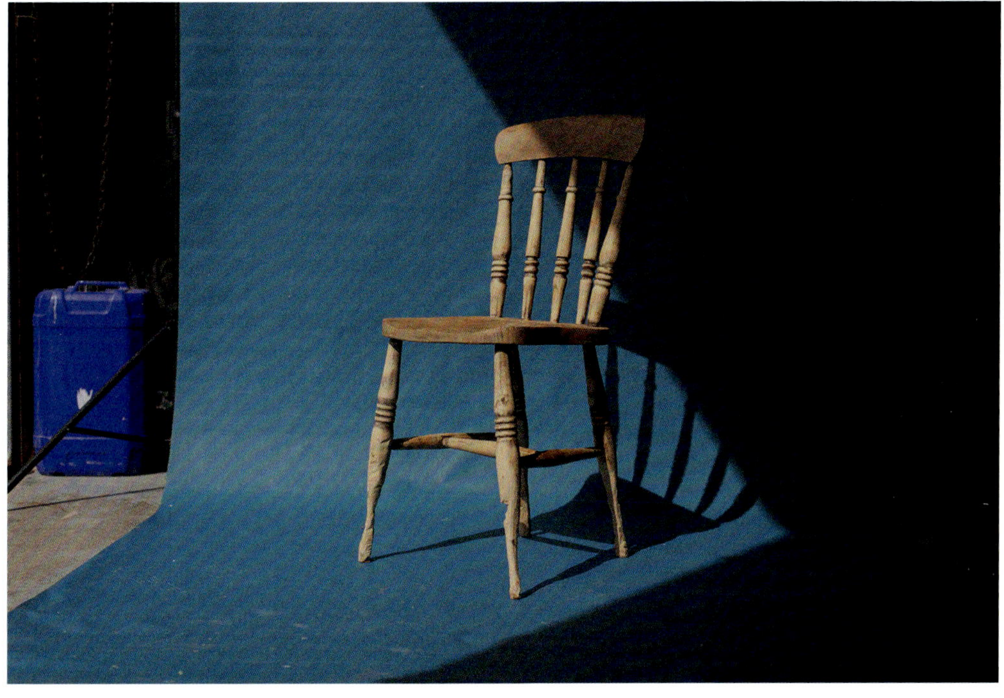

DESERT ISLAND PICS

DESERT ISLAND PICS

Initiated by Stephen Bull, Desert Island Pics is a series of discussions with practitioners about photographs that interest and have influenced them. Bull organised many in partnership with Photoworks in the 2010s, and has adapted the format for this Annual; here, he explains some of the thinking behind the project.

The idea for Desert Island Pics developed about 15 years ago, from my work with found photography. My series *Meeting Hazel Stokes* was chosen from existing snapshots of a theatre usherette briefly meeting stars backstage, and its themes of encounter, performance and image selection led me to wonder what would happen if I asked people to choose the photographs that they would take to a desert island. Central to this idea was performing the encounter as a live event with an audience, the photographs projected as I discussed them with my castaway (following the pattern of a parlour game going back to at least Victorian times and best-known via its radio version). A page of thoughts in my diary shifted to a potential real-life event when I started talking about the concept with others. That's where Photoworks came in. I had worked with Photoworks on various projects since the mid-1990s, and in early 2012 – after Photoworks and the Brighton Photo Biennial merged – Celia Davies suggested I formally propose the project as a series of events for that year's biennial.

It's interesting to reflect on my proposal from May 2012. What was going to be called *Deserted Gallery Photographs*, *Biopics*, or *Desert Island Pics* already had much of the structure in place – after my welcome and a short introduction to the castaway, the eight photographs would be discussed for around 45 minutes, followed by a brief concluding dialogue and two final questions. Before the last question, asking the castaway to choose one image from the eight, the penultimate question became which format the photographs would take. Some guests wanted their images to be presented in traditional galleries, others printed in books, another asked that they be tattooed onto their body. One castaway wanted the photographs printed, mounted and framed as large as possible, so that they could fashion them into a makeshift raft and navigate their way back home.

With the proposal approved, I began work, sketching out the staging and buying a small inflatable palm tree from a joke shop to suggest onstage the imaginary desert-island location. The palm tree became an important tradition and, after each event, the castaway and I would pose for a photograph with it – creating another series of images. The first two *Desert Island Pics* were at the wonderful Marlborough Theatre in Brighton, with an audience capacity of 50; castaway number one was on Sunday 7 October 2012, during the biennial's opening weekend, with the artist Anna Fox, followed a few weeks

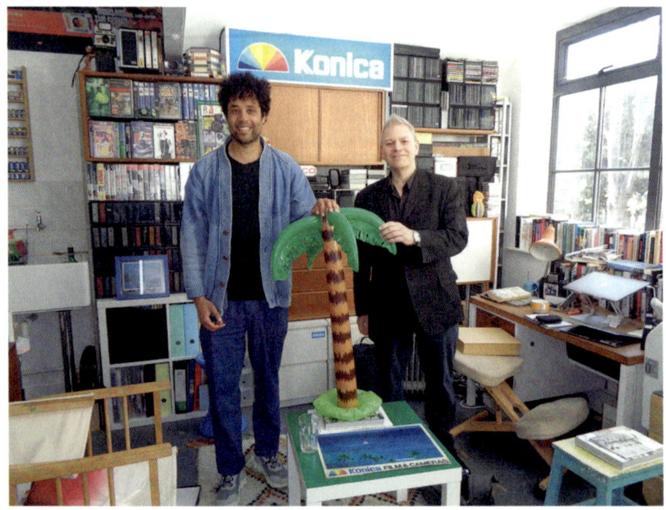

Stephen Bull and Johny Pitts photographed at Pitts' studio; Image © William Morris.

later by photography critic Sean O'Hagan. Both events were sold out and packed in, with some audience members perched on the edge of the stage.

The choices of photographs were fascinating and sometimes unexpected, revealing much about the approach, work and life of each castaway. Often the pictures had never been seen or discussed before, other times they were classics, on which a new light was shone. The idea had been made real and it seemed clear that the *Desert Island Pics* project should continue. Over the next six years, I worked with Photoworks on many more *Desert Island Pics*. The project was, and continues to be, a compelling and rewarding collaboration and I'm grateful for the support the organisation has provided. Through *Desert Island Pics*, countless connections have been made – connections between me and the castaway, connections across their choices of photographs, and connections bringing organisations together.

There have been many extraordinary moments: Brian Griffin's engaging takeover of the stage at Derby's Format Festival; Jeremy Deller in 2014, predating his radio version by some years; the London Art Fair with Alison Jackson, who understood so well the performative format and the narrative created by the selection of images; Susan Meiselas at Photo London, Somerset House, excerpts of which are included in this Annual. The final *Desert Island Pics* for a while was with Donovan Wylie on 24 October 2018 at the University of Brighton, where I'm a senior lecturer; in 2024, the event returned, in the same room, with my colleague Fergus Heron as guest. The palm tree that time was twice the size (as if it had grown during the hiatus), and the event seemed to revive interest in the project, coinciding neatly with the preparations for Photoworks' 30-year anniversary celebrations.

Earlier this year, and exclusively for this Annual, I met three more castaways, this time recording our conversations. It was a pleasure to join Johny Pitts in his London studio, where he was so generous with his thoughts, time and cereal bars. Lauren Joy Kennett suggested meeting at Picnic in St Leonards, a unique photography space complete with its own (real) palm tree. Eileen Perrier, who I have known since we were students together, was on my wishlist of potential castaways back in 2012, so it was an ambition fulfilled to speak with her. Transcripts from these new encounters appear in this Photoworks Annual and, as ever, their choices are fascinating and revealing. Join me with the guests of the past and the present as we discuss their *Desert Island Pics*.

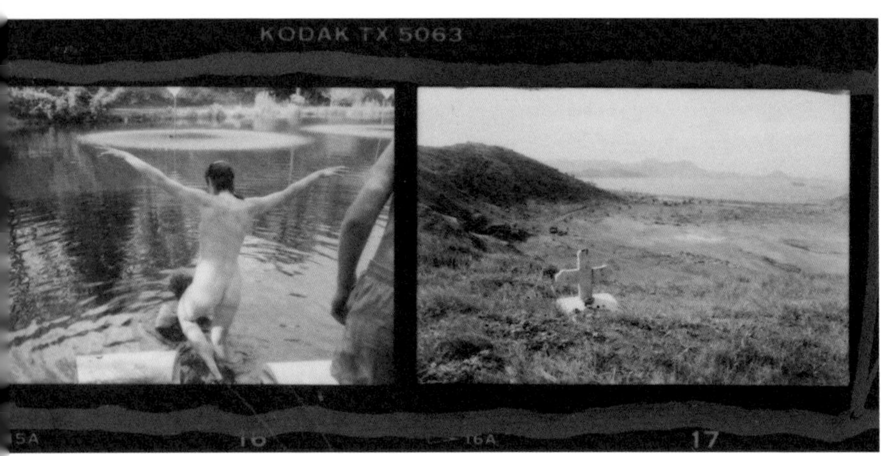

In the 1970s Susan Meiselas ran photography workshops for children in New York, South Carolina, and the Mississippi, while documenting strippers at New England fairs and carnivals in the summer holidays. She went on to photograph the insurrection in Nicaragua and human rights issues in Latin America, then in 1992 began to gather a visual history of the Kurdish people. In 2015-16, she made work with women in refuges in the UK. Meiselas has been a full member of Magnum Photos since 1980, and was married to filmmaker Richard P Rogers. Meiselas recorded her *Desert Island Pics* with Photoworks in 2017, in a pop-up event at Photo London. "Am I ready to be on a desert island?!" she said. "I think I might be considering the universe if I was there. I'd probably take as little as I could, just try to take myself away from everything, so I'd take these few photographs as memories."

Route 12, Wisconsin,
from The Bikeriders, 1968
by DANNY LYON

We're so flooded now with images, and we have mentoring, internships, awards, festivals, fairs. But the late 1960s and early 1970s was an isolated time to be working. I didn't feel myself to be a street photographer, and that was very prevalent; Danny Lyon's *The Bikeriders* was where I saw an immersive approach, and a sense that this could be another way to explore the world. This picture also symbolises my own search for the open road, wanting to not know what's on the other side. It's about the adventure. Danny jumped right on the back of one of those motorcycles and joined the spirit of the road; he tried to give us a feeling of the complex relationships the bikers had. There are interviews in the book, though interestingly the text is at the back. So you experience it as a visual narrative, then dive in deeper if you want.

Lena on the Ballybox, Essex Junction, USA,
1973 from Carnival Strippers
by SUSAN MEISELAS

This picture was taken in the early 1970s, in the midst of the women's movement. The idea of a woman on this auction block at a state fair was startling. I was just gaping, as was everyone else around me. You can see the power dynamics with the men around her – the guy selling the tickets, the manager, the little doorway that was the entry point 'for men and men only'. For me this was about being a woman, recognising another woman attracting men. Most [women] were choosing to do precisely the opposite, not to be the object of the gaze. And so that drew me to her, but I was excluded from that place. So the next mission was to figure out how to get in. This was the work that made me feel there was a possible purpose – and a way – to be a photographer. I mean, I'd been teaching photography in public schools to 10-year-olds. It was a completely different idea then to just 'be' a photographer.

Dick and Susan on the beach in Wainscott, USA, 1995
by NANCY BERNER

People always talk about the woman behind the man, but very rarely the man behind the woman. I have this picture in my studio; for me, it's about what it really means to have a creative life with another creator. It is a rich life – having to let go of the person you care the most about in order to go out into the world, but then having somebody who believes it matters whether you come back. That's also a very, very essential part of going

Two frames from contact sheet, 1980s © Susan Meiselas.

down that 'open road'. My sister Nancy took this photograph and I love it. I'm not somebody who makes selfies, but I'm really happy this image is there for me.

Ché, 1963
by RENÉ BURRI

We always know René because he photographed Ché, but to what extent is he remembered separately from the pictures he made? For me, René was very special; when I joined Magnum, he was one of those extraordinarily generous spirits. When I first went to Magnum in Paris, I landed very early and went to our office off Rue Christine. René was sitting in the kitchen and immediately welcomed me in. Every time he would come through the New York office, he would bring Swiss chocolates. He had a love affair, in a way, with Cuba and with Ché, and then Ché went on to become a symbol for so many people. That's part of the magic of photography; in that moment, he understood Ché so well, not imagining how commercialised his image would become. When you're making a frame, you have some notion you're controlling it, but the fact is – it has its own ongoing life.

Hyères, France, 1932
by HENRI CARTIER-BRESSON

There's this idea of patience for the moment – it's not just a frozen, perfect landscape until the cyclist comes by; you're trying to learn as you look. There's that tension between an aesthetic approach and the social, political context in which you're also trying to capture the real dynamics at play. You don't always know what will unfold, but you still place your body, capturing a moment and anticipating it. Cartier-Bresson obviously anticipated it. He went near the steps, he looked, and then there it was. Maybe he waited for another bike to pass? I'm also a cyclist and you know photography and cycling both demand anticipation. By being the cyclist, you also have to anticipate moves. Anticipating three-dimensional spaces is a terrific way to think about what photography is.

Two frames from contact sheet, 1980s
by SUSAN MEISELAS

This is very personal. My process, in this period, was to go from where I was familiar to a place that was unknown, and I would intentionally leave film in the camera. It was a form of diary. I'm not a writer, so how else could I register these very abrupt shifts? I was very conscious of this idea of moving your body from one place to another. This is one of the combinations that is so stark, because there's my sister about to enter the pond, pregnant with her second child, and then next to that frame on the contact sheet is a hillside in Nicaragua, where there is this horrific scene of a partial body. How can you possibly bridge these two worlds? Yet that's what we physically do when we go places, that is what we're living and absorbing and assimilating in some sense – the contrast while often feeling the contradictions.

iPhone photograph of Justo memorial with
Susan Meiselas' Nicaragua photograph, 2016
by ABBIE FIELDS

Nicaragua still looms large for me. This is the coffin of Justo, who is also in the middle of the three men in that photograph. There are always questions about what photographs are for, and who they are for, and this image in particular had multiple roles. It was my first cover on *The New York Times Magazine*, which was my first engagement with the media. At that time, there was a certain unease for me, because they're in a very performative moment. Justo was very central to my long, long relationship with Nicaragua. I knew he was ill, but I didn't know he would die so soon. I certainly didn't know someone would make this print and place it on his coffin. I have experiences that involve photography, but I also experience how those photographs live in the world; of the eight images I am sharing, this one probably resonates most deeply with me.

Tia from A Room of Their Own, 2017
by SUSAN MEISELAS

I just finished working in the Black Country in a refuge network, on a collaboration with Multistory and a team of creative people. Working with women coming from very different experiences of domestic violence, it was difficult to figure out what to do as a photographer. One day I was out in the garden with Tia, and she just turned away. It is a moment that takes me back to – what is photography about? I'm going back to the core experience of a photograph that comes from a moment someone gives you, and not necessarily consciously so. Maybe it's also about engagement, about trusting your own engagement and not being afraid of where it takes you. It all goes back to that same 'open road', not knowing what's over the horizon, but staying open to the unpredictable.

Born in Aden, Yemen, Nick Waplington studied art at Trent Polytechnic and the Royal College of Art in London. From 1984 to 1999, he regularly visited his grandfather on Broxtowe Estate, Nottingham, taking photographs of friends and neighbours which he went on to publish as *Living Room* (1991) and *Weddings, Parties, Anything* (1996). He has since published numerous other books, and in 2001 exhibited his work at the Venice Biennial. Waplington discussed his *Desert Island Pics* during the 2014 Brighton Photo Biennial. "You know the pictures that you like tend to change with time," he said. "So what I tried to do was take myself on a journey through my own visual photographic experience." When asked how he'd like to take the images to the desert island, he suggested he get them tattooed. "Then I could be really cool, I could have Abbie Hoffmann really big on my back."

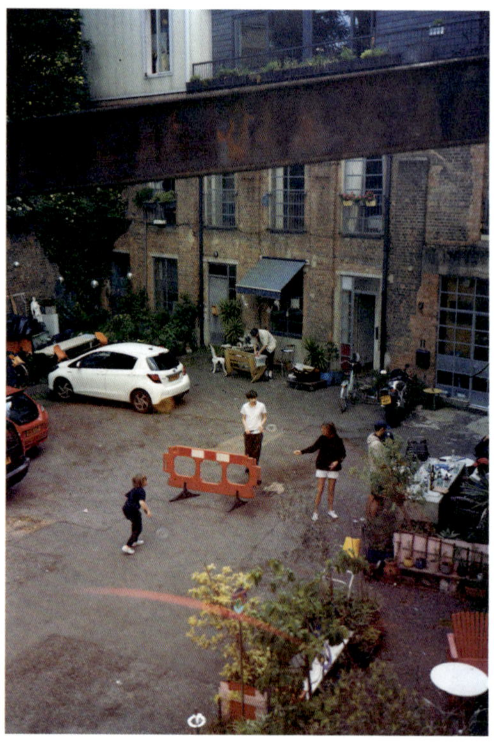

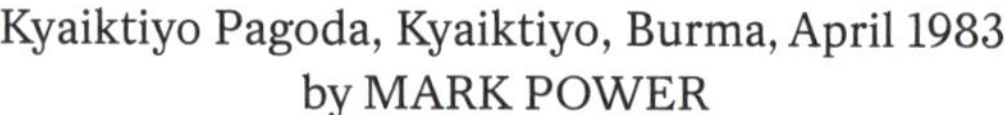

Kyaiktiyo Pagoda, Kyaiktiyo, Burma, April 1983
by MARK POWER

When I was doing my art foundation, I had only ever seen photographs in books. I had never actually met a real photographer, until Mark Power came to teach us one day in I think 198 This photograph is locked in my mind. I loved the story behind it – this is in Burma, it was difficult to get there, the rock is covered in gold leaf, and the monks who live on top believe it won't fall off unless it's the end of the world, and then it won't matter anyway. And I loved the silhouette of the monk playing against the rock. It was a powerful image, in a time when you couldn't go on the internet and just look at anything or anywhere. And the idea that you could travel and take pictures, that it could be an excuse to explore things, that sounded great.

The Chicago Seven: Lee Weiner, John Froines, Abbie Hoffman, Rennie Davis, Jerry Rubin, Tom Hayden, Dave Dellinger, Chicago, September 25, 1969
by RICHARD AVEDON

This is the Chicago Seven during their trial in Chicago in 1969. They were arrested for inciting a riot at the Democratic Party Conference in 1968, at the height of the Vietnam War. Avedon had thought about how to make work that dealt with the turmoil of the 1960s, and come up with this head-on, 10×8, brutal format, where he used a white background to separate the subject matter from the environment, and where he tried to eliminate all shadow. And then they are printed life size. The political series from 1968 to 1975 is, for me, his greatest work. I love this image. These are yippies, the link between the beatniks and the hippies; they saw themselves aligned to the Black Panther movement and the possibility of real, radical change in the USA. Now it seems delusional, but I like that kind of delusion. You know it's OK to be Left.

Nostalgic Depiction of the Innocence of Childhood, 1990
by MIKE KELLEY

By this time, I had got to the Royal College of Art and had started to meet people whose ideas about art practice were completely different to mine. One of the major players in the more left-field art world at the time was Mike Kelley. He thought that people's ideas of pictures of childhood were too sanitised and too clean. What's going on in this picture is actors pretending to be babies, playing with cuddly toys, poo everywhere and whatever. Obviously people found this offensive, then he would just take the offence and use that again in his work. This was a long way from Trent Polytechnic and concerned photography! There is a notion that if we want our work to be positive, we need to clean things up, we have to somehow make the work palatable. In actual fact, you should just let things be and put them out there.

The Yard No.9 from Africa © Nick Waplington.

Eating My Words from Eleven Color Photographs, 1966-1967
by BRUCE NAUMAN

For me, this comes from that same period, of learning about other ways of using photography to talk about the world. He's got white bread, he's written words on the bread, and he's jamming it in, he's eating it. There are different levels of interpretation of what's going on, beyond the simple joke and the physical aspect. He made this series in the studio and they're not elaborately staged, but it's interesting that his shirt matches the tablecloth, which seems to connect with the jam. He's an artist who worked with language a lot, and by eating his own words he is both destroying his creative process and creating work at the same time. It's about, I don't know, everything and nothing at the same time. Currently it's like you have to have a theme, and you've got to follow that theme, but I don't care about that. I'm interested in everything. I want to absorb and then utilise and push it back out. I'm very interested in failure. And text is an ongoing thing with me, I'm trying to incorporate text both with essays and written text on pieces of work, playing with language is something I'm very interested in.

Viral Landscape No.4, from the series Viral Landscapes, 1988-89
by HELEN CHADWICK

I saw this in the V&A in the late 1980s and I was just blown away. She had combined three disparate elements and created something that was beautiful, intellectually engaging and unlike any kind of photograph I had ever seen. The virus part is her own blood, which she photographed under a microscope, then laid on top of pictures of the cliffs of the Pembrokeshire coast. There are so many different ways you could interpret this. For me, this image was part of a whole process of deconstructing what I had been taught, going from this very structured social documentary course at Trent Polytechnic to this feeling of "Do whatever you want as long as you're doing something" at the Royal College. For some students, that failed miserably but for me, because I was very focused, it worked.

Diptych from Case History, 1997-98
by BORIS MIKHAILOV

Just when I was disengaging with documentary, out came this book, *Case History*, by Boris Mikhailov. Wow! It was documentary that was both social poetry and hard-hitting, without the sentimentality I dislike in documentary photography. And when Mikhailov shows these images, he doesn't frame them. They are very, very large prints, almost badly printed, that he just clips up. You're very confronted by them. Here we've got these glue-sniffing children in Ukraine; I remember sniffing glue at school in the late 1970s, if you were at a comprehensive school in Britain then, it was just rife. But I hadn't thought about it for years until I saw these pictures. And, you know, I was at the local skate park yesterday and there were 10-year-olds sitting around smoking marijuana. You think this is somewhere else and it isn't your work, but it's 200 metres away. It's important art engages that.

From the series RFK Funeral Train, 1968
by PAUL FUSCO

This is from my favourite book, RFK Funeral Train by Paul Fusco. Fusco had travelled from New York, where Robert Kennedy was a senator, to the Arlington Cemetery in Washington, where he was buried after his assassination. The train moved slowly through the countryside, and Fusco sat on one of the foot plates and photographed everyone who came to pay their respects, Black and white people together, at a time when America was quite segregated. The pictures were all shot in one day, from morning to evening, and they're just extraordinary. When you think of the 1960s, you think everyone was a hippy, but here it looks like the 1950s. You realise that the notion of the 1960s we have been sold was only for a very small minority; these people were poor and working class. If I were getting these images tattooed, this is the one I'd be really careful with. That's the tattoo that would remain.

From The Allies Capture Ruined Naples, published in Life Magazine, 18 October, 1943
By ROBERT CAPA

This was taken during the Battle of Monte Cassino, and it shows the medics operating on the troops. One of them is my granddad. He had always told me about this SS officer brought into the operating room; he had 80% burns, so they tried to give him a morphine injection, but he said "I am the SS, I don't feel any pain." This always made my granddad cry. Then, recently, I asked him about it and he pulled out this old copy of Life magazine and said, "That's me!" I checked all the facts, and everything matches up. I never really liked Robert Capa much before. I thought he was one of those macho dudes with a cigarette who went around looking for girls, then took a few pictures before hitting the bar again. So this threw me, and it's good to be thrown, isn't it?

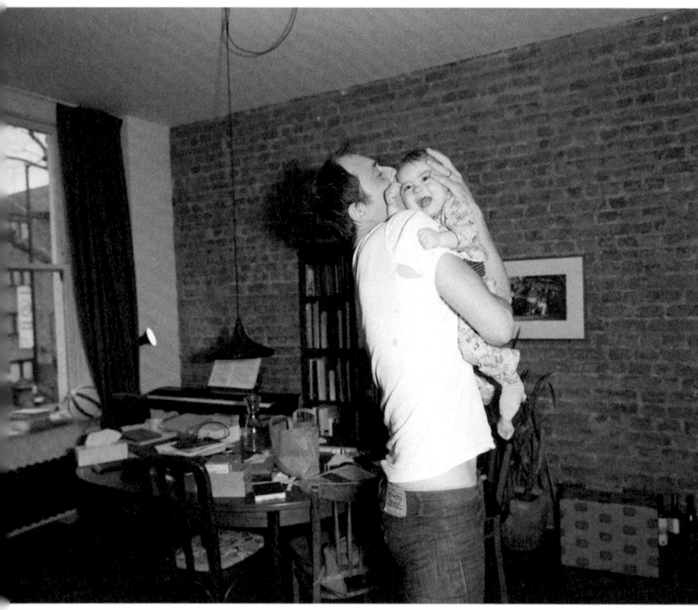

Philip and Thea, December 2015 © Olivia Arthur.

Olivia Arthur studied photojournalism at the London College of Printing and began working as a photographer in 2003, after moving to Delhi. Her books include *Jeddah Diary* (2012), *Stranger* (2015), and *Murmurings of the Skin* (2024); in 2010 she co-founded the Fishbar photography publisher and space with her husband, Philipp Ebeling. Arthur became a nominee member of Magnum Photos in 2008, and a full member in 201 Arthur gave her *Desert Island Pics* at a Photoworks event at London Art Fair in January 201 “It was really hard to choose eight when we have, obviously, many, many photographs,” she said. “It was also hard because I like to look at the whole body of work – I'm always drawn to work made in that way, and I like to make my own work that way. So often I knew I wanted something from a body of work, but I wasn't exactly sure which one.”

Pooh in Bed, Bombay, 1975
by PABLO BARTHOLOMEW

I started my career in photography in India – my family moved there, so I had the opportunity and it was wonderful. It's where I found my feet in photography. I started doing small stories for British newspapers, and I met Pablo quite early on. He is maybe best known for winning the World Press Photo awards in 1984 with his picture of the Bhopal Gas Tragedy and he gave me a lot of advice when I was starting out. So years later, when Philipp and I were starting Fishbar, we asked Pablo to be our first exhibition, showing his and his fathers' work. I have this on a poster on my kitchen wall above the table – I see it every day.

Untitled, 10 Minutes One Afternoon in Whitechapel, 2004
by PHILIPP EBELING

I saw this before I met Philipp. It's part of a series of seven photographs from 10 minutes of snow in Whitechapel, which won the Observer Hodge Award. I saw it online somewhere when I was still in India, and then, not long after, I found myself invited to do a one-year residency at Fabrica, in Italy. We were six photographers, and among them was Philip. This image captures something in his photography that's been very inspiring for me, and that's the simplicity of just seeing something beautiful. I had to go away, to see things further away, then come back, but others see the things that are right in front of them. I hope I'm doing that much more now, discovering what's around me.

Girl on Footstools, A Life Full of Holes:
The Strait Project, 2005
by YTO BARRADA

I saw this work while I was still at Fabrica, and it was very inspiring. It's a very gentle approach to telling a story about a place; a lot is left to the imagination. Barrada doesn't necessarily explain what all the pictures are, just gives little suggestions. I was very drawn to her way of seeing and this work influenced me a lot when I was making *The Middle Distance* – I made a journey along the border between Europe and Asia, which was also about longing for life on the other side, and at the same time, the changes and the things going on in that place. The girl looks almost like she is on a throne, and is dressed up as a bride. I was looking at women my age, I suppose, at that time in your life when things start to change.

Rosie Ricketts and her Son, 2010
by PETER VAN AGTMAEL

In 2008, I was nominated to join Magnum, along with Peter, and we both started this long journey to becoming members. It took us five years together, so he was kind of my classmate but also brother in this stressful period. Our work seems quite different – he comes from a background in war photography in Iraq and Afghanistan, but his work goes beyond just going to those places. It's the thoughtfulness and even academic side of his approach that I find really powerful. His work is very gentle and thoughtful, and this picture captures that for me. It shows Rosie Ricketts and her son, getting ready for a ceremony; her husband has been killed, but rather than the drama of that, this is a tender moment. Peter is great with people, he has great respect, and that comes through in his work.

Joe Petersen, from the photobook Rich and Poor, 1985
by JIM GOLDBERG

Joe's text reads: "It's kind of stinky. Living in this hotel. I don't have nothing, only $10. I keep waiting for someone to come in my door and give me money, but nobody ever will." I love the way Jim incorporates text – these pictures are only shown with the text, it's not that the text is separate. *Rich and Poor* was shot in what they call a hotel, a place where people rent a room, and there's a lot of poverty. I chose this one particularly because of this feeling of hope but at the same time resignation; this combination of having some kind of hope, and yet at the same time being realistic. Jim is definitely a photographer who has tremendous respect for his subjects, and you see it very clearly in the work.

The Great Unreal, 2005-09
by TAIYO ONORATO and NICO KREBS

I met these two at an event at Fotomuseum Winterthur in about 2008, they had a portfolio of their work and I was very struck by it. The way they work together is a lot of fun. It's very analogue, either done in front of the camera or in the darkroom, and staged but they show you it is staged. For this series, they made these road trips across the US and took pictures, and then they played and created things. They messed with the iconography of the US road trip. This picture is very different to the others I have chosen, but I love this book, it's one of my favourites. It's important to keep the fun in photography, and part of the fun of it is that they are laughing at themselves as well. I'm a documentary photographer, I don't make this kind of work, but I wouldn't rule it out!

Iran by the Caspian Sea, 1956
by INGE MORATH

Magnum runs an annual award for young female photographers, the Inge Morath Award, and in 2007 I won it. I don't think I would have applied to Magnum if I hadn't. Then, in 2012, there was an exhibition with past winners and we all got along very well, so we decided to plan an adventure, to make some tribute to her. We found out she had tried to photograph all the way along the Danube River, so we took that as a starting point; eventually, we took an exhibition of her work by truck along the Danube, all of us going along and making new images. It was quite an experience! She was quite a pioneer, and she was also an evocative writer. This image reminds me of her journal, when she's travelling alone, photographing and feeling kind of lost in the middle of nowhere.

Philip and Thea, December 2015,
by OLIVIA ARTHUR

This is Philip and my daughter, Thea. I love the way he is holding her, and also it captures our feelings that year, having a child and trying to figure out how to be photographers and parents, juggling all these things. Of course we take many pictures on our phones, the same pictures everybody takes of their kids. But I made this on a 4×5 camera and processed it myself. I've enjoyed coming closer to home. It seems kind of silly these days, when it is so easy to make good pictures in so many other ways, but I needed it. I've been a bit overwhelmed by the photography world, and the photobook world has just exploded. The geek in me wanted to get back to processing film in the bathroom, and remembering when photography was very uncool. It's been another way of coming home.

Recipient of the first Ampersand/Photoworks Fellowship in May 2021, Johny Pitts went on the road with the poet Roger Robinson and created the work *Home is Not a Place*. A meditation of what it means to be Black in Britain, it went on to be shown in Graves Gallery, Sheffield (Pitts's home town), Stills Edinburgh, and The Photographers' Gallery, London. Pitts is also known for his book, *Afropean*, a travelogue around Black Europe. He discussed his *Desert Island Pics* with Stephen Bull this spring. "I want to start with a disclaimer," he said. "If I was really going to be stranded on a desert island, the photographs would be different. They'd all be pictures of my family, which maybe aren't particularly visually interesting but are important to me. I've chosen eight photographs within the conceit of the premise that I can say something maybe slightly interesting about."

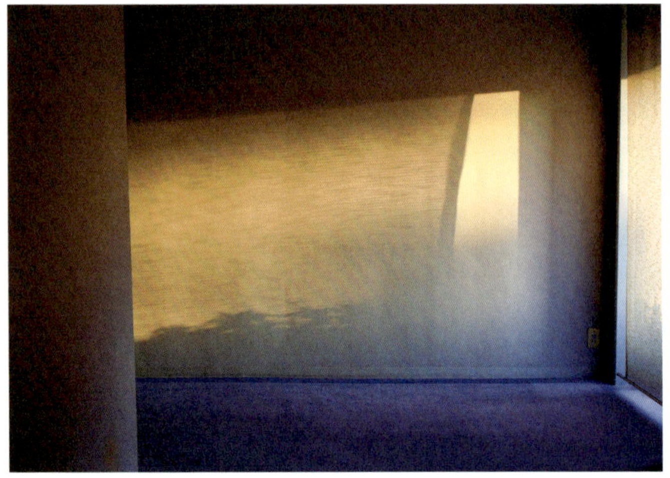

Portrait of Stephen Simmonds, 1997
by RICK GUEST

This photograph is included in the inlay of one of my favourite albums, *Spirit Tales* by Simmonds, a Swedish singer-songwriter partly of Jamaican heritage. I picked it up in the early 2000s, at a moment in my life where I was lost. I had just quit college, I'd been sacked, I spent a year travelling the old industrial parts of Sheffield, and in one record store I found this album. That inlay changed my life and gave me a visual language for the experience I'd had growing up mixed race in Europe at that time, feeling not British but more European. That's where my work with *Afropean* began. The art direction was by Anna Bergfors, formerly known as Mat Cook, who was a big graphic designer of that time; it was like a second-hand art school education, all the beauty and dedication and craft in this little inlay in a CD from the bargain bin.

Acid Rain (Mercy Mercy Me, Marvin Gaye), 1977
by MING SMITH

Ming Smith was a model for many years, then moved behind the camera to become a photographer and was part of the Kamoinge Workshop for African American photographers. This is one of her rarer colour photographs and the framing is off, or maybe it's a double exposure; it shows you how something felt rather than just how it looked. The atmosphere of the image really speaks to me. It's about being on the edge of failure but not failing and makes me think of what Paul Gilroy called Black Atlantic vernacular culture – the idea you're playing around with vernacular photography, almost looking amateurish, but encoded with an atmosphere and retaining just enough formal beauty to hold it together. I also think this photograph honours Marvin Gaye, its namesake, being politically and socially conscious, but somehow finding a way to create beauty, which is certainly what Gaye's 'Mercy Mercy Me' did.

Untitled [Woman carrying flower box],
from São Paulo Anotações, 1982
by GEORGE LEARY LOVE

George Leary Love was an African American photographer based in Brazil; he was married to Claudia Andujar, who is also a great photographer. He was very experimental, would play with end roll burnouts and use expired film – again, it's the edge-of-failure aesthetic, but he's just a master of colour. There's a whole history of colour photography, coming through William Eggleston and Stephen Shore, but there's also an alternative history that comes from South America, and Love didn't want to produce a kind of culture safari. He was always trying to remind you that there is a gaze at work here, and a technology, and not to just take the images for granted – somebody is looking, using a device!

Kitakyushu Prince Hotel; c2023. © Johny Pitts.

Canopy, 1958
by SAUL LEITER

There are so many great Saul Leiter images, but this is my favourite. I think it might be one of the greatest photographs of all time. It's colour but it's taken on expired film, and that reduces the palette so it's almost monochrome. It's from his book *Early Color*, which was published so beautifully by Steidl; the first thing I noticed was that it's street photography but it's vertical (orientation), which is unusual. Then there's how he deals with negative space. I remember thinking, "I didn't know that was allowed" when I first saw it, it just blew my mind. He's doing everything wrong, in a way, and yet there is a great photo.

Box Walking, from God
Forgotten Face, 2011
by ROBIN MADDOCK

For me this photograph sums up Britain in the 2010s. You've got the rain, the drabness, it's an austere image. You've also got the shipping container and – since the 2008 financial crisis and the rise of all this anti-immigrant sentiment – I see so much symbolism in that, in the idea of globalisation but, going back, the British Empire. There's this little woman trying to steer the weight of empire in a different direction, back to an imagined past. Maddock is a funny guy and in a lot of his images you see humour, but he's also a real visual poet. I like the distance too, I've never liked this idea that, in street photography, you've got to be in people's faces. The idea of the poetry of distance massively inspired my work.

Rue de Thionville, 1987
by ADAM BARTOS

I discovered Adam Bartos through Anna Bergfors. He's one of the few people taking what Eggleston did and pushing it a stage further in terms of finding beauty in banality. He's amazing at photographing cars. I realised that, when I was taking photographs, I was often cropping out the cars – I could appreciate a 1970s saloon, but I just didn't see the beauty of modern cars. He was taking photographs in the 1980s and found something about their form interesting. There's also a lone figure, which is in many of my choices; it makes me think of (cultural critic) Mark Fisher, who talks about the secret sadness that lurks behind the 21st century's forced smile.

Ryotsu Port, 2007,
from Sado Shina Shina Aruki, 2001–2014
by HIDEKO TAKAGI

Takagi is a Japanese photographer, born in 197 I discovered her work when I was in Tokyo. When we think about Japanese photography, we often go to the *Provoke* era and black and white, but she uses colour, and I see in her work the colours I associate with the reality of Japan. I'm a nerd, but she shot it on Fujifilm Superia Premium, which was specifically developed to work with colour in Japan. For me, her colours sum up this post-bubble moment in Japan, the faded future and optimism. She's what really got me thinking about the tyranny of the single image, though, when actually it's a series of images that often makes work powerful.

Kitakyushu Prince Hotel, c2023
by JOHNY PITTS

This is from ongoing work about my experience of living in Japan in the 1980s. I grew up in working-class Sheffield, but then had this blip where my father, who was an African-American singer, got a role in an Andrew Lloyd Webber musical touring Japan. I got whisked from a terrace house in Sheffield to Japan at the height of its bubble economy; there were prototypes of flying cars, we were staying in five-star hotels. It was incredible! But then I went back in 2013, and it was futurism in stasis, all slightly sad-looking and aging. I've started trying to trace back and, walking in this hotel, had an amazing feeling of the presence of my dad. There was a steam bath just round the corner; I must have gone with him there as a child. Something about the blank wall or the way the sunlight fell had stirred a memory. It's funny – I must have stored the memory of this wall, and the atmosphere it emitted, deep in my subconscious all those years!

Sorry I'm Not Sorry explores Lauren Joy Kennett's experience of living with undiagnosed autism; it was commissioned in 2023 as part of In Focus, a partnership between Photoworks and Aspex Portsmouth as part of the national Explorers initiative, dedicated to increasing the visibility and representation of neurodivergent artists. *Sorry I'm Not Sorry* went on show at Aspex in 2023, and was co-published by Photoworks and Jane & Jeremy in 202 Kennett's conversation with Stephen Bull took place in May 202 "I loved the idea of it, but when it came to it, I found it really challenging," she said. "It felt like a deep study of myself, which I'm not sure I was prepared for. I'm not completely sure the photographs I've chosen are the ones I would take, but when I look at them, I realise they are all kind of saying the same thing. And that wasn't purposeful at all."

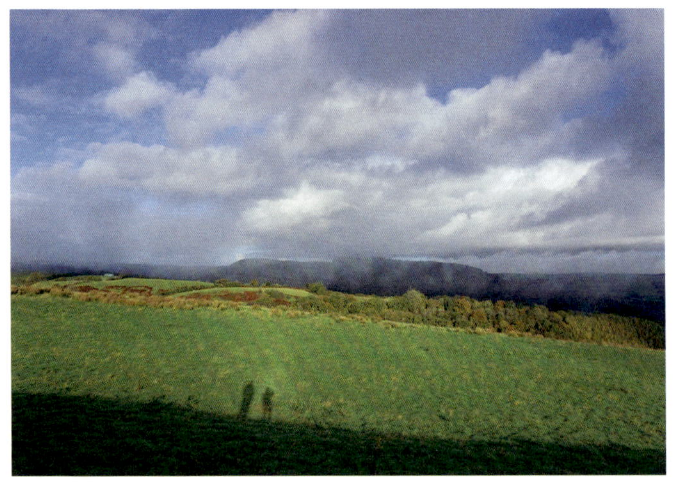

Self-Portrait in a Blue Bathroom, London, 1980
by NAN GOLDIN

I came across this photo years ago, before I knew anything about photography and before I knew who Nan Goldin was. I really connected with it. It feels so powerful in its intimacy, but it's also distant. It's saying so much, but what it's saying is also ambiguous. It feels cold and clinical, then you have this small, naked portrait of a woman who has caught herself in the mirror. She's studying herself. I now know how different it is to a lot of the other work she makes, which makes it even more interesting to me. A bathroom can be a place of escape and solitude, and a place where you examine yourself. It's a place where you take off your clothes and there's a mirror, so you are kind of forced to look at yourself. It's a place where you can go and sit with yourself and your own mind.

Untitled, Providence, Rhode Island, 1975–80
by FRANCESCA WOODMAN

This one doesn't have a title, but it's like a dream sequence, or I guess a nightmare. There's a door that's unhinged, but there's no doorway, and there is a window that is shining light into the scene, but Woodman is hiding behind the door. The bottom half of her body is revealed, and there's a slight motion of the foot, but we don't know whether she's moving behind or trying to emerge – or if the door is falling on top of her, or she's trapped. The nude bottom half of her body feels incredibly vulnerable, and the image feels very much like a fragile mind. Without the body, it would still be a powerful image, but it wouldn't be speaking to the human. It's about being there and not being there.

The Spirit Leaves the Body, 1968
by DUANE MICHALS

This is the second image in a sequence of seven, and it is incredibly powerful for me. It's painful and tender, although it could also be frightening if we're talking about death. I find the splitting of the human form kind of familiar, a lot of times I have experienced things from outside myself, like I haven't been in my body. I feel it relates very much to my work about late autistic discovery – there was this past me who wasn't who I thought it was. I wasn't who I thought I was. There's been a lot of letting go of what's gone and moving into a new life, like a death and a rebirth.

Untitled, 2021 © Stephanie Kennett.

Hilton Head Island, Southern California,
USA June 24 1992
by RINEKE DIJKSTRA

Dijkstra doesn't give you a title – I mean, there is a title, but it doesn't give you much about the actual image. We're looking at a young woman in an orange bikini standing on the beach, and she looks like that painting of *The Birth of Venus* by Botticelli, but she's so vulnerable. She's got this body she isn't comfortable with yet, but she's completely exposed. It's that time in your life when you're somewhere in between being a child and an adult, and for that feeling of discomfort in yourself to be captured on camera, it's incredibly powerful.

Sharon D Butts, from Rich and Poor, 1977–1985
by JIM GOLDBERG

I love this series, the combination of the image and the statement from the person tells you so much, so much more than you would get from the image alone. This image shows Sharon holding her son above her head, and she's wearing a vest that says "Evil woman", but I feel like she looks like a superhero. Her statement is saying, "What I really want is a real home with nice furniture and also a van to drive, and I would like to give my son what I didn't get in life, which includes love", but even without her real home and nice furniture, you can see she is giving her son love. She's in a kind of victory pose, holding him above her like he is her priority and she'll hold him up above everything else.

Waiting for Trains While Playing with Trains, 2009
by JUSTINE KURLAND

This picture is another dream, but it's childhood, imagination and freedom, and being a tiny person in an enormous world. Justine took her son and they lived out on the road; he had a great fascination with trains, so they went to incredible spots to watch trains come past. I am mother to an autistic son, his special interest in dinosaurs and this is how I imagine he experiences his reality. He IS a dinosaur. I love their mother and son connection, and the freedom of being on the road. I don't have that capacity; I struggle with organisation and directions and travel, but I'm incredibly drawn to it. There's another aspect too, which is when I met my son's dad, he invited me to come to America with him, and I just got to sit in the passenger seat and be driven through these incredible landscapes. It felt like the start of another life.

Hydrangeas, 1999
by ALESSANDRA SANGUINETTI

I love the contrast of the brutal concrete wall with the enormous hydrangea bush in front of it, like there's this beautiful thing covering up this ugly thing. And then there's a young girl, wearing what looks like a nightdress, hiding her face behind the blooms of the hydrangeas. It feels like a dream, like you can imagine hiding yourself behind those enormous flowers and breathing them in, and it taking you somewhere completely. I feel closer to the natural world than the human world, like I understand it more and it speaks to me, so I guess that's what I'm seeing in this.

Untitled, 2021
by STEPHANIE KENNETT

This is a photograph by my mum, taken at the top of the hill above my childhood house in South Wales. It's a silhouette of my mum and dad, with sunshine and clouds; they look like tiny people in the landscape. They've lived in this house for 50 years, and they go on the same walk each day, no matter the weather. They're always inspired by the changes. At the moment, they are looking to move somewhere smaller and less remote, because it's a lot of work to maintain the house. But this photograph is the image I have of them in my mind. My mum and dad helped me to see, they're the reason I understand the world visually. They are just full of wonderment. My whole childhood was, "Wow, look at the way that curtain is moving in the wind!", so if I could only take one image, it would be this.

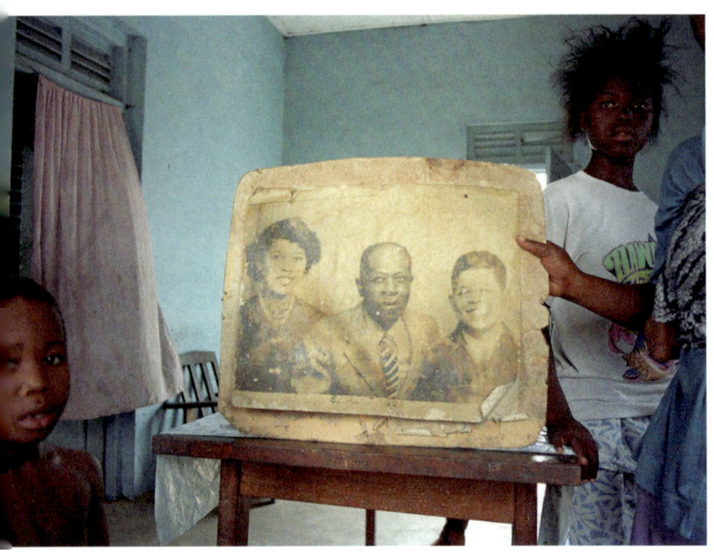

Eileen Perrier graduated from Surrey Institute of Art and Design in 1996 and from the Royal College of Art in 2000. She has previously had solo shows at institutions such as Autograph and Whitechapel Gallery, and has been included in group exhibitions at The Photographers' Gallery and Somerset House. Perrier was a senior lecturer in photography at the University of Westminster from 2005 to 2022 and is currently an associate lecturer at the London College of Communication.

Perrier was first on the list when Stephen Bull began organising *Desert Island Pics* 15 years ago, but somehow their conversation never happened – until now. Their long-overdue *Desert Island Pics* took place on 13 May 202 "It's interesting that most of the images I selected are black and white, and I was surprised how many early photographic processes are included," said Perrier of her eight. "If I had to have a physical print, OK – it has to be the Joy Gregory, because I already have that in my home."

Untitled, Ghana, 1995–96
by EILEEN PERRIER

This is a picture I took in Ghana in my grandmother's home. It's a colour photograph that includes within it a black-and-white studio picture of my mum's first cousin, Aunty Teresa (with her father and brother). She and her husband are both half Ghanaian, half English; they were born and grew up in the East End, then moved to northwest London. In the early 1980s, they went back to Ghana for about three years. At a restaurant, someone said Aunty Teresa looked like a family member and took her back to the family house. On seeing this photograph in the house, they realised they had found their family on Aunty Teresa's side. They told her about my mum and said, "When you go back to the UK, you must find her." Of course, Aunty Teresa has a copy of this black-and-white photo in her house in London. So in 1987, when they returned from Ghana, Uncle Abraham presented a small copy of it to my mum, and that's how we stayed in touch. That was quite amazing, and demonstrates the power of photography and legacy.

Portrait, 1976 from The Black Triangle:
The People of the African Diaspora, 1985
by ARMET FRANCIS

Born in Jamaica and based in London; Armet is a founder of Autograph ABP. He produced this amazing book, *The Black Triangle: The People of the African Diaspora*, which I came across in a Black bookshop. The cover portrait really struck me, and I wanted to find out more about the Black Triangle. He was exploring the transatlantic slave trade – moving people from Africa to Europe, the Caribbean and America. He travelled from the UK to Jamaica, Africa and America, and I believe this portrait was taken in Senegal. Up until seeing this book, most of the Black photographers I knew about were African American. I hadn't seen a body of work like this – it was compelling. Currently an archivist from DACS Art360 is helping Armet archive his negatives, after we successfully applied for funding. I'm hoping some of his work, negatives and transparencies may be stored at Autograph. If that works out, it'll be great to know that some of his legacy will live there for perpetuity.

The Brasher Sisters, Lyn and Stella,
Southampton, May 1974 and 1999 from The
Free Photographic Omnibus 1973-2001
by DANIEL MEADOWS

After graduating, I was fortunate to have Anna Fox and curator Val Williams support my work. They exhibited my *Red, Gold and Green* (1996) series as part of the Shoreditch Biennale in London, in March 199 Val gave me a copy of *National Portraits*. Daniel Meadows travelled around in a double-decker bus in the 1970s, taking free portraits and processing them in the bus so people could come back to collect them. I found that really amazing. Subconsciously, it inspired my own mobile studio series, where I took portraits using a 5×4 camera and instant film. I focused more on Victorian-style imagery and *cartes de visite*, but in hindsight, this influenced my work – with people coming forward and being provided with a copy of their image.

Untitled, family portrait, Ghana; 1995. © Eileen Perrier.

Baby's Breath, from the series
Language of Flowers, 1992–2000
by JOY GREGORY

I came across this series after my son was born, the first time his dad and I went out after his birth. We visited Zelda Cheatle's gallery for Joy's opening. I wasn't planning to buy anything, but I loved this image and ended up purchasing it. I loved the name Baby's Breath, the delicacy of the plant in the cyanotype, and the fact it marked our first outing as new parents. The cyanotype process made me think of Anna Atkins. I knew Joy's work from my time at Autograph, but I thought the way she made images in the 1990s was interesting. She wasn't doing what might have been expected of a Black female artist – her work wasn't centred solely on identity. It was conceptual. Early in my career, discovering her work was inspiring. More recently, she included my work in her book *Shining Lights: Black Women Photographers in 1980s-90s Britain*, which was an honour.

Yoga undergraduate Peter Dodoo, student of Mr Strong,
Ever Young Studio, Accra, Ghana, c1955
by JAMES BARNOR

I love this photograph because I love yoga! Part of a series of images James took of Peter Dodoo, it feels very different visually from the subject matters he's best known for. I met James once at Autograph, when curator Renée Mussai introduced me to him. It's great that his work was rediscovered by Autograph and Clémentine de la Féronnière. He was a renowned Ghanaian photographer, worked for Drum magazine, and did extensive work in the UK but then he seemed to disappear. I didn't know anything about his work until meeting him. I love his studio portraits. His fashion photography is beautiful, and there's humour and cheekiness in some of his shots, for example with models around Piccadilly Circus. His images stand the test of time. Since 2022, I've qualified as a yoga instructor, and I'll lead a yoga class at my solo exhibition at Autograph this summer.

Sesema, 1972
by JD 'OKHAI OJEIKERE

"Sesema" is Yoruba slang – it's a hairstyle common among young women. JD 'Okhai Ojeikere was a Nigerian photographer who documented African hairstyles – mainly cornrows or hair wrapped with thread – because he recognised they might start disappearing after women began to wear wigs in the 1950s. I just love all these visual records of the various styles. I've had some of them done at my local hair salon, but when I went last week to a different hair salon, with stylists from East Africa, they didn't know how to do this particular style. I know a Nigerian hairdresser called Pat; hopefully she can do it for me next week. When I was a kid, my mum used to wrap my hair in thread – not as elaborate as these styles! This work inspired me, even indirectly, to document women, and eventually men, and their hairstyles and fashion in London; between 1998 and 2003, I photographed people at the Afro Hair & Beauty show.

From Dwelling:
In This Space We Breathe, 2017
by KHADIJA SAYE

I remember Khadija from when she studied at Farnham – I was a visiting lecturer, and we stayed in touch. I was collecting photography from students of diverse backgrounds, from their final major projects, because there was always this narrative, "I was the only Black student on the course." I had experienced that myself. I wanted to show the work from these students in one place, so they were aware that they were not the only one! Khadija would update me; she talked about doing a residency. Then the next time I heard her name was when the Grenfell Tower fire happened in 201 It was devastating to know that she had passed away. Then I learnt her work was showing at the Venice Biennale, I thought, "Ahh, her career was just taking off." She created these stunning tintype portraits – mystical, spiritual, and containing elements outside the photographer's control. Beautiful work.

Even This Will Pass, 2013-14
by AIDA SILVESTRI

Aida produced this work in her final year at the University of Westminster. A part-time student, originally from Eritrea she is now based in the UK. For this series, she photographed and interviewed men and women from Eritrea who had come to London by car, plane, lorry, boat, train, even on foot. Each person is blurred in the photo. She used stitching to trace their journeys, with different coloured threads for each, mapped out on the portraits. I was so proud of her – this work is powerful, sensitive, personal and clever. She captured individual stories while preserving their anonymity. The portraits are out of focus, but in the format of ID photos.

FUTURE TENSE

In this short article, I suggest that the future of photography is already here and that we are essentially experiencing the long afterlife of photography. For some time, the photograph has been a computational simulation, and its circulation establishes the condition of the networked image. Over the next 30 years, we will see a super-convergence of AI-assisted digital image generation and CGI modelling and rendering, packaged in software capable of performing analytical, predictive and averaging tasks in the production and circulation of visual imagery. The distinction between the still and moving, the graphic and photographic image will be replaced by a seamlessly pliable image displayed in real time on novel screen formats.

This is business as usual, as the history of profitable technical appliances and software amply demonstrates. However, the problem with thinking of the future in terms of technical development is that it gives little thought as to how technologies will be used, or what societies want to do with them. In the case of the image, the question for the future is what kind of reality technologies will produce – and in whose interests.

In the dominant techno discourse, the trending answer to the future for all things is artificial intelligence (AI). Governments, universities, corporations, manufacturers and media practitioners are promoting as well as reacting to the idea that, in the near future, AI will totally shape the way we live. However, AI is neither a utopian nor a dystopian dream, although still represented as such in popular drama and fiction. AI is the computational engine of an industrial, commercial, civil, medical and military mode of reproduction already in place and functioning. Over the past 30 years, largely by stealth, a fourth industrial revolution (4IR) has been completed, through greater convergence of technologies, computing, robotics and biotechnology. Now the earth is girded by a vast network of computer networks, supported by satellites, signalling relay stations and fibre-optic cables, connected to data factories storing and processing information, relying on continued extraction on a scale previously unknown.

Whichever way you look at it, we are living through a transformative period of the Anthropocene, in which uncertainty, insecurity and precarity are differential but defining features of everyday human experience. The dominant feature of 4IR is automation, in which more and more human functions are carried out by machine systems. Now we are witnessing the automation of culture and with it the predominant European ways of seeing, established since the Renaissance and encapsulated by oil painting and, subsequently, photography. We don't have to project the future; the future is already here. What is happening is the outsourcing of seeing to computational systems and there is an urgent need to understand the values written into machine vision. What can the machine see and what does it occlude?

Computer systems process data at speeds humans cannot. The scale of computer calculation is being applied to more and more functions previously carried out by analogue and mechanical systems, including the way we see. By a combination of large data sets and human labelling, algorithms are being trained to recognise, detect, analyse, predict and generate visual images. The important point to note is that the large image data sets are made up of pre-existing images scraped from the internet. These are images not from the future, but from the past.

I asked ChatGPT (who doesn't these days?), to predict likely developments in photography, artificial intelligence, climate change and capitalism over the next 30 years. Couched in a hybrid of encyclopaedic fact and soft, equivocal, marketing language, the algorithm provides a typical technology-obsessed set of answers to photography in the future. As one would expect, it hedges its bets in an uneasy, if not queasy language of averaging. In the future, the visual image will be hyperrealist, virtual, augmented, holographic, immersive and autonomous. Image technology will be wearable, implantable, embedded and mind-controlled.

Much of what ChatGPT predicts has been predicted by technophiles over the past 30 years at least and, of course, this is what ChatGPT is regurgitating. The list goes on in more specific ways. The kit for making images will have a lot of AI-trained software on board. Cameras will have AI assistants that, in real time, suggest editing of compositions, lighting, background changes and object removal. More fanciful predictions suggest the creation of interactive, multi-sensory experiences, capturing, creating and experiencing reality in new ways allowing you to "feel" an image rather than just see it – interactive "living photos" that change over time or react to viewer emotions.

Already on the R&D drawing board for AI are ultra-advanced assistants, personal companions, emotion-aware software and conversational holograms. Sound familiar, or see it at the movies? Our devices will be smart and connected. Some of the possibilities are already in production; others will be realised, and still others will be obsolete before their time. For those familiar with critical new media theory, such ideas can be traced back to the 19th century.

This is the era of the synthetic image, the infographic, in which we will marvel at the immediacy, scale and seamlessness of image definition and flow, but will be mindless, bored and distracted, seeking solace in an imaginary authenticity. Meanwhile, the automation of the average functions of the human sensorium will continue relentlessly if the capitalist mode of production remains unsocialised and unregulated.

Here are four perspectives, running against the dominant grain, from which to think about the future of the visual image.

1 Regarding photography solely as a tool, as the apparatuses of cameras and imaging techniques has produced – and continues to produce – a narrow, historically determinist and fetishistic view of technological development. There is nothing inevitable about what we invent and what we apply it to.

2 Photography is not a unitary object, but rather, as others have said, there are many photographies, and they are not all sub-categories of the same essentialising, indexical apparatus of the light-reflected image. A better starting point for considering the future of photography is to regard it as situated practice within an assemblage of technical, social and institutional systems, each of which have effects upon each other, and which determine practice and meaning.

3 The complex assemblage that is photography has an equally complex relationship to who owns and controls the means of reproduction and how this shapes what is and what is not possible to represent. The future of visual practice is, therefore, inescapably political, in which the liberation of the image and images of liberation will have to be struggled over.

4 The future of photography, or, more accurately, of visual imaging, lies in uncovering its past. The history of photography is largely that of capitalism, colonialism and patriarchy – and the marks of these systems of oppression and exploitation remain inscribed within the photographic image. Visual-imaging practices of the future will need to engage with, analyse and reconceptualise the history of photography. We also need to seek collective meaning in photo sharing, to know what is represented and what remains unrepresentable, in order to grasp the image's relationship to meaning. Amid the proliferation of image-making, we need to reduce the number of significant images, to see image-making as applied knowledge in everyday life.

NO COUNTRY FOR OLD MEN
AMIN YOUSEFI

It is hard to predict what photography will look like in 30 years, especially when I have yet to experience three decades of life. I was born when the world was on the brink of the digital revolution and leaving behind the analogue age. I remember reading my father's analogue camera manual while I took photographs on his cellphone, a strange mix of past and future in my hands. At 16, I used a Cybershot camera to macro the mundane beauty of flowers in our garden, or an insect clinging to a window – small, simple moments. A couple of years later, when I entered my BA in photography, the programme was designed to use film cameras for the first two years, transitioning to digital in the latter half. The constant back-and-forth between digital and analogue left me disoriented. Then, while I was questioning whether we had truly left the world of mechanical tools behind, the world introduced a new way of creating images through artificial intelligence image generators.

What will the future look like? In the world of photography, this question may sound obsolete. However, with the emergence of AI, the question has resurfaced in a different form. Some have enthusiastically boarded the fast-moving AI train, embarking on new experiments and generating optimised results. The pace of this optimisation has accelerated so rapidly that even the creators struggle to keep up. Unlike in photography, where for instance, faster and more portable cameras led to capturing instantaneous images or the concept of the "decisive moment", the rapid evolution of this new medium moves at such an unusual pace that its historical narrative will no longer follow a linear trajectory.

When any tool can effortlessly create something that would have been considered a masterpiece in the previous century, what kind of art will we make? How will we define "value" in a piece of art? A simple answer might involve measuring the time, skill, technique and delicacy invested in creating the work. Yet this perspective has lost much validity within the long evolution of art, particularly following movements such as conceptual art, in which traditional notions of value were fundamentally challenged.

Howard Becker introduced the concept of art fields in his 1982 book *Art Worlds*, and his insights remain relevant today. Yet the landscape has shifted dramatically. AI platforms are no longer confined to the traditional spaces of galleries and museums. At a fundamental level, images are now being created through algorithms, which in turn offer a new way of evaluating art. The question of which artist will gain recognition is no longer solely in the hands of galleries; the algorithms of virtual platforms increasingly determine it. Take two identical images posted on Instagram with different advertising strategies – watch how these two photographs can follow drastically different paths and outcomes.

These new technologies enable almost anyone to produce images closely resembling the work of Rinko Kawauchi or Jeff Wall, but it seems misleading to suggest that anyone can truly become a Kawauchi or a Wall, in this prompt-ethean era, simply by generating similar images. They can only present themselves as Wall or Kawauchi, not as their authentic selves. Instead, the universal accessibility provided by these tools lets artists question and explore what it truly means to produce contemporary art in dialogue with established figures. By consciously embracing or deliberately rejecting these tools, artists can craft works that expand and redefine the boundaries and meanings of both the medium and contemporary art.

In Plato's *The Ion*, Ion claims to be inspired by the gods when he recites poetry. Socrates challenges him, asking if he truly understands the meaning of the poems or if he is merely mimicking what others have written. Socrates proposes that Ion's recitations are not the result of his own wisdom but are like a "magnet" that passes the divine inspiration from one person to another. He suggests that Ion is not a creator but a channel for something outside himself, much like an instrument through which inspiration flows.

The channels remain, though they are no longer gods or spiritual forces speaking through a human throat. Some 2,400 years after *The Ion*, this claim is unchanged. Yet creativity, which once emerged from years of practice and research exploration, is now reduced to feeding a prompt and an imported image into a machine: "Turn this picture into Studio Ghibli art." Generating something in the style of Studio Ghibli is not enough to make someone creative. "Real" creativity nowadays seems to mean selecting a humorous, historical, trendy or famous photograph and proudly displaying the computer's output.

PHOTOGRAPHY AFTER PHOTOGRAPHY AFTER PHOTOGRAPHY

HELEN STARR

Photography is a medium that stops time. It is a technology that captures a moment of pause, when reality stands still. People often speak of ghosts – the way the shock of finding a loved one's body imprints itself on the mind's eye, creating an ephemeral overlay that haunts a room long after the moment has passed. You blink and it's gone, a fleeting thread connecting the now to the past, as the mind processes grief and memory through the heart (burn). Writers such as Octavia Butler and Ursula Le Guin leave similar imprints on the mind's eye, crafting worlds that linger and haunt long after the last page.

As a world-building curator, I think a lot about the blink of an eye, how the opening and closing of the lens becomes a portal to another realm. World-building is a way of remaking reality through the imaginary. And the imaginary can be understood as a cartographer's tool, mapping not just place, but feeling, memory and possibility.

Using various technological tools, lens-based artists such as Matthew Barney, Gregory Crewdson, Hayao Miyazaki and Hidetaka Miyazaki engineer experiences that trigger episodic memory – our embodied, emotional, scene-based memory – rather than semantic memory, which is tied to facts or knowledge. In other words, they don't simply tell you about their cosmos, they make you feel as if you have already lived inside it.

Episodic memory is how our minds understand our reality through felt presence, fragments, and déjà vu. It is how we understand qualia – the experience of things such as the redness of a sunset, or the beauty of light playing across the surface of a dewdrop. Game engines excel at generating the feeling of presence, or co-presence, as your body navigates this interactive synthetic space. Whether that presence is embodied by a playable character or a non-playable character, both types of interaction draw the player into scripted AI worlds on a deeply immersive level.

In modern AI – especially in machine learning and reinforcement learning – games are still used as training grounds. AI agents learn through video games, which provide complex, controllable environments in which to practise long-term strategy and adaptive behaviour. These environments, in turn, have influenced the development of procedural AI tools, offering new ways to create richer, more generative experiences of presence. As early as the 1990s, pioneers such as Rebecca Allen and Auriea Harvey recognised the potential of classical AI to construct game engines capable of managing 3D virtual worlds full of imaginary beings, interacting with each other and with visitors.

When corporate engines such as Unreal and Unity became functionally accessible in around 2014–15, a new generation of artists was empowered with the tools to both design and capture their own virtual worlds. This marked a significant evolution in virtual photography, which had previously relied on in-game screenshots of environments created by game designers and developers. With Unreal and Unity, artists gained the agency not only to design but also to control the worlds themselves, placing artistry at the forefront. They no longer simply captured frozen moments; they built entire universes in which to freeze those moments.

Leveraging AI technologies with finesse, these artists began creating immersive worlds as personal as they were innovative, visualising their unique cosmologies through movement, sound and interactive design. Artists such as Anna Bunting-Branch, Lawrence Lek, Ayoung Kim, Danielle Brathwaite-Shirley, Kinnari Saraiya and Sarah Al-Sarraj embraced these emerging tools to design richly-layered virtual spaces drawn from their cultural imaginaries. Each world carries a distinctive aesthetic, shaped by how the artist codes the play of light, shadow, and form within their virtual realms.

This new approach to world-building allows these artists to map innovative forms of collective presence within their time-stopped realities, immortalising bespoke AI-driven characters mid-story. Each captured image becomes more than just a still; it is a personal archive, a visual document of these highly-individualised, culturally-rich narratives. With every click of the virtual shutter, these artists challenge traditional notions of authorship, expanding the boundaries of how we experience, interact with, and reflect on virtual worlds. They invite us to reconsider not just what virtual worlds can be, but what we can become within them.

These shifting realities, captured through sensory worlds, offer a glimpse of a pluriverse – the coexistence of multiple, often conflicting, perspectives. Much like the varied genres of photography, it rejects singular truths. Instead it invites an exploration of diverse, layered existences, in which each world and story can coexist simultaneously, unbound by a fixed understanding.

THE JANUS OF PHOTOGRAPHY
ÁGNES BÁSTHY

Technology is often said to be Janus-faced. In my interpretation, one face is turning towards truth and liberation, while the other is turning towards power and social control. Since photography is a child of technological progress, it has inherited this feature. If we try to predict the future of photography, or its role in the future of society, we have to consider this fact. Therefore, it's never easy to anticipate technological change.

When we take a look at the face of photography that represents social control and power, we see manipulation, surveillance, abuse and revenge. This was here from the beginning; it's enough to evoke the case of the Paris Commune. Since then, photography has become a helping hand to the police and military service. We all know that photography is the mother of surveillance technology, which we have been surrounded by for many years and which is getting more intense, sharper, deeper and closer in these days of surveillance capitalism.

The other face of Janus turns toward truth and liberation, which in many senses is also the mission of art. I'm sure that the artisanship of analogue photography will stay with us, because of its beauty, its materiality and its solid durability, which seem not to be among the strengths of digital technology. The latter will never substitute prints and analogue images, for the same reason virtual reality can never replace or defeat material reality. Ironically, even if an atomic war in the next 30 years entirely abolishes humanity, printed photographs will stay, maybe in the form of Borges's *The Library of Babel* or their digital versions in the data banks as in Franco "Bifo" Berardi's adaptation of the story. Anyhow, they will provide evidence not just that humanity existed, but how it existed – if photography can be protected against fatal manipulations.

Will photography be able to defend its integrity? What does that mean? What kind of ethics should be developed? If today many people can't distinguish a photograph from an artificially generated picture, it's entirely plausible that, in 30 years' time, nobody will be able to. The only way for photography to keep its integrity is not just as an art but as a source of evidence. The meaning of 'human' is in transition, but we can protect photography as a precious mirror, which can help us to reflect on our humanity and history, and which has always been the visual tool of conscience and memory. This is not about documentation per se, because that's a very problematic idea. It's about the human intention of expression, based on human experience and reflecting on our agency.

Photography is a truly modern medium, which can picture the richness of our world very fast compared to other media. Being fast is an evolutionary advantage, but overproduction, overconsumption and exhaustion are the features of capitalism. The relationship between art and distraction has been a problem since modernity, and it is intensifying. We have to rethink and relearn how we can truly see and not just consume photography, on a personal and institutional level. Being slow is a luxury, but it shouldn't be; it's a route to pleasure and meditation, a mood of care and deep focus. It relates to the question of consciousness as well, but over the past few hundred years we have been too busy producing and consuming to find out who we are. This behaviour has led us directly to an era in which a minority try to persuade the majority that digital technology can replace us, humanity.

In the ongoing but sadly slow process of humanity's self-discovery, which includes so many setbacks, the use and abuse of photography will be entirely embedded in the social and power structure in which we live. Meanwhile, our perception of this reality will still be shaped by this technical medium.

Bibliography

- Walter Benjamin: *Das Kunstwerk im Zeitalter seiner technischen Reproduzierbarkeit* (*The Work of Art in the Age of Mechanical Reproduction*); 1935
- Jonathan Crary: *Suspensions of Perception – Attention, Spectacle, and Modern Culture*; MIT Press, 2001
- Peter Osborne: *Anywhere or Not at All: Philosophy of Contemporary Art*; Verso Books, 2013

WHAT DOES THE FUTURE OF PHOTOGRAPHY HOLD? EMILY JUNE SMITH

A younger photographer, I grew up when smartphones were invented. I am part of the generation known for having a screen in hand, more associated with looking down than looking around. Yet I find myself drawn towards analogue photography, time-travelling backwards to the beauty of actually holding my image, not a pixellated assortment of a file. I enjoy the imperfections of analogue, of seeing the small white marks left from dust on a negative, and wondering where that dust might have come from. I like seeing a slight hue of green in the shadows.

I am not afraid of AI, the alien that people believe is currently invading art. Photography has always changed over time, from analogue to the rise of digital technology and social media, to AI and its perfectly imperfect rendition of life. Currently if you ask AI to make an image, it creates oddly beautiful, distorted visuals. At the moment, what photographers and AI have in common is that, just like art and human life, they are perfectly imperfect. What I do fear is the negative impact AI could have on photography.

Over time, AI's imperfections will be ironed out, I think, due to the corporate world and its need for perfection. AI will become a seemingly perfect creation, only giving right answers and 'perfect' images. That's when we will lose this balance between AI and art, and when it could push art into a new era. Surrounded by 'perfect' images, created by a click of a button, people could come to favour the clean, perfect view of AI. It could change people's perspectives on the raw messiness of art.

This preference could easily become a whole movement, like Dadaism or surrealism. It could mean we finally lose analogue photography altogether. Art would become completely digitised, constructed by numbers and codes, no longer holding the fingerprint imprints of the artist. I fear the fight to find the imperfectly perfect within photography again, its humanness.

I have always believed that being an artist consumes you completely. It takes pieces of our hearts, souls and minds and transfers them into art, something AI could never do. Art is beautiful and messy and human. In a world in which society told us to fear imperfection, it would take a special person to fight the grain. Fortunately, such people are usually the artists. As an artist, I hope I never create perfect work. I hope that the future of photography will always be imperfect.

172 LOOKING BACK TO LOOK FORWARD: PHOTOGRAPHY, CONNECTION AND THE BOTSWANA ARCHIVE

Thirty years ago, the photographic landscape in Botswana was shaped – like much of Southern Africa – by the residue of colonial documentation and the shadow of apartheid-era politics. The cameras, mostly held by white foreign hands, framed our people through a gaze shaped by power and access. Those images, while vital to the historical record, often overlooked the complexity of Batswana lives, reducing them to spectacle, or capturing them through ethnographic distance.

Take, for example, the extensive documentation work of Sandy Grant, a white Scottish journalist and photographer who lived in Botswana for decades and became one of its most prolific chroniclers. His photographs, which span key moments in the country's development, are now treasured for their historical value. But what does it mean that one of the largest visual records of Botswana was created not by its people, but for them, without a full awareness of the politics of image-making, authorship and legacy?

For too long, Black and Indigenous Batswana were subjects of photographs but not their authors. The archive, both in Botswana and in the wider Southern African region, bears the traces of this imbalance. Photographic collections remain locked in institutional or personal vaults, inaccessible to the public and the very people captured within them. And yet, photographs are not neutral objects – they carry memory, power and potential. What does it mean when your national memory is shaped by someone else's lens?

The connections between Botswana and South Africa offer an illuminating thread. During apartheid, Botswana served as a quiet refuge for many fleeing the South African regime, including artists, intellectuals and political activists. That cross-border movement created a shared visual language, existing in exile, silence and shadow. Yet much of that history remains undocumented or scattered. Today the border remains porous, both culturally and artistically, and this connection continues to shape a new generation of photographers working between Gaborone and Johannesburg.

Photographers such as Thero Makepe exemplify this generational shift. With roots in both Botswana and South Africa, Makepe's work interrogates heritage, masculinity and belonging through a deeply personal lens. "If used correctly, the personal archive can help subvert dominant narratives of place or culture," he explains. "The history of Tswana and Sotho people who migrated from other places in the 1950s, 60s and 70s is overlooked in the grand national narrative of Botswana, so my use of family archives helps to counteract that."

Documentary photographer Fifi Monosi, another vital voice, centres on everyday life in Botswana, often focusing on those historically erased from the archive, including queer and trans communities. "In a country where queer and trans lives are often silenced or stigmatised, I have seen photography become a powerful tool to affirm existence," she says. "It's about saying, 'You were here and you mattered.'" Her work is not simply about representation, but about reshaping how we see the archive itself. "I choose to see the people I photograph not as subjects, but as collaborators. It becomes a shared space of storytelling, trust and agency."

As a white photographer working from Botswana, Stuart James Arnold is acutely aware of the historical power imbalances with which his practice engages. Rather than evade this he meets it head on, with care, return and refusal. "Being an outsider with a camera is loaded," he says. "Responsibility doesn't come from talking. It comes from showing up, shutting up and sticking around." His decades-long commitment to analogue photography isn't a nostalgic gesture, but a political one. "I say no to galleries that want to fetishise poverty, to curators who want the exotic without the politics, to collectors looking for tidy stories they can hang on a wall."

For Arnold, the archive isn't a romantic past – it's a contested present. His analogue land-based work rejects digital immediacy and echoes a concern with care and accountability. "Analogue photography will outlast the current hype machine because it was never built for trends," he states. "You can't fake the marks of time, handling, or dust. Not with prompts, pixels, or pretend nostalgia." For him, photographic honesty lies in its imperfection, and that becomes more vital, not less, as we move deeper into an AI-saturated era.

This reclaiming of narrative is not merely aesthetic, it is political. It challenges the archive, not just as a storage of images, but as a battleground of authorship, access and memory. Who owns the image? Who gets to be seen – and who decides what is worth remembering?

In imagining what photography might look like 30 years from now, I am drawn not only to emerging technologies – AI, deepfakes, immersive 3D archives – but also to the question of cultural stewardship. We may very well have digitised searchable, blockchain-protected archives that allow for greater transparency in image ownership and intellectual property. In that future, perhaps a young Motswana photographer will find an image of their great-grandmother in a transnational database, fully credited, contextually preserved and linked to oral histories. But for that future to exist, we must lay its foundations now.

That means investing in local photographic education, digitising and repatriating archives, and honouring the contributions of Black photographers whose work has long gone unrecognised. It also means making room for multiple gazes: queer, feminist, youth-led, Indigenous. The archive of the future must not only be technologically advanced, it must be ethically sound, plural in voice, and accessible in practice.

Connection, as Photoworks reminds us in its 30th year, is both a gift and a responsibility. In the past, the connection between Britain and Botswana was marked by colonial ties and extractive gazes. Today, connection means collaboration, co-authorship, and solidarity. Tomorrow, it could mean something we haven't yet imagined – an entirely decentralised archive, curated by its subjects, where photography becomes not just a record but a tool for justice, healing and futurity.

Botswana, with its youthful population and dynamic cultural scene, holds an exciting role in shaping that future. Our images are no longer silent. They speak – of memory, of resistance and of possibility.

BILATERIAN
KATE SIMPSON

In the future, which is not the future but an inaccessible image, we will walk around galleries in pairs. Sometimes a hand will be held in a hand and one will feel bigger than the other. That is how we will tell each other apart. Sometimes we will pull ourselves away from images to look into each other's eyes and find that we can only focus on one eye at a time. This will seem duplicitous, like an image taken with two eyes that comes out as one. Sure, diptychs exist, but they come together, like the past and the present, aesthetics and effect. I will have been thinking about images for some time: how humans imbue their work; how humans bond through images. After visiting the exhibition that depicts the future on a shattered planet, we will walk over the shards of a shattered planet. The sun will set. Everything will have two sides. We will call the shards images and they won't seem as violent. They will shine like bias. I will say I liked the exhibition, but I could tell all the artists were bilaterians: their bodies could be split down the middle. I will say I worry about symmetry – that we will not be able to stop splitting and splitting apart; that having two sides means one is a downside. And sure, diptychs exist, like the present and the future, like aesthetics and their after-effects. As the sun sets, you will ask what happens when the future becomes accessible: when it can be held; when it no longer feels bigger. I will say that artists are bilaterians and they compose like bilaterians. You will ask if the image is an initiation or an event. I will say it is neither. The image is sight split into shards: it is one atom bonded to two. The future is what happens when you flip the shard over and it shines.

CONTEXTUAL NOTE

In *A Foray into the Worlds of Animals and Humans* (1934), the biophilosopher Jakob von Uexküll coined the term 'umwelt' ('surround-world'), which describes how individual creatures are each enveloped by sensory experience. The theory of 'umwelt' means all animals have a private, phenomenal world that can never be accessed. This, in turn, means objectivity can never be attained.

A year ago, in April 2024, I visited Pinault Collection's Punta della Dogana venue, in Venice, which had been completely given over to the work of Pierre Huyghe, an artist interested in the post-human and its 'sentient milieu'. It was there, walking around darkened rooms, that I encountered UUmwelt – Annlee (2018-24), a 'co-production of imagination' between the human and non-human. On a towering screen, a series of amorphous images were being produced by a computer interface that captures the brain activity of a person imagining Annlee, 'herself an imaginary character'. I watched as the semblance of a body metamorphosed, endlessly blurring in and out of being. The work was a fleshy digital composite. It was engineering: biological, technological, cultural. It was life considering itself.

The first bilaterians, animals with bilateral symmetry, are thought to have appeared in the Ediacaran period, over 540 million years ago. Humans, as bilaterians, are the most dramatic ecosystem engineers to have existed since then, within the bilaterian clade. We are transforming the planet in the blink of a geological eye. Thirty years from now, we will likely have surpassed a 1.5°C temperature rise. Humans, locked into their own 'umwelt', are actively invoking higher temperatures, and the ramifications will be felt by all other species in their own 'umwelten'.

As we look to the future of photography, we look to images as reflectors of human bias. Images cannot be objective realities: they are reflections of the self; they reflect the vision of a single species. Images demonstrate how the present is being perceived by us, and how the planetary future will largely be shaped by that perception.

DANIT ARIEL
Artist, writer, Photoworks curator
@danitariel
photoworks.org.uk

OLIVIA ARTHUR
Artist
oliviaarthur.com

ĀRUN
Artist
aavanam.in

ÁGNES BÁSTHY
PhD candidate in the Doctoral School of Sociology at Eötvös Loránd University, Budapest, Hungary
elte.hu

STEPHEN BULL
Artist, writer, senior lecturer at the University of Brighton
brighton.ac.uk

JULIA BUNNEMANN
Curator (Deutsche Börse Photography Foundation Prize), The Photographers' Gallery; Photoworks curator 2018–25
@jbnnmnn
thephotographersgallery.org.uk

BEN BURBRIDGE
Professor of visual culture at University of Sussex; Photoworks co-editor and co-curator 2003–18
@ben.burbridge
sussex.ac.uk

JULIETTE BUSS
Co-director at Corridor; Photoworks head of learning and engagement
@juliettebuss
photoworks.org.uk

DAVID CHANDLER
Photoworks director, 1997–2010

GABRIELE CHIAPPARINI
Artist
@gabrielechiapparini

CELIA DAVIES
Landscape designer; Photoworks director 2013–17

ANDREW DEWDNEY
Co-director of the Centre for the Study of the Networked Image and emeritus professor at London South Bank University
centreforthestudyof.net

TANLUME ENYATSENG
Writer, creative director, cultural producer, founder of the Banana Club collective; former Photoworks P+ writer-in-residence
bananaemoji.com

LOUISE FEDOTOV-CLEMENTS
Photoworks director since 2023
@mazmanian
photoworks.org.uk

ANNA FOX
Artist, professor of photography at the University for the Creative Arts, Farnham; Fast Forward: Women in Photography research project lead
annafox.co.uk
uca.ac.uk
fastforward.photography

LINA GEOUSHY
Artist
linageoushy.com

NATALIA GONZÁLEZ ACOSTA
Artist; Photoworks digital manager
nataliaga.com
photoworks.org.uk

MOHAMED HASSAN
Artist
mohamedhassanphotography.com

SAYURI ICHIDA
Artist
sayuriichida.com

JANE & JEREMY
Independent publisher and design studio
jane-jeremy.co.uk

MYAH ASHA JEFFERS
Artist
myahjeffers.com

RINKO KAWAUCHI
Artist
rinkokawauchi.com

LAUREN JOY KENNETT
Artist
laurenjoykennett.com

BILLY HC KWOK
Artist
billyhckwok.com

KALPESH LATHIGRA
Artist
kalpeshlathigra.com

GORDON MACDONALD
Artist, co-editor of Hapax Magazine; Photoworks head of publishing, 1999–2011
@editorgordon

NEETA MADAHAR
Artist
neetamadahar.com

ALIX MARIE
Artist
alixmarie.com

CAMILLA MARRESE
Artist and visual designer
camillamarrese.it

SHOAIR MAVLIAN
Director of The Photographers' Gallery; director of Photoworks, 2018–22
@shoair_m
thephotographersgallery.org.uk

ANNE MCNEILL
Director of Impressions Gallery; Photoworks founder and director, 1995–96
@annemcneill215
impressions-gallery.com

SUSAN MEISELAS
Artist and president of the Magnum Foundation
susanmeiselas.com
magnumfoundation.org

EMMA MORRIS
Arts professional and consultant; Photoworks director, 2010–13
@iamtheemmamorris

JACK MOYSE
Artist
jackmoyse.myportfolio.com

HENNA NADEEM
Artist

PIERO PERCOCO
Artist
percoco.fail

EILEEN PERRIER
Artist
eileenperrier.com

JOHNY PITTS
Artist, writer and TV presenter
johnypitts.com

LÚA RIBEIRA
Artist
luaribeira.com

JOSIE SAUNDERS
Photoworks programme producer
@jozsaunders
photoworks.org.uk

JOACHIM SCHMID
Artist
lumpenfotografie.de

THABISO SEKGALA
Artist
Sekgala's estate is represented by goodman-gallery.com

ANNA SELLEN
Artist
annanas.co.uk

KATE SIMPSON
Editor, writer, poet, critic
kateelspethsimpson.com

THEO SIMPSON
Artist
theosimpson.co.uk

EMILY JUNE SMITH
Artist; Photoworks digital youth engagement producer
emilyjunesmith.com
photoworks.org.uk

DIANE SMYTH
Writer, editor; Photoworks Annual editor
@dismy
photoworks.org.uk

HELEN STARR
Afro-Carib cultural activist, curator and producer
@themechatroniclibrary

ALISON THOMSON
Freelance copy editor
alison@alisonthomson.co.uk

NICK WAPLINGTON
Artist, represented by hamiltonsgallery.com

PHOEBE WINGROVE
Artist; Photoworks learning and engagement administrator
phoebewingrove.com
photoworks.org.uk

AMIN YOUSEFI
Artist; Photoworks assistant curator and P+ editor
aminyousefi.com
photoworks.org.uk